8245

A history of Venezuela /

D1236350

A HISTORY OF VENEZUELA

A History of
VENEZUELA

BY

GUILLERMO MORÓN

of The Academia Nacional de la Historia
Venezuela

EDITED AND TRANSLATED BY

JOHN STREET

Lecturer in Latin American Studies
Cambridge University

ILLUSTRATED

LONDON
GEORGE ALLEN & UNWIN LTD
Ruskin House Museum Street

FIRST PUBLISHED IN 1964
SECOND IMPRESSION 1965

PRINTED IN GREAT BRITAIN
in 11 on 12 point Pilgrim type
by EAST MIDLAND PRINTING CO. LTD.
BURY ST. EDMUNDS

TRANSLATOR'S PREFACE

Guillermo Morón was born in 1926 at Carora, Lara State, in Venezuela, where he first went to school. Later he studied in Barquisimeto and Caracas, specialising in Social Science, before working in Madrid, Spain, for his doctorate in history, which he received in 1954. He also studied philosophy, in London, and the philosophy of culture and Classics in Germany. Meanwhile he taught history and literature in Caracas, from 1947 to 1951, and had a period as a lecturer in Spanish American culture in the University of Hamburg (1956-58). At present he is a professor of the history of Venezuelan culture in the Andrés Bello University, Caracas. He is also a member of the Venezuelan National Academy of History and editor of Shell Venezuela's publication *Revista Shell*. Guillermo Morón's energy and breadth of interests are illustrated by his published works, which include biographies and volumes of essays on historical, philosophical, literary and political topics as well as his *Historia de Venezuela*, which first appeared in 1956 and has had two more Spanish editions since that date.

This English edition is based on the third Spanish edition, published in 1961, but it is not a direct translation. The text-book form of the original has been abandoned for a narrative presentation, which has necessitated minor changes in the organisation of some chapters. At the same time much of chapters I and II and parts of other chapters have been abridged, without losing the development of the author's ideas. Also, two completely new chapters have been written in order to bring the book as nearly up to date as is practicable. Guillermo Morón wrote the first of these which deals with events and politics in the confused period since the death of the tyrant Gómez in 1936 (chapter VII); while the second is an analysis of the Venezuelan economic scene written by the economist Dr. Manual Rodríguez Mena, of the Universidad Central, Caracas. I have tried, in the translation, to give a reflection of Guillermo Morón's own style and method—the unexpected metaphor, the patriotic soliloquy—which appear especially in the introductions to the chapters.

Venezuelan historians in general have too often written according to a preconceived thesis and without sufficient documentation. Traditionally, history has been a literary exercise; and where this view is changing, it seems to do so for the worse: history now is often concerned with purely contemporary politics, whatever its ostensible subject may be. Hence the exaggerated reactions of some historians to work by colleagues of another political persuasion. At present, in Venezuela, a book, for example, on the nineteenth century is read as a contemporary political tract—and this may be the intention of the author. There are few impartial books about Venezuelan history, but Guillermo Morón's is as well-documented and balanced as any, and has certain clear advantages over most others written by Venezuelans.

The book has real perspective on the Colonial period: no harsh judgments about the Spanish régime; no concentration of interest on one period or hero, as is so common. The Independence period, from 1811 to 1830, has been given more attention by historians than all the rest of Venezuelan history together; but Guillermo Morón keeps a much more reasonable measure. Bolívar, the greatest hero of them all for Venezuela, receives here fair treatment, although his Argentine counterpart, San Martín, perhaps receives less than justice. But when one remembers the work of other Venezuelans in this connection (for example, Vicente Lecuna), one learns to respect Guillermo Morón's moderation.

Guillermo Morón's view of the nineteenth century in Venezuela is conditioned by his realisation of the futility of the thirty-five revolutions which took place between 1830 and 1901, splitting the nation and "wasting the people's vital energy". (Interview in *El nacional* of Caracas, May 23, 1963.) His political beliefs are revealed by his yearning for the rule of peace, education and culture: the Marxist's might become apparent from his concentration of interest on the role of the 'people' in the nineteenth-century *pronunciamientos*.

The ground of almost contemporary history following the death of Gómez, which Guillermo Morón breaks, is almost virgin to historians, and the author deserves credit for publishing opinions and interpretations which will almost certainly bring him strong opposition from those who do not agree with his politics. The presidential periods of Generals López Contreras and Medina Angarita seem to Guillermo Morón full of hope and promise for the future of democratic government in the country; whereas to others they are marked as periods only slightly better than the years of Gómez. The present president, Rómulo Betancourt, and his party, Acción Democrática, appear to many to hold out the strongest hope of a peaceful solution to the problem of the bitterness between the extreme right and the extreme left; but Guillermo Morón, whose main thesis is concerned with this question of national co-existence, of internal peace, remains unconvinced of the certainty of this hope. No-one knows how the future will turn out, and at this point we have passed out of the legitimate field of history, as Guillermo Morón implies in the title of a section of chapter IV: "Too recent history". Yet, hopeful patriot that he is, he feels bound to provide us with an inkling of the possibilities the future holds for Venezuela.

I have frequently consulted the author about the problems his book presents to the translator, and I believe that I have respected his intentions. I should like to make it clear that the blame for any disparity between this text and the Spanish one is mine, as is the responsibility for the contents of this preface.

John Street

Cambridge, August 1963

ACKNOWLEDGMENT

The author wishes to express his thanks, for their help with this edition, to Dr. Manuel Rodríguez Mena, of the Universidad Central, Caracas, to Sra Carmen Delia de García, of the Asociación de Escritores Venezolanos, to Miss Mary Green, of the *Sunday Telegraph* and to the photographic collection of Shell Venezuela. And, of course, to Dr. John Street, the editor and translator.

CONTENTS

CONTENTS

ILLUSTRATIONS

CHAPTER ONE

The Aborigines

I. INTRODUCTION

IN some remote parts of the country, the forests beyond the Orinoco and those of the western side of Lake Maracaibo, live peoples which we call natives, aborigines or Indians. These are the ancient inhabitants of Venezuela, today reduced to less than a hundred thousand individuals all told. Some of them live in communities close to and even surrounded by the "creole" population, that is, the white folk normally considered as the Venezuelan people. They form a minority with a life completely different from that of the rest of the Venezuelans, both in productive activity, in their daily tasks, and in their outlook on life, so remote from that of a civilised people.

An example will give us an idea of the situation of the Venezuelan Indians at the highest point of their development, where they have in part succeeded in adopting creole culture and in attaining a higher level without losing their own tribal state. In a recent study Walter Dupouy writes: "The Indian communities of Anzoátegui have a cultural level similar or close to that of the ordinary poor peasants of the country. This is owing to their long contact with the creoles, from whom the Indians adopted or adapted a part of the low-grade culture of the country district, a culture itself partly Indianised. They keep alive their own Carib language, which they use normally among themselves, and they speak Spanish when talking to creoles. But it appears that the children and young folk no longer know their mother tongue, a lamentable fact which we were able to observe among the group of Mapiricure. They cannot read and write, although here and there are young people who have been to school and who therefore can . . . Their economy is based on primitive cropping of small plots, with some slight attention to breeding goats, pigs, donkeys and poultry."[1]

The above picture synthesises the way in which, over the four centuries of Venezuelan history, the Indian has gradually disappeared. Slowly and painfully a part of the race became assimilated into the life of the new Venezuela; but the great majority disappeared during the Spanish conquest of the country. The Indian of Venezuelan history, who played a part in the formation of the creole, that is, in the making of what Venezuelans are today, gradually became part of the nation through the process of miscegenation; the Indian of pre-hispanic times, the lord of the land before the Spanish occupation, disappeared. What remains today is the Indian as a problem, the minority which still retains its own low level of culture, but which will eventually be assimilated, as is at this moment happening in the case of the Indians of Anzoátegui, Zulia and elsewhere, as the general culture of the nation advances over them.

The share of the native race in the formation of the Venezuelan people must be gauged by the mixing of blood and of culture during the first three centuries of creole history, centuries which comprise the basic period in the making of the present-day Venezuelan nation. There is no doubt that certain details of folklore and of economy spring from the aborigine. This contribution is not to be scorned, any more than any other ingredients of the amalgam. But it cannot be maintained that Venezuelan culture, so far as historical civilisation is concerned, is based on native culture. It is true that agriculture was known to the Indians, and the Venezuelan peasant is still struggling to surpass the indubitably primitive methods inherited from them. It is true that artistic expression can be appreciated in the elaboration of pottery and of basket-work. It is true that some folk dances owe their origin to the dances which tribal religions employed in their time. But nothing of this gives form or shape to present-day Venezuelan culture. Venezuela is at an advanced stage of intellectual culture thanks to European, indeed Spanish, moulds. It is essential to realise this historical truth.

But it is also right to show the contribution of the aborigine,

---

[1] 'Noticias preliminares sobre la comunidad indígena de San Joaquín de Parire, Estado Anzoátegui,' in *Boletín indigenista Venezolano*, no. 1, Caracas 1953, p. 95.

even though it was influential in only two spheres because of the limited possibilities of the stage of culture to which the Indian had attained. One is evident in the torrent of blood which the Indian poured into the creole, especially over the first three centuries, and the other in the minor details of culture expressed today in the national folklore.

Experience has shown that it is impossible to maintain aboriginal cultures in co-existence with creole culture, but that on the contrary the former must be incorporated into the latter. This may appear unjust if regarded from an emotional point of view, but not so if one follows the lesson of history, of human progress. Only through miscegenation has the aborigine joined civilisation, for one cannot call civilised those inaccessible groups which still live their primitive life, not even those groups which practise a way of life like that of the creole peasant. This truth must be respected for its historical weight, with no attempt to produce reasons of an exclusively sentimental nature. The fact that there exist as isolated examples particular individuals capable of living within the framework of a superior intellectual culture—there is no other suitable expression—shows that the race is capable of becoming civilised when it finds appropriate conditions. But these conditions are precisely those offered by the homogeneous group, the creole group. It does not, therefore, appear to be possible for us to advance the Indian, to civilise him, while at the same time conserving his political community structure nor his economic and social position. The intense pressure of the proximity of the creole, the progressive degeneration of the Indians' own way of life, the obliteration of their native customs and language owing to their adoption of Castilian and to the practices of society as ordinary Venezuelans understand it, will decide the fate of those Indians who still remain.

The war of extermination was cruel, and the treatment on an inferior plane offered by their protectors to the Indians until a short time ago turned out to be unworkable. If the war perfidiously destroyed, the protection merely debased. Neither method has anything to recommend it and therefore scholars and politicians today are seeking a new approach to the problem, even though in Venezuela it has lost its former importance. One first, very general, conclusion has been reached: the Indian, the minority, must be incorporated into the life of the nation. But how? This is the real question today, and so far it remains without answer.

Should the Indian communities be preserved? No one can seriously desire this. The communities must gradually disappear, their demise helped on by well-planned and organised political action, such as seems to be emerging today. It must be hoped that in the near future—when the forest has been conquered and the land filled with towns and cities—not one group will remain which still speaks the Carib or any other aboriginal language, and the problem of the Indian will be a purely ethnological one. To aim at the opposite is to seek to turn back the process of culture to stages already left behind by Venezuela.

The Indian forms a part of Venezuelan history, since he is one of the ingredients in the mixture of race and culture, and in this way occupies a place which no one can deny him. But he must be completely assimilated and entirely integrated into the Venezuelan way of life, and miscegenation is the historic method of this incorporation.

To sum up: the question of the native has two aspects, one historical and the other contemporary. The first is the contribution of the Indian to the formation of the Venezuelan people, through the process of miscegenation. From the sixteenth century to the eighteenth, a period during which there existed large numbers of natives, creole man in one way or another came into close contact with the groups of primitive inhabitants, and miscegenation took place. The result was imperceptible assimilation, which has given the blood of the Venezuelan people a large, though unverifiable, proportion of Indian blood. Certain purely cultural characteristics of the Venezuelans of today are also aboriginal, although there has been no such contribution to intellectual culture. No general idea, no way of behaviour—morality, law, religion, literature, language—comes from the natives. This racial mixing has brought into being a new form and an adaptation of Hispanic culture which is the basis of modern Venezuela.

The second aspect of the Indian question concerns the minorities which remain. The first thing to recognise is the need to incorporate these minorities into the nation's productive life. Their preservation and increase would cause a lack of balance in the country. But the process of incorporation, always slow, must take place in accordance with the social conscience of modern civilised man.

2. THE OLDEST INHABITANTS

Where did the American Indians come from? This question has been discussed since they were first discovered by Europeans. The early chroniclers, following the notion of a dispersal of peoples after the Flood, sometimes linked the American Indians with Asiatic origins, even with the sea-faring Phoenicians. Modern anthropologists generally accept it as likely that the American Indians originated in Asia, and possibly in Australia, Melanesia and Polynesia; but there is also a view that man originated in America just as other branches of the species originated elsewhere. And the Indians, in America, although they were one race, were by the time of the Spanish conquest divided into many groups at very varied levels of civilisation.

The Indians of Venezuela did not reach a high level of culture: they have no written history before the Spanish conquest. Little is known yet about the Venezuelan Indians of palaeolithic times except that life was very primitive and it is likely that the people lived by gathering what food they could find. Later there appear to have been three successive invasions: firstly one of similar food-gathering Indians; secondly, embracing the coast and with some penetration of the interior, came the Arawaks, a people living in stable communities; and thirdly the Caribs, whose main characteristic was their war-like nature, and who forced the Arawaks to retreat from large stretches of the coast and interior. These invasions seem to have come from two sources: the sea and the tropical forest; but the various tribal groups migrated in such diverse directions that it has become almost impossible to decide from which area any particular group originally came.

By the sixteenth century many tribes had settled in definite areas, though others still wandered through the *llanos*, the hot plains, and penetrated the savannahs, while yet others slowly ascended the rivers, stopping here and there on the banks before moving on. Sixteenth-century Spanish accounts relate that the most densely populated parts of Venezuela were Paria in the east, the Venezuelan Andes and the western shore of Lake Maracaibo, and the North-East. The Caribbean coast was less full, but possessed many small groups. The missionaries in the eighteenth century found many tribes living along the banks of the Orinoco, cultivating crops on the neighbouring *llanos*.

Before the arrival of the Spaniards the people of Venezuela included various "nations" of Indians: that is, groups of tribes related by language and customs, but living separately and without any notion of common nationhood. The tribe, therefore, was the basic unit of society. It consisted of Indians living in the same place, united by language and customs as well as by religion. Occasionally tribes of Indians living in the same area would become allies for war, as for example in face of the Spanish invaders. These tribes might belong to the same nation, or might have no such link; but in any case the union did not imply that they had any political organisation in common.

A tribe was usually led by a chief, who was its head both in peace and in war. He was sometimes advised by a council of warriors or elders, and he might be elected from among the bravest or be recognised as the wisest, or he might be hereditary chief. Religion was closely connected with the government of the tribe, and so the priest was usually a member of the council, or might even be the chief. The tribes of the food-gatherers of the *llanos* were very simply organised and each consisted of few Indians; but the fishing Indians of the rivers had much more complicated customs, which required a real exercise of internal authority, over such matters as fishing or hunting, the building of huts, and other social and religious usages. The chief was therefore leader in war and administrator in peace; and this double role was best established in the great tribes of the Andes, the coast and some of the higher land. The need to preserve certain lands for hunting and others for harvesting increased the organising skill of the chief, who thus gained in importance and prestige.

The Indians' economic life was a step beyond the primitive, and had advanced as far as could be expected where there was no knowledge of the wheel or of metal, those two things most necessary for the development of a culture. An attempt at a general classification can be made by dividing the tribes according to the main economic effort of each. The food-gathering tribes, the most primitive, lived hard, wandering without shelter, eating what they could collect without previous preparation and also game and fish. By the sixteenth century most tribes were sedentary, practising agriculture; but the level of culture varied from the slash-and-burn technique of the Orinoco tribes to digging, irrigation and building of terraces as practised in Mérida. The staple foods were maize and various roots, such as the yucca from which cassava was made in the *llanos* and manioc on the Orinoco, the Río Negro and other places. The plot (*conuco*) also produced some condiments, such as red pepper. This type of small cultivation in plots practised by the natives was copied later by the whites, and passed on to the mixed breeds: it has become a constant factor in Venezuelan sociology. Some fruit trees were also cultivated, and cacao and tobacco, which were to become decisive products in the development of the country. Cotton too was grown, although the Venezuelan Indians could not weave, but used the product for making nets and hammocks. The Andes region had the best agriculture, whereas in other regions, mainly on the coast, agriculture had reached a middle stage of development, and among the Orinoco Indians it was still at the lowest level. Some tribes practised apiculture, and many domesticated the wild hog or kept poultry, local fowl such as the *paujil*, the *guacharaca*, or a species of turkey and duck.

Certain crafts were practised too, ranging from basket-work and pottery to work in precious metals, although this latter was little advanced. Indians moulded and baked clay and used the results both for ordinary household purposes and also in the shape of idols. The best work was done in and around the Andean region.

The Caribs were notable navigators, both on the sea and along the rivers, and other tribes, such as those in the Maracaibo district, were also sailors. Trade increased, and canoes were built to carry as many as fifty men. Trade goods included clothing, drugs, salt, cotton, skins, rubber, cacao, gold and even slaves. A primitive token system arose in some parts, where for example disks made from shells were used in trading.

The social organisation of the Indians varied from tribe to tribe. The more sedentary tribes built large villages, whose inhabitants could be counted in thousands. Other villages consisted of only half a dozen huts, while some villages were housed entirely in one large hut. The present-day Motilones live three or four hundred together in such a house. Marriage customs varied very greatly, as they still do. War for some tribes was a way of life, particularly for the Caribs, who prepared themselves for it by courses of dancing and mock fighting. Their weapons were bows and arrows, clubs, blow-pipes and spears; they used shields and prepared and used poisons such as curare. Whether a people is warlike or not depends largely upon circumstances such as rivalry, competition for land, and so forth; consequently it must be remembered that not all Caribs were warlike, nor all Arawaks peaceful. Indeed, some Arawaks were at least as warlike as the Caribs. Cannibalism was practised as a rite, as was war itself on occasion. Eating parts of the body of a distinguished enemy or even a member of one's own tribe was a way of conserving and increasing the vital force of oneself and one's tribe, and it was accompanied by the appropriate ceremonial.

The Indians had games, some played with balls as in Central America, and some ran races. All had dances, traces of which remain to this day; these were not merely recreations but had also a ritual significance, such as the celebration of victory. Music was provided by clay and bamboo trumpets, drums and maracas. Alcoholic drinks were made from fermented maize or fermented cassava mixed with honey. The two types of religion prevalent were animism and shamanism: the first attributed the possession of a spirit to all things, while the second concentrated on magic exercised by a witch-doctor in order to ward off evil. Slavery was known and practised by both Arawaks and Caribs as a means of providing a supply of labour for the land.

During the seventeenth and eighteenth centuries the Indians of the interior gradually came to adopt some of the refinements offered by the Spaniards. In this period of transculturation they learned to use new utensils, animals and such things as firearms and steel knives.

3. THE INDIANS TODAY

There are still many groups of natives in Venezuela, some of them semi-civilised and others living in inaccessible regions such as the Guayana forests, and parts of the *llanos* and the western mountain ranges. They keep their customs, although some tribes speak Spanish as well as their own language, and have adopted some civilised habits such as the wearing of clothes. The rights of these minorities are protected by special laws, and an active interest in the position of the Indian is shown by the government, by anthropologists and sociologists, and also by the educated section of the nation. Attempts are being made to discover exactly how these minorities can be incorporated into the life of the country by raising their cultural levels, that is by spreading the use of Spanish and bringing these people into closer contact with the rest of the nation. Indians today still retain their primitive way of life, even those who live among the other members of the nation and are called civilised. Some individual Indians truly are civilised, and this proves that the race is capable, given the opportunity, of living on a higher cultural level than its native one. In fact the Indian has very gradually been growing into Venezuelan life, and it is therefore to be expected that the remaining minorities will also in time be assimilated.

The decrease in the number of Indians in Venezuela can be seen from the figures of the Censuses of 1936, 1941 and 1950. The total numbers of Indians at these dates were given as 103,942, 100,600, and 98,823 respectively. In 1950 about 40% of the Indians were judged to be inaccessible, out of contact with civilised centres. The total population of Venezuela at the Census of 1950 was given as 5,161,543. About twenty-five tribes exist in various parts of the country, and the greatest concentrations of Indians are found in the Amazon Federal Territory, with 39,010, and the State of Zulia, with 29,020.

Interest in the Indian problem has become greater in recent years, and Venezuela is taking part in an international movement of protection for natives coupled with the attempt to incorporate them into normal society. The most important organisation dealing with this question in Venezuela is the Comisión Indigenista Nacional, founded in 1947, given official standing in 1948 and made a special care of the new Ministry of Justice in 1950. This Commission deals with all questions relating to the Indians, not only matters of government but also purely scholarly research. In the short time since its foundation, the Commission has worked hard and well, for example resolving labour problems, supervising administration, helping with the census of natives, and undertaking anthropological and sociological research.

There exist, too, Indian missions established by the Catholic

Church from the sixteenth century onwards. Four are now in operation: one run by the Capuchins on the Caroní (State of Bolívar) another, created from this first in 1954, in the Delta Amacuro Federal Territory; a third on the Upper Orinoco, under the Salesians; and the fourth, run by the Capuchins, is the mission of Guajira-Perijá, with jurisdiction in the State of Zulia. They work under the terms of a law of 1915 which laid down that their task was to incorporate the natives into the normal life of the Republic of Venezuela.

In 1951 the Commission was successful in obtaining a government decree making it necessary for any visitor to the native territories to have a special permit. The government maintains a lively interest in the native population, and is trying to find a practical solution to its problems.

CHAPTER II

The Discovery and Conquest

I. INTRODUCTION

WHEN the word "conquest" is mentioned a violent reaction takes place inside every Venezuelan, every American creole. The constant teaching of more than a century is behind that reaction, which has not been altered by recent studies which find the colonising effort of the Spaniards praiseworthy. Yet it must be remembered that the process known as the conquest, which occupied the whole sixteenth century, is at the same time responsible for laying the foundations of the Venezuelan way of life.

The men who carried out the conquest of Venezuela, despoiling the lands of the numerous native peoples who inhabited it, destroying their villages, demolishing their culture and extirpating their very race, were men who possessed those same fundamental human values which characterise the Venezuelan of today. It has been remarked that Indian blood gave a strong tinge to both the conquerors and the blacks they brought with them. Laureano Vallenilla Lanz, the eminent Venezuelan sociologist (1870-1936), wrote: "If one compares, as certain authors have done, the number of natives who escaped the ravages of the conquest with the number of Spaniards, Canary Islanders and Africans who entered the country during the whole colonial period, it can easily be deduced that it was native blood which formed the greatest proportion of the composition of our people, not only in the so-called coloured people but also in the immense majority of the creoles, or whites, and even in the most aristocratic families which, especially in the later years of the period, thought of themselves as pure-blooded descendants of the conquerors."[1] But if this is true biologically speaking, the opposite was the case in the

---

[1] Laureano Vallenilla Lanz, *Disgregación e integración*, Caracas, Tipografía Universal, 1930, p. 129.

matter of culture, where the forms of thought, the habits and spiritual nature of the conquerors predominated. The psychology, character and cultural aptitudes of the Venezuelan are moulded on those of the conqueror, though they show great changes due to the influence of the native and the negro and of the new habitat.

Who were the conquerors? They were Europeans, Spaniards with a long medieval tradition, who were at the time closely involved in the Renaissance. The weight of religious beliefs acted upon them together with an uncommon spirit of liberty. They could organise a society of men who were capable of governing themselves, but they were aware of a superior binding power: the King. Above the King, God. But facing the King, each individual man. It was this political complex which determined the dual attitude of the sixteenth-century conquerors.

The discoverer and conqueror embarked on an enterprise which was organic and systematic from the cultural standpoint. On the one hand politics came into play, since the attempt was being made to put the power of a nation called Spain into a concrete form: Spain, still in the process of integration, searching for the right formula to turn herself into a dominant power. On the other hand there were also economic needs, which could be satisfied by the winning of wealth— gold—and the expansion of trade. Thirdly, the enterprise clearly had the nature of a religious crusade, a projection of the Catholic faith.

But the individual, the conquerer with a name of his own, the common soldier, although he participated in this directed enterprise, had urges which were more essential, more vital, and closer to his own daily needs. When one remembers that the mass of the small conquering armies, and even the majority of the "captains" who led them, were unimportant folk, members of the so-called inferior classes on account of their economic and social status, one can understand the popular enthusiasm aroused by the war of conquest. The ideal of the soldier was to get rich, or to excel in heroic actions, or merely to live a life of excitement.

Ambition was one of the motive forces of the conqueror: ambition for riches, for power, for heroism or even for conversion of the natives. Which of these ambitions was predominant? On the whole there seems to have been a balance, although there are numerous examples which can be used to support the claims of one or another of them. More than one conqueror entered the lists for pure love of fighting, and more than one for pure love of liberty.

It is important to understand the last point: the feeling for liberty was strong in the conquerors. This seems a paradox, since their job was to reduce to submission or to kill entire peoples. All war is cruel, and wars of conquest are more cruel than any other. The Spanish conqueror needed the new land for his deeds of prowess and for his life, which was one long deed of prowess; the natives were an obstacle to the realisation of those deeds. The Conquerors did not scorn the native race as such, for they entered into the closest contact with it and produced a mixed race; but they did understand the impossibility of any cultural co-existence. If the Indian became assimilated, he became another member of the conquering group. Here, in the ability to live together with the cultural convert—the Indian must learn Spanish, how to cross himself and to wear clothes—is to be found the first stage in the transformation of the Spanish conqueror into the founder of a new way of life.

The conqueror, plebeian, ignorant, but possessor of a way of life able to dominate others, settled in the country. He was fierce, proud, and Catholic. He destroyed peoples while desiring to create others in his own image. He oppressed the whole land in his eagerness to attain his own liberty. He had the necessary means and he used them. As for the conquest itself and the settlers of Venezuela in the sixteenth century, they can best be understood through the words of Rufino Blanco Fombona in his valuable interpretative essay. He wrote: "It was not numbers which won the conquest, nor boldness, but a superior race beat an inferior one; a civilisation which possessed the arquebuse, the sword, the bulldog and the horse against another one which only had the arrow and the club, and also lacked animals for use in war or for transport. It has been said with reason that if the Indians had known the use of iron, the Europeans would not have been able to subdue the empires of America."[1] If we substitute the word "culture" for "race", in

---

[1] Rufino Blanco Fombona, *El conquistador español del siglo XVI*, Madrid, Ediciones Nuestra Raza, 1921, pp. 123-4.

order to avoid anthropological difficulties, we have an accurate sketch. For if there are not superior races there certainly are superior cultures.

2. THE DISCOVERY OF VENEZUELA

The discovery of what is today Venezuela was carried out between Columbus' third voyage to America (1498) and the last conquering expeditions into the interior in the west, in 1550. This process revealed the geography of the territory to the newcomers, although the full discovery in fact continued slowly through the sixteenth, seventeenth and eighteenth centuries, and indeed some forest areas in remote parts of the country have still not been visited. However, 'discovery' is normally used to mean the first contact made by Europeans with the new land, and particularly the voyages along the coast made by the first sailors to visit it. This was the first stage of the history of Venezuela, when one world entered into relations with another.

It was on the third of his four voyages to the West Indies that Christopher Columbus (born about 1446 probably at Genoa; died 1506 at Valladolid) saw the mainland which came to be called Tierra Firme, in the eastern part of Venezuela, in the region of Paria. Possibly he found the whole north coast of the Orinoco delta and the coast from there to a point opposite the island of Margarita in the north of Sucre. In 1498 Columbus sailed from San Lúcar de Barrameda, in the south of Spain, and reached the south of the island of Trinidad on July 31st. The next day the mainland was sighted, although it was thought to be another island, and according to the account of Las Casas it was named Isla Santa, Holy Isle. For some days the flotilla of three caravels sailed through the Gulf of Paria, between Trinidad and Venezuela, sighting some Indians, a few of whom Columbus captured. Columbus himself made a landing on August 9th somewhere in the south of the peninsula of Paria, and then he left the Gulf, making for Hispaniola, on the 13th, and sighted Margarita on the 15th. To begin with Columbus did not believe that he had found the mainland, but after his voyage along the length of coast he became convinced that he had found a *"tierra firme"*, and a very large one, unknown until that time.

Christopher Columbus in 1492 had succeeded in gaining the support of the Spanish sovereigns, Ferdinand and Isabella, for his attempt to reach India by a voyage westwards round the world. On his first two transatlantic ventures (1492-3 and 1493-6) he had discovered several West Indian islands and established a town, Santo Domingo, in Hispaniola (now the island of Santo Domingo), which became the centre of colonising activity in the earliest stages of the settlement of America by the Spaniards. From Santo Domingo the government of the Indies, as the area newly discovered was called, was carried on for some time.

After the discovery of the Venezuelan coast Columbus sailed to Santo Domingo, where his brother Bartolomé was in charge, and from there, in October 1498, he wrote a detailed letter to the Spanish monarchs telling them of his latest success, and sending them a map of the new lands. He told them of the gold found in these regions, and especially of the many pearls, which he had seen round the necks and arms of the Indians. From his observations of the waters, land and rivers, Columbus advanced the theory that the Earthly Paradise must be in the interior of Paria, but also was led to consider scientific problems. He was an early scientific geographer, who used his calculations, for example, to prove that the shape of the earth is that "of a pear, which is round except where the stalk grows, where it grows outwards, or like a very round ball on one part of which is placed a woman's nipple; and the part of the nipple or stalk is the highest and nearest to the heavens." But he also shrewdly noted how the islands he had found were longer from east to west than from north to south, and attributed this fact to the direction of a current in the sea. The exception of Trinidad, he thought, must be because the island had formed a part of the mainland at one time.

Other explorers followed Columbus, making contracts with the Crown of Castile, as had Columbus himself. Normally the Crown granted to the leader civil and criminal jurisdiction over the expedition and any land discovered. The leader or his supporters financed the enterprise, while the Crown drew a percentage of the profits. The Crown had in fact given Columbus almost exclusive rights to the exploitation of the Indies, but, realizing its mistake, made contracts with other explorers, who soon opened a route along the Venezuelan coast to beyond Cabo de la Vela.

Alonso de Ojeda had been on Columbus' second expedition, and with the protection of Bishop Fonseca, who had general charge over the affairs of the Indies, he undertook in 1499 a long expedition on the Venezuelan coast. He was the first to prove that the territory was part of a continent, and the first to observe the many Indian villages at all closely. He went from the Orinoco delta to the Gulf of Venezuela and Curaçao, exploring and naming various features. With him went two important cosmographers, Amerigo Vespucci and Juan de la Cosa. In 1502 Ojeda returned, with a permit to settle a part of the territory and with two commercial associates, Vergara and Campos of Cadiz. They made various attempts to settle, fought with some of the Indians and traded with others for pearls, but they could not gain a permanent hold; and in the end Vergara and Campos imprisoned Ojeda, who eventually gained his freedom, returned to Spain and took up again his profession as an expert mariner.

The Crown contracts stipulated that the coast actually discovered by Columbus must not be visited by the new expedition, but no-one respected this clause. Ojeda had contravened it, and so did the next explorer, Cristóbal Guerra, who with his brother Luis and the mariner Pedro Alonso Niño sailed along the Venezuelan coast in the second half of 1499. This was a purely commercial enterprise, dedicated to trading for pearls, gold and slaves and to armed robbery where possible or expedient. They used trade goods such as needles, glass, and pieces of cloth, in these transactions. On his return to Spain, Cristóbal Guerra was imprisoned for his misdeeds and forced to return the Indian captives to their native lands.

Vicente Yáñez Pinzón, a fine sailor who had accompanied Columbus on his first voyage, left Spain in December 1499 and reached the coast of Brazil, then turned northwards and sailed up the eastern coast of Venezuela, arriving back in Spain in September 1500. He saw the River Amazon and the mouths of the Orinoco, which had, however, been visited by Ojeda already. On his return to Spain he was rewarded with the title of governor of the lands he had discovered, but he never took possession and instead followed another exploratory route. At about the same time Diego de Lepe followed Yáñez Pinzón's previous route, making a trading trip. Rodrigo de Bastidas set out in 1500 on a long voyage along the routes already known, during which he anchored at many points along the Venezuelan coast to load Brazil wood (used for the extraction of a dye), to trade for gold and pearls, and to study the land. He was accompanied by the cosmographer Juan de la Cosa. Bastidas reached as far west as Santa Marta and Cartagena, in what is now Colombia.

This activity produced a good body of knowledge of the coast of Tierra Firme, and permitted the continuation of exploration both along the coast and into the interior. In 1500 Juan de la Cosa drew a map giving for the first time a complete outline of the Venezuelan coast. The actual name of Venezuela, which has been attributed to Vespucci, does not appear before the date 1528. Vespucci had written a description of his voyage with Ojeda, telling of the lands, the Indians and their customs—although Columbus had already written such a narrative.

3. THE CONQUEST OF VENEZUELA

"The Conquest" is a term used to describe the whole process whereby the Spaniards struggled with the Indians to seize the land and established themselves in it by founding towns, engaging in agriculture, and setting up a political organisation. It continued throughout the sixteenth and seventeenth centuries.

After the discovery of the Venezuelan coast voyages began to be made from Spain and Santo Domingo to capture slaves and to obtain gold, pearls and Brazil wood. In the period from about 1502 to 1530 many adventurers approached the coast simply to rob, although at the same time there was a movement of colonisation, especially in the island of Cubagua and in Cumaná. In fact, the first centres from which the mainland was to be conquered were in the islands of Cubagua and Margarita. Trinidad was explored, but not at this stage settled.

Cubagua, a barren rock, became famous for its pearls, and all the early explorers visited the oyster beds there. From 1510 some Spanish pearl-fishers were established there, using Santo Domingo as their commercial centre. They had to bring their water from the river of Cumaná, now called the Manzanares. By 1520 about three hundred had settled and built houses in Cubagua, founding a township which became known as Nueva Cádiz, and which for the next twenty years was one of the most prosperous in the Indies, with its population of a thousand and its huge profits. Everything consumed had to be imported, even firewood, but houses and public buildings arose and the island became an independent administrative unit. Nueva Cádiz, holding jurisdiction over the island of Margarita and the mainland Cumaná coast, may be regarded as the first Spanish political and social experiment in Venezuelan territory. The town was governed by a mayor elected yearly by the *Cabildo* (Town Council); and government was regulated by ordinances and was in direct contact with Spain. In 1543 the island was evacuated because of earthquakes which had taken place the previous year; and this brought to its culmination the decay begun by the exhaustion of the oyster fisheries and the ravages of pirates.

Margarita began as a source of provisions for the people of Cubagua, who even cultivated crops and kept some cattle there. But in 1525 it was made an independent province under Marcelo de Villalobos, a judge established in Hispaniola since 1511. He died before taking possession, and in 1527 his daughter Aldonza was confirmed in the governorship, although as a minor she was represented by a guardian, and she governed only through lieutenants. Her successors governed the island until the end of the sixteenth century from Asunción, the capital. Asunción received new settlers when Cubagua was evacuated, but the majority of the people from that island went to found the town of Nuestra Señora de los Remedios, later called Río de la Hacha, on the Cabo de la Vela. On Margarita there grew up an important settlement of mixed race.

Trinidad was conquered by the same Spaniards who subdued the eastern part of Venezuela. In 1515 it was visited by Bono de Quejo, a Basque, who opened it up to exploration. In 1530 it was granted as a governorship to Antonio Sedeño, a Royal Treasury official in San Juan, the capital of Puerto Rico, but in spite of his efforts he could not establish himself there owing mainly to the resistance of the Indians. From 1535 Trinidad was left to the visits of slave-hunters, although its Indians began to visit Margarita frequently for trade, and became accustomed to contact with the settlers there. Thus it remained, and fresh attempts to subdue the island in 1553 and 1571 were unsuccessful.

Expeditions to the coast and the interior of the mainland

were also made, some of them purely warlike and others of a missionary nature. In Cumaná the Indians waged incessant war against the intruders, and destroyed an early Franciscan mission. Lands cropped by the settlers of Cubagua were protected after 1520 by a fortress built at the mouth of the River Manzanares. An expedition led by Gonzalo de Ocampo with the object of founding a town failed, and the members went to swell the population of Cubagua. The Paria coast provided a similar picture, and the only certain thing is that it was frequently visited by expeditions seeking gold, pearls and slaves.

From at least 1513 missionaries were established on this eastern coast, but by 1515 the Indians had rebelled and destroyed the Dominican mission; yet in the same year six Dominicans and six Franciscans went to Cumaná. More came, and by 1519 two monasteries existed and five more containing four monks each were to be constructed. Their task was to protect the Indians from slavery and other ill-treatment. But the two monasteries were wiped out by the Indians in 1520, and the government of Santo Domingo sent a punitive expedition which ravaged the land. It was during this episode that Fray Bartolomé de las Casas, the "Apostle of the Indies", met a bitter defeat. As part of his campaign for better treatment of the Indians, he had gained royal permission to colonise the whole Venezuelan coast from Paria to Cabo de la Vela with farmers brought from Castile, and by means of peaceful persuasion he hoped to convert and pacify the natives. Some of his settlers were killed together with the missionaries in the risings of 1520. The cruelty of the repression removed any hopes for the success of his scheme in the future.

The whole north-east of the country gradually succumbed to armed conquest. Among the various expeditions arose the legend that great riches were to be found on the River Meta, well inland. Diego de Ordaz, appointed governor of a large tract from the Orinoco westwards, ventured up the river and took possession of the land, but came into conflict with other explorers and was made prisoner before being sent back to Spain via Cumaná, Cubagua and Santo Domingo. He died on the voyage home, possibly poisoned by his captor. The only result of his incursion was the reconnaissance of the Orinoco up to its confluence with the River Meta. Jerónimo de Ortal, companion of Ordaz and his successor as governor of Paria, struggled for five years from 1523 on the coast and the rivers, in the forests and the *llanos*, to reach the rich goal of the Meta. He did not succeed, but fought with Antonio Sedeño, who abandoned Trinidad and sought his fortune on the mainland. At one point they became allies, but could not agree, separated, and fought again. Ortal founded no towns, but split up his men among the Indian villages, where they stayed long enough to start a race of mixed blood, to wipe out some tribes and to subdue others.

Sedeño was in rebellion against the legitimate governor, Ortal, and also against the Licenciado Juan de Frías whom the government of Santo Domingo sent to pacify the conquerors. Eventually Sedeño penetrated the *llanos* seeking the Orinoco and the Meta, and although he died, his band continued, under quarrelling captains, crossing the whole eastern zone until they came into contact with the German subjects of Charles V who were opening up the west of the country. Another group were reported in 1548 to have crossed the hostile country from Margarita to Colombia, taking two years over the adventure.

The great expeditions led by the Germans took place in the western regions of Venezuela; and they were led to the far south-west by the legend of El Dorado, which played the same role among them as had the legend of the Meta among the explorers of the east. This German enterprise arose through the close connections of various German commercial and banking firms with Charles V, both in matters of finance and even in family affairs. The Welsers in particular, but also the Fuggers and the Ehingers, had gained Charles' gratitude through the provision of important loans and other services, and they saw the commercial possibilities which participation in the enterprise of the Indies would have for them. Hieronymus Seiler and Henry Ehinger, who in 1528 were the agents for the Welsers in Spain, made various contracts with the Crown concerning ventures in the Indies. Through one such contract German miners were to be recruited for work in Hispaniola, and through another negroes were to be imported for work in the mines; but the third and most important agreement in effect granted to the Welsers the exploitation of a province called Venezuela, stretching from Cabo de la Vela in the west to Maracapana in the east, and delimited north and south merely by the Atlantic and the Pacific. Naturally these terms were vague, since only the main points of the Caribbean coast were known.

This agreement, in the form of a *capitulación* such as was commonly made with the Spanish explorers, is interesting since the German subjects of Charles V are treated in regard to the Indies on the same level as his Spanish subjects. The Germans are allowed to name a royal governor, one of them is to be an Adelantado, and in all respects the venture is a typical Spanish colonial enterprise. A royal decree of 1530, signed in Augsburg, laid down that Seiler and Ehinger were merely the agents of the Welsers, who were the principals to whom the agreement of 1528 referred.

García de Lerma had been appointed governor of the contiguous territory of Santa Marta, and the Germans made an agreement to pool their resources with his. Lerma was to be captain of the joint expedition, which would subdue the Spanish rebels of Santa Marta first, and then the army would proceed to conquer Venezuela. German money would support Castilian arms. In October 1528 the expedition sailed for Santo Domingo. There Ambrose Ehinger, the Germans' agent in Hispaniola, took over command of the Venezuelan enterprise and became first governor of Venezuela. Santa Marta was already pacified, so the expedition sailed directly to Coro, landing in February 1529 at this miserable little port to the north-east of Lake Maracaibo.

Ampíes already was colonising the islands of Curaçao, Aruba and Bonaire, where he had rights, and had founded Coro on the mainland in 1527, where he had no rights. He was forced to give way to Ambrose Ehinger, who made the village legally a town and set it up as his capital. From 1529 to 1546 a succession of Germans nominally governed Venezuela, although in fact they spent most of their time scouring the country. Colonial administration was almost totally lacking, and no real town was founded, but only transient army camps here and there. A series of lieutenant-governors replaced in Coro the Germans, while these were out seeking gold, slaves and El Dorado. The fact that the Germans sought quick wealth and did not colonise made the enterprise different from most others. Even the soldiers, most of whom were Spanish, had to pay for their arms, horses and food, and the goods of dead soldiers were seized by the Germans to cover their "debts" to the firm. If the goods were not sufficient, the survivors were forced to pay the debt off. Naturally the troops became rebellious under such treatment, and their protests only ended with the end of the German régime. The Welsers had indeed established a monopoly of trade in Venezuela and neighbouring places, and made considerable profits, for example by selling bread bought at half a peso in Santo Domingo for two and a half pesos in Venezuela. The soldiers were always in debt. The whole German effort was founded on inhumanity: complete monopoly over a province which hardly existed, and the systematised indebtedness of its settlers. This was in complete contrast to the organised, legal character of the Spanish conquests, working as they did from the concepts of properly established town and citizenship. The German system saw in each man only a customer, and not a human being able to help in founding a new society.

The Welser régime was brought to an end by a royal decree of 1556, but in practice it ended ten years earlier. Juan de Carvajal arrived at Coro in January 1545 as interim lieutenant-governor and rebelled, seizing authority and establishing himself with an army inland at El Tocuyo. The Welser governor, Philip von Hutten, returned in June 1546 after a five-year absence with an expedition to the south. One of his captains, having quarrelled with another companion, Bartholomew Welser, joined Carvajal and prejudiced his mind against the Germans. Carvajal knew that he possessed no legal authority, and got rid of the legitimate governor von Hutten by trapping and killing him together with Welser and some Spanish soldiers. But the tyrant fell before the courage of Juan Pérez de Tolosa, who reached Coro in 1546 having been appointed *residencia* judge of Venezuela and Cabo de la Vela; that is, he was empowered to judge the actions of the various officials of these areas. Pérez de Tolosa marched straight to El Tocuyo, captured Carvajal and tried and executed him for his many crimes. The judge reorganised the province and left Juan de Villegas in charge while he went to reorganise Cabo de la Vela, where he died. Villegas governed well and in 1548 was appointed governor by Charles V, still in the name of the Welsers, although he continued to govern according to Spanish norms and the example of Pérez de Tolosa; it can therefore be said that the Welser régime ended in 1546.

The western region of the mainland, as has been seen, began to be settled from the islands of Curaçao, Aruba and Bonaire, just as the east had first been penetrated from the eastern islands. Coro, on the mainland, lived on the poor produce of plots growing maize and gourds and a few other things. It had some income from the sale of gold and slaves brought back by expeditions into the interior, but it did not flourish. It had no pearl-fisheries, and when the pearl-fishers of Cubagua migrated in 1542 they passed Coro by and went on to Cabo de la Vela, which possessed rich oyster beds. The city which arose on Cabo de la Vela became the centre for the exploration of the Guajira Peninsula and the coast of the Gulf of Venezuela and for trade with Río de la Hacha. By 1540 to 1550, as a result, the coastal routes of Venezuela were open, from one end to the other of the country. By 1546, too, the German governors with their Spanish captains and troops had explored the present States of Falcón, Zulia, Lara, Portuguesa, Cojedes, Yaracuy and Apure in a bloody search for wealth and dominion. Small groups of twenty or even fewer occasionally explored the forests, rivers and plains on their own account.

Ambrose Ehinger, governor of Venezuela from 1529 to 1533 explored part of the Maracaibo district and set up a camp called Maracaibo which soon declined. A second incursion of his with fresh troops brought from Santo Domingo went westwards and followed the River Magdalena into the mountains. There were savage fights with Indians, but also much booty. Ehinger died in 1533 while still exploring, and his men returned then to Maracaibo and Coro.

Nicholas Federmann, acting governor in Ehinger's absence, set out in 1530 on an unauthorised expedition to find El Dorado. He wrote an interesting account of his travels along the foot of the Andes in Venezuela, but on his return to Coro was sent back to Spain by Ehinger under the accusation of overstepping his powers. After Ehinger's death the Welsers appointed George Hohermut (known to the Spanish colonists as Jorge Espira) as governor, and Federmann became his lieutenant. He was sent to Cabo de la Vela to discuss the boundary with the province of Santa Marta, but once again went off on his own initiative, exploring the Guajira Peninsula and entering what is now Colombia. The governor of Santa Marta made him withdraw, so he returned to Coro before setting out for the south, where he entered the *llanos*. Eventually, after fierce fighting

with Indians and suffering great privations, this expedition
crossed the Colombian Andes and reached the high land of
Colombia at Bogotá in 1539, where they met the Spanish explorers Gonzalo Jiménez de Quesada and Sebastián de Belal-
cázar. Federmann, a really great explorer and organiser, died
in 1542, at odds with both the Welsers and the Spanish Crown.

Hohermut undertook an exploration between 1535 and
1538 of the *llanos* and the mountains, crossing the Apure and
the Arauca and reaching the interior of Colombia. Of 361 men
only 90 returned, but they were laden with 5,000 pesos of gold.
Hohermut died in 1540, and in the same year von Hutten, one
of his companions, became governor and set afoot an expedition, from 1541 to 1546, to seek El Dorado. He travelled extensively in the south, south-west and south-east, and even reached the River Guaviare, well outside Venezuelan territory, before returning to meet his death at the hands of the rebel Carvajal in 1546.

The judge Juan Pérez de Tolosa, after settling accounts with
Carvajal at El Tocuyo in 1547, sent his own brother Hernán
with a band of a hundred men on an expedition to the Andes.
Hernán penetrated to the Colombian plateau, as far as Cúcuta,
before returning in 1550 to El Tocuyo. The region to the south
of Lake Maracaibo, San Cristóbal and Mérida, was under the
jurisdiction of Pamplona in Colombia, founded in 1549, and
did not at first form part of Venezuela. Mérida itself was founded in 1558 by an expedition from Pamplona led by Juan Rodríguez Suárez, and these settlers went further north into Trujillo, meeting there with colonisers from El Tocuyo.

The two great movements of conquest, eastern and western,
converged on the central coast and valleys, gradually founding towns. Most of present-day Anzoátegui, Guárico and
Apure, however, were not settled until the seventeenth century. From El Tocuyo the movement of conquest reached out
to the east, in a long campaign against the fiercest resistance
from warlike Indians, especially the Jirajara and Caracas
tribes. A first spear-head of conquest thrust through Barquisimeto, the Lake of Valencia and Borburata, where it met the
sea. A second conquered the valley of Caracas, and the veteran
Diego de Losada founded there the town of Caracas in 1567.
Guaicapuro, the local Indian chief, a figure of extraordinary
warlike power, defended his land and culture ferociously un-

til killed by Francisco Infante. Guaicapuro has become an emotive symbol equal to any great Venezuelan soldier and patriot. From Margarita Francisco Fajardo had attempted to settle on the coast near Caracas in 1555 and 1557, but was only recognised by El Tocuyo in 1559. Fajardo, the son of a governor of Margarita and of the chieftainess of the island's Indians, used to advantage his mother's family links with the mainland Indians, and was able to make some settlements and open a few mines. This central conquest was directed by governors already established in Venezuela, and is therefore another stage of the whole movement. The first such governor was Juan Pérez de Tolosa (1546-1548), but his successors through the century consistently pushed on the occupation of the land.

The southern region, the immense Guayana territory, was first explored by Ordaz in 1531 and Alonso de Herrera, sent by Ortal, in 1534. The Orinoco was followed as far as the Meta, whose lower courses were also explored; but no settlements were made. In 1576 the Jesuits penetrated the area, and Dutch adventurers in 1579, with some small effects on the Indians. Gonzalo Jiménez de Quesada sent his brother to conquer Guayana, and was granted its governorship which passed on his death to Antonio de Berrío, the husband of a niece of his. Berrío after 1590 tried to conquer his province, where he founded a town called Santo Tomé de Guayana forty leagues up the Orinoco on the western bank. Another expedition led by Domingo de Vera in 1595 attempted to settle in Santo Tomé and its district, but ended in failure. Many died in the forests, and others migrated to other provinces already settled. Only some parts of the banks of the river were really conquered. In 1568 and 1569 other expeditions had fruitlessly reconnoitred parts of Guayana, though one expedition resulted in the foundation of the town of Nueva Córdoba in 1569 by Diego Fernández de Serpa. With this was laid the foundation of the province of Cumaná.

One last conquest was made between 1636 and 1640 by Juan de Urpín among the Cumaná Indians in the region of Barcelona, a town which Urpín founded. But in the sixteenth century still the centres of settlement had sent out secondary expeditions to subdue neighbouring areas, such as the expedition from El Tocuyo of Alonso Pacheco Maldonado, which conquered the Maracaibo region and founded the town of that name in 1569.

To sum up, the conquest may be regarded as a process with four stages: the first being the search for gold, the second the movement of settlement begun mainly by Pérez de Tolosa, the third the subsequent secondary spread of occupation, and the fourth the further settlement due to missionary activity especially in the *llanos* and the Orinoco region. The motives behind the conquest were of course complex. In general, however, there was the fever for riches, the search for gold, pearls, slaves or even Brazil wood, symbolised by the Meta and El Dorado; but there was also to a large extent a thirst for knowledge of the land; and undoubtedly there existed, consciously or unconsciously, in the conquerors a desire to bring the new lands into the fold of their own civilisation, as typified by the Catholic faith. Even though the conquest was bloody and cruel, many of the conquerors worked hard to convert the natives to the Spanish, Catholic way of life; and these were not only the missionaries, but also the tough soldiery

CHAPTER III

The Colonisation and Settlement of Venezuela

I. INTRODUCTION

THE process of the settlement of Venezuela in the sixteenth and seventeenth centuries is the topic which has been least studied by historians, even though there exist whole archives of documents on the subject. Therefore modern readers have only a partial knowledge of the way in which the colonists settled down in the land and began that new life imposed by the unfamiliar conditions. It is necessary to go to the documents to find out how and where the towns and villages appeared; because it is not enough merely to know the dates of the foundation of the towns, but it is essential to find out the details of the management of the land, in the widest sense. We need to understand one thing in particular: when does the Spaniard become the American?

Until towards the end of the seventeenth century the mainstay of the new provinces was an economic institution called the *encomienda*. This was the handing over of a certain number of Indians to the *encomendero*, the master, who in return for their labour on his land or their tribute to him undertook to protect, civilise, convert and in all ways look after them. Once the land had been subdued the conqueror became tame himself, and turned into a planter or rancher and thus the *encomendero* acquired social power and became the support of the whole life of the country. But what is not clear is how landed wealth was able to develop on top of the system of *encomienda* concessions. It seems likely that the *encomenderos* formed a class of gentlemen farmers, which was overwhelmed by a more powerful class of landowners. But it is important to emphasise the role of the *encomenderos* as settlers, penetrating as they did into every region and assimilating the native peoples, whom they bent to their wills. The *encomendero* civilised the country: he was the seed from which sprang the larger class of creoles, who made themselves masters of the land.

The sectors of the territory which by 1650 were already brought to political life, populated with towns, townships and hamlets, fertilised and enlivened by cattle-breeding, stretched from the corners of the Andes, at San Cristóbal, to Paria, with salients into the *llanos* and along the Orinoco—in effect, the country which a Venezuelan can traverse today without touching the forest zones. It was the domain of the *encomenderos*, who bred cattle, cultivated the crops, and lived active lives. By this date there began to operate a new organised force, the missions, whose aim was to complete the assimilation of the natives who were still spread out within the boundaries of the province, and to go beyond the frontier, to the south, where neither the conqueror's sword nor the *encomendero's* spade had yet penetrated. Indeed this force began its work from the population already settled in a district, and soon produced a multiplicity of new villages in the east and in the *llanos*, and in other regions too. These mission villages did not become civilised through the gradual apprenticeship of the Indians, but as a result of a sort of cultural mixed breeding. The missions, even against their own rules, were the most important means by which the native was assimilated into the creole way of life, since they collected together groups of Indians and this facilitated the process. The mission was a kind of *encomienda* held by friars. Both the secular and the religious *encomendero* were obliged by law to look after the Indians, but both came up against the reality of the fact that the aboriginal cultures could not persist side by side with Hispanic culture.

It is interesting to note how both these institutions, which basically were very similar, came into conflict over their material interests: both the *encomenderos* and the missionaries claimed to govern the Indians for economic ends, and brought accusations against each other before the Crown. Since it possessed the better weapons—spiritual ones—the mission or religious *encomienda* won, supported as it was by a Catholic state.

As for the settlement of the country, the process of mixing culture and race, the incorporation of new lands into the creole culture, this was carried forward by the *encomenderos* during the first two centuries, and the task was completed by the missions from about 1650 onwards.

Both institutions, *encomienda* and mission, were successive attempts to solve legally and humanely the problem of the disparity between the life of the natives and the life of their conquerors. The thought behind this showed very great moral sensitivity, which was shattered by the collision with practical difficulties. As is usual in all that men attempt, the day-to-day dealing with the facts blunted men's imagination; and the Indians suffered.

The negro settlers did not affect the issue, since they did not represent any special problem to the Spanish nation nor to the individual conqueror. They were brought in as slaves, and this soon created doubts and therefore the introduction of laws on the subject. The numerical proportion of negroes did not greatly affect the racial composition of the settlers. Certainly, the Venezuelan was given a tinge of African blood and culture, which stimulated and invigorated the general mixture; but this bore no comparison with the torrential infusion of native blood. The negro as a settler was only important in certain restricted areas where there were mines or where the soil was favourable for one main crop, cacao. In towns there was a negro quarter which gradually became diluted and was absorbed into the general population. Whereas on the coast negro areas were important, in towns inland the negro was scarcely in evidence.

In fact the settlement of the country was carried out by the miscegenation which the Spaniard practised with the mass of the native population, with the small added influence of contact with the negroes. Both the *encomenderos* and the missionaries brought with them culture and organising ability, which they diffused among the *encomienda* Indians and the negro slaves and which had the most profound influence in the raising of the population to the level of creole culture.

The earliest truly Venezuelan history can be glimpsed in the fusing of peoples and cultures which took place in the *encomienda* towards the end of the sixteenth century, and in the mission village towards the end of the seventeenth century. Here were to be found the peasant, the artisan, the priest, the "artist", and the citizen, all making a new Venezuela. The town, in which tastes became refined and where power resided, cannot be explained in a vacuum, and needs to be seen against this background of the cultivated land and the remote village.

2. WHITES AND INDIANS

Although there were early attempts to establish settlements, it was really only after the foundation of El Tocuyo that there was a movement of colonisation. Two methods were used: the foundation of towns together with the distribution of house plots, and the creation of large farms for agriculture and stock-raising. When a town was founded, the soldiers present were given plots according to their merit, and were expected to build houses on them. Fields were also allocated for farms nearby. The leaders were granted large estates. From the beginning Indians were employed to build the houses, till the soil, and perform the daily tasks. These Indians were divided among the soldiers in *encomienda*, so that the conqueror was responsible for the welfare of the natives, who generally had first to be subdued. The *encomendero* was granted the Indians living in a certain area, and although this did not in law imply that he was given their land, in practice that land usually came to be considered as the property of the *encomendero*, who set up his farms there so that he could employ his labour force on the spot without having to transfer it elsewhere. The *encomienda* had been established in Hispaniola by Columbus, in practice though not in law, and Diego de Ordaz in 1532 had given an *encomienda* in Venezuela; but it was only at the settlement of El Tocuyo and Barquisimeto that the institution became properly established.

The Laws of the Indians included legislation on the *encomienda*. For example Law 1, Título 8, Libro 6 laid down that Indians should be collected in villages so that close contact with Spaniards should civilise them; and another law stated that the grants of *encomienda* Indians should consist of the native chief plus his subjects, who must be kept together. The *encomendero* received the grant for his own lifetime and for the life of one successor. The New Laws of the Indies in 1542 reiterated former prohibitions against the enslavement of the Indians, and laid down certain limitation on the use of Indians in *encomienda*: only males could be employed in the fields, and only those over twelve years of age, and then only for three days in the week. In return, they were to be paid a small wage and to receive housing and religious instruction. But these provisions were far from universally respected, as is proved by the need for fresh decrees for Venezuela in 1609, 1627 and 1662. The Franciscans complained about abuses, with the result that a decree of 1672 forbade personal service by Indians; but it was ignored and had to be reissued in 1676. It was enforced in 1679 by the governor Francisco de Alberro, who saw to it that Indian women were freed from labour, the men only made to labour three days a week, and that the small wage was paid to them. At the same time he freed Indians who had been brought forcibly from the *llanos* and made to perform labour. In 1686 a decree forbade in stronger terms all personal service by Indians, and the next year this was enforced through Venezuela.

In return for what was even in law almost free labour, the *encomendero* had to pay to the Crown a poll tax on each Indian, pay the cost of all religious services for his flock, protect the Indians in all ways, paying for their clothes, medicines and other needs, serve in the local militia and pay for other troops if needed, see to the roads in his district, and pay for the visits of investigating officials and bishops.

At the date when this institution was abolished in Venezuela, 1687, there were round Caracas 37 *encomiendas* with a total of 537 working Indians. For the first two centuries of colonial rule the *encomienda* had been the basis of the country's economy, and when it ended the settled Indian villages disappeared: the Indians had either fled to the remotest places, or had been exterminated or else had become, as was most common, part of the mixd mass of the population.

Clergy of various orders had entered the country at all times, but the first missions to settle for long among the natives were not established until after 1560. The Crown granted a certain region to a particular order for its missionary work, and the territories thus granted were still in the hands of the natives, atlhough possibly already traversed by explorers. A mission usually established itself close to the settled frontier, with the object of penetrating further into the wild territory from this base. The friars had first to learn the native languages; then they set out, accompanied by a few Indians already used to the white men, and established a small mission village in the interior. One friar would stay there, teaching religion and getting the local natives gradually used to wearing Spanish clothes and accustomed to a more civilised life. The various mission villages comprised the mission, ruled from the Prefecture or base. In each village the individual missionary ruled, although self-government by the natives was the declared aim, so that the Indian chief's authority was accorded apparent though not real respect. Once the natives were fully civilised, the village was supposed to pass under the authority of the normal powers of the country, that is to say the bishop and the secular administration. By this process, especially in the seventeenth and eighteenth centuries, extensive territories were added to settled Venezuela.

As early as 1513, 1515 to 1519 and in 1561 attempts had been made to set up missions in parts of Venezuela, but with no permanent success. Franciscans and Capuchins established themselves in Cumaná in 1650, and were assigned separate fields of work by the Crown. Again, in 1693 the king ordered the Capuchins in Caracas to set up a mission in the Maracaibo district, which was done by two friars in the next year. In 1749 this field was divided into two Prefectures, Maracaibo and Santa Marta. A Prefecture had been established in the *llanos* in 1658, with limits including the Caribbean, the Orinoco, the Meta and Lake Maracaibo. This immense territory was extended to the Upper Orinoco in 1765, and the new area became a separate Prefecture. Twelve Capuchins who reached Cumaná in 1680 began a mission in Guayana, starting in the island of Trinidad, where by 1702 they had five villages, together with three in Guayana proper. Jesuits worked on the rivers Casanare, Meta and Orinoco, and Dominicans, coming from New Granada, set themselves up in the Barinas region before 1644. Of all these mission fields, the most extensive and successful were those of Guayana and Cumaná.

The importance of the missions as agents of settlement was immense. For example, a very great number of the villages and small towns of the *llanos*, Guayana, and the east of the country owe their origin to the missionaries, and their native inhabitants insensibly became part of the Venezuelan people through the work of the religious orders. No important town originated in this way, only villages. But the missionaries also had an economic function: they started the great herds of cattle of the *llanos*, and opened up the interior to agriculture, with the help of the civil authorities and some individual colonists, although it was not the Indians who profited greatly from this movement, but the missionaries themselves and the new Spanish and creole population.

The War of Independence against Spain in the early nineteenth century brought to an end these missions, some of which were already dying as the natives became assimilated into the ordinary life of the country. This had happened to the mission villages of the *llanos*, which had become so mixed that during the eighteenth century they became ordinary villages. The Guayana missions were flourishing at the time of the War, but they were completely extinguished. The main reason for this was that the missions, run by Spanish priests, declared for the mother country and put their wealth in cattle at the disposal of the royalists. The patriots naturally took any opportunity of using the cattle for themselves, and even killed the missionaries in some places, as at Caruachi in 1817. This was not an anti-religious movement: the friars were simply regarded as enemies who might give considerable help to the royalists.

One example will show how the missions were affected. Santa María de Yacuario was founded in 1730, and its population gradually increased to 481 in 1788 and 661 in 1817. In that year the friars were killed, and from then the figures fell: 256 in 1820, 37 in 1833, nil in 1849. A century's training failed to fit the people to fend for themselves; and this can be regarded as evidence that mission training did not fit the Indians for life in white communities. Only complete miscegenation ever brought the Indians fully into the culture of the hispanicised Venezuela.

Yet the problems arising out of the destruction of the missions were soon recognised. Bolívar, the Liberator, when President of Great Colombia (which included Venezuela, Colombia and Ecuador), in 1828 passed a measure intended to aid the reestablishment of missions in Cumaná, Barcelona, Barinas, Maracaibo and Guayana. In 1858 there was a move to bring European priests to help run the missions in Guayana, while in 1890 the Archbishop of Caracas decided to find fifty missionaries for the various regions, and in 1893 certain remote districts were designated mission territories, especially in the furthest parts of Guayana. The Capuchins of Caracas were put in charge, and they were to bring out fifty more priests from Spain. The government's efforts culminated in laws of 1915 and 1921, which made the Catholic missions dependent on the

D

Ministry of the Interior and laid down rules for them. Each mission was obliged to have a church, a school, a hospital, and a house for the missionaries.

The missions now are organised in four large units. The Apostolic Vicariate of Puerto Ayacucho has been in existence since 1953, under the Salesians, and from 1932 to 1953 this mission laid its foundations as an Apostolic Prefecture. The Capuchins have the Apostolic Vicariate of Machiques (since 1943), working in the Venezuelan part of Guajira and in the Sierra de Perijá; and from 1922 they have run the Apostolic Vicariate of the Caroní, in the State of Bolívar, and in the Delta Amacuro Federal Territory until 1954, when the latter area became the district of the newly created Apostolic Vicariate of Tucupita.

A collection of all the legislation ever issued concerning the Indians of Venezuela has lately been published.[1] All governments have tried to resolve native questions, but certainly in colonial times practice was never in accord with the spirit of the law. Under Spanish law, the Indian was a minor, who had to be protected, whereas the Republic too hurriedly released the Indian and treated him as a full citizen. Both methods failed to bring the Indian into civilisation, but at least both showed deep concern for his welfare. The whole question is at the present time being thought out afresh, so that the laws may be in consonance with the real circumstances of the Indian.

In colonial times there were three sorts of Indian villages, each with a special form of administration. They were *encomienda* villages, villages which had once been mission villages, and mission villages; occasionally a white village would be set up next to a native village, and this resulted in miscegenation. The *encomienda* villages and those which were no longer mission villages payed tribute, and were ruled by a *corregidor* subordinate to the civil authority, who was supposed to protect and encourage the Indians, although this was often difficult. In the seventeenth century the Indians of the Andes district were ordered to be collected into seventeen villages, for greater ease in the task of converting and civilising them; but this "reduction" merely demoralised the natives and led to the loss of their former lands.

The Republic established Indian reserves, where the natives

---

1 *Fuero Indígena Venezolano*, 2 vols., ed. Fray Cesáreo de Armellada, Caracas 1954.

live on their own lands in what are called Communities. They are ruled by a Captain-governor, who represents the old chief, and acts as a police officer in his own area.

3. NEGROES

Slavery has always existed, although it is now forbidden among civilised peoples, and it may be regarded as one stage in the development of a culture. The Portuguese introduced the trade in black slaves to Europe from their African possessions, and a few personal slaves accompanied their masters on the early Spanish expeditions to America. From 1501 black slaves were allowed to be imported into Hispaniola, where they were used in the mines. Bartolomé de las Casas begged the king to allow a few black slaves to be brought in order to spare the Indians from the hard work which was crushing them, but he did not initiate or encourage the immense trade which grew up. The negroes were seized or bartered for on the African coast, and were of very varied stocks, cultures and languages. The Portuguese were the first to enter the trade, but the English and the Dutch soon followed, though not the Spanish, who merely bought and used the slaves.

In Venezuela a few blacks were used in early times in the pearl fisheries, but the Germans brought in the first contingents after 1528, when they made an agreement with the Crown to be allowed to import 4,000. A similar number was allowed by another contract of 1536. The actual numbers imported cannot in fact be determined, but from this time many were used in all the expeditions for rough work, and as time went on more were brought in, with licences from the Crown. In 1560 Sancho Briceño was permitted to import and distribute 200 blacks; in 1592 Simón de Bolívar (an ancestor of the Liberator) obtained permission for 3,000 "pieces", as they were called in the trade, to be imported into Venezuela. In the eighteenth century the monopolistic Guipúzcoa Company brought in various shipments of slaves. Many slaves were imported through contractors who included Portuguese, French, English, Italians and even some Spanish. The English took up to 80,000 slaves a year, and exported more than half to foreign countries, including the Spanish American possessions. In 1713, as a condition of accepting the Treaty of Utrecht, the English demanded and were given by Spain the right to export 4,800 negroes annually to Spanish America for a period of thirty years, and this was a valuable addition to Britain's trade. In 1784 an English contractor was allowed to take 4,000 slaves into Trinidad, and another in 1786 contracted to take 5,000 or 6,000 negroes to La Guaira and Havana. The Spanish Crown made large profits from the sale of the necessary licences, and indeed treated the slave trade as a source of national revenue. It was only in 1817 that King Ferdinand VII forbade the buying of slaves in Africa, and declared free all who came to Spanish ports.

The black slave was of primary economic importance in Venezuela, as in other parts of America. He formed the labour force on plantations, in some mines, and in the home. In Venezuela no actual slave market existed, but the trade entered all the provinces, besides those coastal regions where the negroes are now concentrated most strongly. Slaves were bought for money or bartered in exchange for local products such as meat, salt and cacao. The market was in Cartagena, in New Granada, where the slave-ships unloaded, and where, for example, in 1633 fourteen ships arrived with 800 or 900 slaves each. Conditions on the voyage from Africa and the treatment given by the traders were extremely cruel, although occasional humanitarians attempted to mitigate the evils, as did Pedro Claver (1580 to 1654), called the Saint of the Slaves, who worked in Cartagena to ease the lot of the negroes.

The slaves were used for all sorts of work. In the early days some prospected for mines and worked them for their masters. The first mines in Venezuela, at Borburata and Chirua, were worked by negroes, as were the mines near Barquisimeto, where a real village of about 200 blacks, including wives and children, worked under the supervision of Spaniards. Here a negro called Miguel led a rebellion in 1555 and even tried to take the capital of the district, Barquisimeto, but he and his followers were soon annihilated by Spaniards of the conqueror type. Some mines in the Andes were also exploited by negroes.

But Venezuela was not rich in mines, and the negroes were most needed for work on the land. The large estates of *encomenderos* depended on black slave labour. Tobacco in Barinas, cacao around Caracas and near Lake Maracaibo, cotton in El Tocuyo and Carora, and later sugar cane, all required negro labour. It would be true to say that colonial agriculture was maintained by the negro. The negro could work hard in a tropical climate, and that is what he was made to do. In Spain it was realised that this labour force was necessary for the agriculture of all Spanish America, and an economist writing in 1787 recommended the importation of 10,000 a year to make America flourish, and thought that Spain should seize slaving bases in Africa so that this most precious commodity should not be entirely in the hands of foreigners.

Although the numbers of slaves brought into Venezuela cannot be calculated, Humboldt gave the figure 62,000 for 1812, following Andrés Bello, Luis López Méndez and Manuel Palacio Fajardo. Maracaibo province had 6,000 in 1787, and already in 1555 several hundreds were in Cabo de la Vela. Humboldt's figures do not include villages of free negroes and the very great number of these negroes who had become part of the mixed population.

The negro was bought as a tool, and the price depended on age, sex, physical fitness and experience. The wild negro straight from Africa cost less than the "*ladino*", who already knew Spanish and the jobs at which he would have to work. Besides the mines and fields, negroes worked in houses as servants and even as children's nurses. There is the notable case, for example, of Bolívar's black nanny, Matea. In war, the negro became a hero and fought faithfully for the patriots against the royalists, as did the legendary Negro Primero of the *Llanos* cavalry.

Colonial laws protected the slave in the same theoretical way as they did the Indian. The master was supposed to give the new slave religious instruction. The punishments he might inflict were laid down for each case, including whipping and even death. The master was supposed to build healthy quarters for the slaves, keeping males and females separate unless they were married; he had to provide a hospital for the care of the sick; and he had to look after burials, superannuated slaves and children too young to work. But of course the efficacy of the laws depended entirely on the men who applied them. This status of slaves persisted in Venezuela until March 24, 1854, when President José Gregorio Monagas declared their absolute liberty. On the other hand, even in colonial times a slave might obtain his liberty by buying it under the law of manumission; and the Frenchman Depons, who visited Venezuela in the very early years of the nineteenth century, complained that the law of manumission worked too well, so that the labour force was not so great as it ought to be.

It has been said that the negro part of the racial composition of the Venezuelans has produced in the people a spirit of rebellion, ferocity in battle, inconstancy, flightiness, improvidence, shiftiness, negligence; but these faults can be seen in the Spanish conquerors too, although perhaps they predominate in the negro. At any rate, the negroes mixed their blood with Indians and Spaniards, and injected a very important element into the Venezuelan people. The negro, strong and active, quickly assimilated the intellectual culture of the country and learned the Spanish language and customs. Already in the eighteenth century a large proportion of the town-dwellers was descended from negroes mixed with Indian or Spanish blood. The owner of slaves himself was not above taking a negro woman, not only on the estate but even in the town, and this brought forth an innumerable generation of mulattoes. The lower-class Spaniards lived with slave women, producing large numbers of both mulattoes and *mestizos*, or offspring of white and Indians.

Today, Venezuela's whole coastal zone is dominated by the negro element, but it also spread throughout the whole land, including even the most remote Andes. It is true that there exists no negro problem in any Spanish-speaking country today, because the negro has been assimilated into society without any trouble. In Venezuela this phenomenon of complete assimilation, social, political and economic, is of the greatest importance. Venezuela has a tradition of liberty and equality for all which in some other nations has still to be evolved. The negro of colonial days, a slave and therefore inferior, has given way to the educated man, the "creole" negro, who is one of the unifying links of the Venezuelan people.

CHAPTER IV

Colonial Life in Venezuela

I. INTRODUCTION

THE Spanish author Américo Castro has put forward the idea that history happens in a particular "essential home", and has written: 'All the peoples of the Iberian Peninsula and of Hispanic America, in spite of their very marked differences, live in a very similar essential home, even though they are separated by certain clear nuances.'[1] He is not, of course writing about the concrete environment, but about a style or texture of life, "vividura" as he has named it. There is no doubt that the cultural background of Venezuela is Spanish, as I have insisted in these pages and elsewhere.[2] In spite of this, when one notices differences between a Spaniard and a Venezuelan one must remember that each has had to live according to needs which were at times opposed.

Venezuelan history does not merely begin with the native cultures and then continue with the Hispanic one. This latter certainly contains the main ingredients of Venezuelan culture: social forms, language, religion. What the Venezuelans have made of these things is the meaning of the word "history" for them. The possession of these ingredients, which have undergone the influences of native and negro cultures and other subsequent forces, all this constitutes Venezuelan historical life and brings together Venezuelans in a common society. If we say that the Venezuelans form a Hispanic culture, we speak the truth; but left at that, without further explanation, the expression is not the whole truth. For the Venezuelans have done something with that culture; they have assimilated it to their own immediate interests; they have lived it and converted it into their own history.

[1] Américo Castro, *La realidad histórica de España*, México D F 1954, p. 58.
[2] Guillermo Morón, *Los orígenes históricos de Venezuela*, Madrid 1954, p. 327.

The most interesting moment of Venezuelan history, from the sociological point of view, is to be found in the process of Spaniard turning into Venezuelan. To trace the subtle course of that change, of that birth of a different culture, is a feat of intelligence. The conqueror lost his Iberian home, yet retained his way of life. For how long? Perhaps until the second generation, when the *encomendero* was a creole, born in America. But perhaps it was not until the third generation that there appeared the notion of the "land of our fathers", the homeland, applied to Venezuela, although this did not imply the idea of separate statehood, but only that of land, land rendered human by possession.

Once the process of taking possession, the conquest, was completed, the home was built. The natives could not set up a true society, but the conquerors could, and so could the creole, born in the new country. What we call colonial life is not merely the picturesque parade of the various classes, but the living of all of them together; this living together from one generation to the next gradually brought into being the essential quality of Venezuelan life. It is in the seventeenth century that we may expect to find the change going on: we know all about the coming of the conqueror, and then we can see that in the eighteenth century there exists a society different from that of Spain; but its actual growth, and the process of transformation, which took place over three centuries, have not yet been investigated, and it is there that are to be found the answers to many questions.

In the history of the old Province, in the period which we call the Colony, the living germ of the Venezuelan tradition is seen. Already in the seventeenth century there were groups of men who were able to understand what was happening in the creole world, although the picture did not become clear until the eighteenth century. In the life of those people who by 1670 found themselves bereft of their *encomiendas* there was bitterness, just as there was among the leaders of Venezuelan society in 1728 when the Guipúzcoa Company was given complete commercial monopoly in the country. This bitterness is the result of the feeling that these people were not allowed to count for much in their own homeland, in the land which they themselves had tamed, in the city which their own forefathers had brought to life, and in the moral environment in which they had their being.

When the English in 1590 attacked Caracas, which was then hardly more than the suggestion of a town, they met no resistance except from Alonso Andrea de Ledesma, an old man who had been in the army which founded Trujillo. He sallied forth alone, armed and on horseback, like a Don Quixote. But deeds like this do not constitute a whole history. For that it still needed the smuggling adventures of the half-breed Andresote, carried out with the connivance of the authorities and the landowners and with the help of the Dutch interlopers. The growth of a ruling class was complemented by the artistic insight of a slave who painted a portrait of his mistress.

The royal decree of 1795 which permitted men to buy rank found the ground already prepared, although it met opposition from the higher-class creoles. The coloured people had been rising slowly, like some huge surge in the sea of Venezuela's social history.

Some explanation, too, must be given of the reason why one fiery writer could, at the end of the eighteenth century, almost shatter that society's philosophy: Valverde, who was the interpreter of a feeling for change common to the great men of that period on the verge of Independence. This is what that colonial author said: 'I believe that I have every right to say what I like, good or bad, about Señor Aristotle, as has had anyone who up to now has taken a fancy to write about him; and neither Popes nor Councils nor Inquisition have forced such a man to eat his own words; and unless I am mistaken, all who have followed this path have reaped immortal glory in the republic of letters.' Behind the words beats a spirit of dedication to critical truth, which only appears when man has attained sufficient dignity, elevation of mind and spiritual liberty.

The colony, then, is not merely one moment in the story of Venezuelan history. It is much more than that, much more than a period: it is a whole complex life in which the Venezuelan came to know and respect his own nationhood.

2. SOCIETY

The colonial period lasted for about three hundred years, from the time of the Spanish settlement to the emancipation of Venezuela, in 1811. Colonial society was being built all this time on the basis of the contacts between whites, Indians and negroes.

An enumeration of the various social groups in the country, it must be understood, is only valid for a particular moment in history, for there was no rigid classification throughout the whole of colonial times. Some authors have described the groups in colonial society as castes, because of the inequalities established between them by practice as well as by law. Now it seems preferable to talk of social classes, since this implies a hierarchical social order while admitting the possibility of passing from one class to another in spite of the barriers which existed against the rise of inferiors. This class structure was not founded on political principles, but on historical facts. The idea of democracy, which is a modern theory of political co-existence, has no meaning for the colonial period, as the historian Caracciolo Parra-Pérez has pointed out.[1] 'The term democracy, as understood in the modern sense, is not applicable to colonial society, which was composed of castes and founded on inequality.' But he then remarks that the democracy of the ancients is compatible with the existence of these castes, or rather classes as it is preferable to call them, as in Athens, the pattern of democracy, despite her privileged citizens. Modern political democracy is also compatible with a society organised on a class basis, as is seen in England, and even more clearly in the United States of America, where the negroes are in practice and even in law second-class citizens. Inequality was the basis of Venezuelan colonial society.

One can accept in general the classification of society in use since Humboldt's day, even though it strictly applied only to the last years of the colonial period, when a long tradition was already established. The groups consisted firstly of the whites, if one considers Spaniards as white, for it should be remembered that the Spanish is one of the most mixed races of Europe, especially since the Moorish domination of the Peninsula, which lasted for centuries. These whites were European Spaniards and "Spaniards" born in Venezuela. Then there were the blacks, who formed as slaves the lowest level of the scale, although there were some free negroes. Thirdly the Indians, who were practically in the same situation as the blacks in spite of the laws which recognised their special status; then *mestizos*, off-

---

[1] Caracciolo Parra-Pérez, *El régimen español en Venezuela*, Madrid 1932, p. 61.

spring of white and Indian; mulattoes, offspring of white and negro; and *zambos*, offspring of Indian and negro. Other groups were formed by the crossing of these, and each had a name implying the racial mixture in the members. In fact it was impossible to differentiate accurately between the various cross-breedings, so that it is easiest to talk of a class of *pardos*, coloured people, including all the mixed breeds, and a class of creoles, meaning the whites or those accepted as white. This leaves us with three main groups: the creole oligarchy, the rich and dominant class; the large class of coloured, including all *mestizos*, mulattoes and so forth who were free but not rich; and the class of slaves, including in effect the negroes, the Indians and mixed breeds who were born slaves.

The conquerors founded the towns, divided the land, seized the mines and dominated the natives, becoming their masters. They made Venezuela their home; and it became even more "home" when their children were born there, since the real interest of these lay in the new land and in increasing their wealth in that country. The conquerors were recognised by the Crown as the ruling class, and this right descended from generation to generation. Before the end of the sixteenth century there is mention of a class of creoles, Spaniards born in America, possessors of the land and rulers of the towns. The dominating class consisted, then, of the conquerors and their descendants. Although Spaniards continued to reach Venezuela throughout the colonial period, they were not numerous owing to certain restrictions, and the amount of Spanish colonisation was very small in proportion to the size of the country: this was generally the case in all the Spanish American possessions. These newcomers worked at various occupations, and although they did not always see eye to eye with the creoles, in effect they formed part of the creole dominant class.

The group of black slaves grew even larger as their labour was needed for more agricultural enterprises; while the purely Indian group tended to diminish as the race died out and its members became assimilated.

In the seventeenth century the creole class consisted of two distinct groups. Firstly there were the city men, owners of large estates which they might seldom visit. These were called in Venezuela the *mantuanos*, or, by the lower classes, *grandes cacaos*. Then there were the small farmers, the *cosecheros*, who had little contact with the big towns. The first of these groups were the aristocracy, proud of a purity of blood they never had and of Spanish titles bought with the country's products. There was not enough time for a hereditary nobility to arise in Venezuela. Each town was dominated by a group of families, mainly descended from the original settlers, who held the local council offices. The interests of the leading groups in the various towns did not always coincide.

The opposition between these various classes was most evident in the last century of colonial rule, when the creoles claimed greater consideration from both the coloureds and the Spaniards. They gained privileges in all aspects of life, in church, in the street, in the home. The wearing of certain clothes was forbidden the coloureds; and the right to sit in the choir in church, the right to bear arms and to flaunt titles, were jealously guarded. The numerous legal cases in which creole families were involved show the excessive social cantankerousness of the times, brought on by the growth of the number of coloureds who began to fill the countryside and the towns and to monopolise certain functions. Close intermarriage reduced the great names to a few families in each town. The creoles married their children to relatives in order to retain municipal power in their own hands, and also out of snobbery: a *mestizo* might be descended from slaves.

All the highest posts were held by Peninsular Spaniards. Political, judicial, military and ecclesiastical posts were awarded in Spain to court favourites, to friends of ministers, and sometimes to men of merit; but the creoles were kept out of them—a practice which caused constant quarrels, complaints and ill-feeling, since the latter believed themselves to be more qualified for these posts as the people of the country. In the whole of Spanish America up to 1811, of all the archbishops and bishops ever appointed 700 were Peninsulars and 278 were creoles; of the viceroys 166 were Peninsulars and four were creoles; of the captains-general 588 were Peninsulars and fourteen were creoles. Yet all were Spanish subjects and legally there were no differences between them.

In Venezuela all the high functionaries were Peninsulars. They naturally identified themselves socially with the leading creoles, although the latter accused them of disliking the distinguished families and favouring the aspirations of the coloureds. Any governor who did not gain the support of the *mantu-anos* of the main towns could not govern or live in peace, and the same was true for ecclesiastics. The history of Fray Mauro Tovar is a good example. He was bishop from 1640 to 1654, during which period his arbitrary behaviour kept Caracas in constant turmoil, until he had to be transferred to Chiapa in Central America. Strangely enough, although he was tyrannical with the creoles, it was with the governor that he came into conflict; which proves that the unity of the various groups was not always effective.

In sum, the dominance of the Peninsulars was not absolute: they were the King's representatives, but the exercise of their functions centred round the creoles.

Socially and economically the creoles were the dominant class. By creoles, of course, is meant those considered white, with no tinge of colour, although this is purely theoretical, since the descendants of the conquerors had some colour, however much diluted. The creole oligarchy claimed and obtained all sorts of privileges, behaving as an aristocracy jealous of its prerogatives in face of the central authority and the more numerous lower orders. They had indisputable power by virtue of their importance in the town councils and their possession of vast estates.

Each big town had its own ruling oligarchy, who had local rather than national views. The important families of every town entrenched themselves in the town council and exercised a municipal dominion from it. The rod of justice, the royal standard, the right to process under a canopy, were means of gaining distinction. Each town was a little republic wanting to rule itself. Local political power, ruling the town, was in their hands, and they were the mainstay of local affairs. Simply to list the names of the town councillors of Caracas and other big towns shows how these powers were confined to a few families. In Caracas one meets time and again the names Mijares de Solór-zano, Blanco, Tovar, López Méndez, Toro, Palacio y Sojo; in Mérida Gaviria, Dávila y Rojas, Ruiz Valero, Trejo de la Parra, Paredes, Bohórquez; in Trujillo Briceño, Paredes, Pacheco, Mendoza Uzcátegui; in Coro Colina; and so on. This dominance was supported by wealth, that is the possession of land. The big landowners were in effect the descendants of the conquerors, with riches in cacao, tobacco or cattle, and this gave them power. When wealth became more widespread through the appearance of other profitable occupations and the growth of the small farmer and merchant classes, the superiority of the *mantuanos* began to diminish. At the same time the coloureds began to claim and even to win some privileges. It is no coincidence, for example, that about 1761 the free mulatta Jerónima Garcés should take the mayor of Coro, José Alonso Gil, to law to prove her right to wear a lace-trimmed mantilla.

In general the Spaniards were public servants in administration, defence, finance and the Church. The creoles had most of the municipal offices, but really occupied themselves in agriculture and stock-raising, using slaves or free labour, though some exploited the few mines in Venezuela. There grew up a class of traders who wandered from town to town, and usually these were energetic immigrants from the Canary Islands. The coloureds and lowest-class whites plied various trades: they were the carpenters, blacksmiths, silver-smiths, tailors, builders, bootmakers, butchers, and so on, who tended to do quite well and rise in the social scale.

In the country districts there emerged a large number of independent small farmers who on occasions tried to gain predominance in the towns and who were opposed to all monopoly. A lucrative occupation for men of the most diverse social backgrounds was that of muleteer, an occupation which owed its existence to the breeding of mules, horses and donkeys, the needs of commerce and the growth of agriculture. The muleteer was an important agent in the spreading of fashions and ideas. The wheat of Tunja and Vélez, the honey and the biscuit of Ocaña, the cotton cloth of El Tocuyo, the cattle of the *llanos* circulated through the efforts of the muleteers, who travelled in troops with their animals over all roads, sometimes evading the *alcabala* (sales tax), and smuggling tools, silks and books in their panniers.

The coloured people began to appear in the earliest days, when soldiers and other Spaniards on Cubagua and Margarita cohabited with Indian and negro women. Very few Spanish women accompanied the conquerors and first settlers, so the white man usually took an Indian or negro woman: it was in effect a masculine invasion which produced mixed breeding. In the new towns the soldier took a woman from his *encomienda* Indians, either as a concubine or as a legitimate wife, and for this reason the towns were the first centres of miscegenation. The offspring joined the father and followed him in war, so that cultural mixing was quickly accomplished, with the Indian mother usually forgotten. In the first century few Spanish women came to the country, and when they did they were willing to marry the Hispanicised sons of the conquerors, who took their fathers' names and language, knowing nothing of the maternal customs and tongue.

In the Indian villages set up by the missions or by the civil authority miscegenation also took place. These native villages were founded near to Spanish settlements, and this facilitated the process. Most Venezuelan villages and townships had such an origin. On the large estates the labourers and soldiers, particularly the masters, cohabited with Indian women and slave negresses, and the same happened at the mines. The sensualism of the Spanish race has always been more powerful than its prejudices and religious dogmas. In the eighteenth century Venezuela contained nothing but coloured people: the dominant creoles were simply an economic class which had not escaped the miscegenation any more than had the others.

There is no doubt that the Spaniard was the founder of Venezuelan society, since he brought the culture which is now Venezuelan. But his blood did not stay pure, and became mixed with that of Indians and negroes: this is the important fact so far as the Venezuelan race is concerned. The writer Arturo Uslar Pietri has given a penetrating, if perhaps not altogether exact, analysis: 'The Venezuelan *mestizo* is the confluence of the three racial elements. His sensibility is delicate; his gift of adaptation, rapid; his intelligence, lively and swift; he is very intuitive, ambitious, egalitarian, superstitious, violent, generous, improvident, poor in popular art, sensitive to music, an enemy of systematisation, of order and of hierarchy: It is the *mestizo* soul which provides the nation's psychology and characterises its history: a nation tormented by its two basic passions, equality and faith in the coming of a saviour.'[1]

3. POLITICAL AND ADMINISTRATIVE ORGANISATION

Spain ruled her possessions in America and the Philippines through a special organisation whose head was the Council of

[1] Arturo Uslar Pietri, *Obras selectas*, Madrid 1953, p. 854.

the Indies, and which shouldered the enormous burden of governing in the name of the King these immense and disparate territories. The so-called colonies were in fact regarded as integral parts of the national territory and not merely as colonies. The basic unit of the empire was the province, a name used vaguely at first to mean the land granted to a discoverer who would explore and settle it, and later used as an administrative term meaning a *gobernación*, or a division ruled by a governor. Various provinces or *gobernaciones* might be grouped to form a Captaincy-general (as was to be the case with Venezuela) or the more important Viceroyalty.

The earliest Venezuelan province was the *gobernación* awarded to the Welsers in 1528, which included a large part of present-day Venezuela. Various other such *gobernaciones* were set up in different parts of the country at different times from very early days, but not all survived to be united in 1777 into the Captaincy-general then established. Of those which did, and which were independent of each other until that date, the most important was the *Gobernación* of Venezuela, created for the Welsers in 1528. It was the biggest, most populous and most advanced province of the area. Its capital was finally fixed in Caracas after early experiments at Coro, El Tocuyo, Barquisimeto and Valencia. It fell under the judicial authority of the Audiencia (high court, with certain administrative functions) of Santo Domingo until 1717. From then until 1723 it was under the audiencia set up at Bogotá, the capital of the new Viceroyalty of New Granada. In 1723 the Viceroyalty was suppressed and Venezuela returned to the care of Santo Domingo until 1739, when, with the re-creation of the Viceroyalty the province returned to the Audiencia of Bogotá until 1742. Then it passed again under Santo Domingo until 1786, when the Audiencia of Caracas was set up.

The province of Cumaná was created in 1569 from the remains of various others which had not survived. The province of Guayana was created in 1591, although it had in fact been in existence before then. Its capital originally was Santo Tomé, which in 1768 removed and became Angostura, now named Ciudad Bolívar. The province of Margarita, orginally given to Villalobos, passed to the Crown in 1600. The province of Trinidad was created for Sedeño in 1530. It was eventually seized by the English in 1797, and the Treaty of Amiens in 1802 left it in

An old native of the state of
Zulia

A peasant of the Barlovento
region of Miranda State

A medicine man of the Baras
tribe from the Frontier region of
Venezuela, Colombia and Brazil

A peasant woman of the
Venezuelan Andes, Mérida State

FRANCISCO DE MIRANDA

JOSÉ ANTONIO PÁEZ

JOSÉ GREGORIO MONAGAS

ANTONJO GUZMÁN BLANCO

British hands. The province of Maracaibo was constituted in 1777, but it was carved from the previously existing provinces of Mérida and La Grita. All these provinces had judicial histories somewhat similar to that of Venezuela. After the creation of the Captaincy-general of Venezuela they all remained in it as administrative units, and to their number in 1786 was added a new province, that of Barinas.

The early provinces were ruled by a governor who was both civil and military chief, and was usually given the title of *adelantado*, which was superior to that of plain governor. Later, the provinces were ruled by ordinary governors, who were the highest officials until 1777. Each of the six provinces had its governor, recommended to the King by the Council of the Indies, but appointed by the King alone. There was no fixed term of office, but by the end of the colonial period it was usually not longer than four years.

The governor's actions were ruled by the Laws of the Indies, and the Council of the Indies supervised his administration and even his private life. Judges were sent out to investigate the governor's conduct if necessary, and at the end of his term he and his staff underwent the *residencia*. This meant that a judge appointed by the Council opened an enquiry in the capital of the province so that all complaints against the administration could be heard, and at the end the *residencia* judge declared the governor guilty or not guilty of misdemeanours. Appeal to the Council was supposed to be allowed, but there was the case of the *residencia* judge Juan Pérez de Tolosa who both condemned to death and executed Carvajal, in 1546. Certainly the *residencia* restrained the abuse of power. An interesting example of a *residencia* is the case of Mateo Gual, governor of Cumaná from 1753 to 1757, who was judged by the governor of Margarita, Alonso del Río y Castro. Del Río was sent to Cumaná in 1759 to take over power as *residencia* judge of Gual, although another governor had taken office already. When the enquiry began Del Río sent officers to the chief towns to collect complaints against the old governor and his officials. Various charges were made: for example, that there were no prisons in the towns; that there were not enough butcher's shops; that the land was not being cultivated. In the end the sentence was that Gual should pay a minute fine for not establishing the prisons, and the other charges against him were not proved. Gual, as was usual, defended

E

himself; but the case is extraordinary, for his record in administration and in general was good and he only had a small fine
to pay. Some governors ended in prison and were ruined as a result of their *residencia*.

Lieutenant-governors acted in the name of the governor in
the various towns of the province, and there was also a number
of other minor officials under him, such as the justices of the
small towns and villages.

The political system bred strong regional feeling in the Venezuelan provinces, so that a native of one was almost a foreigner
in another. Each province tried to remain independent, although by the eighteenth century they formed two large
groups, the western including Venezuela and Maracaibo, and
the eastern including Guayana, Cumaná, Margarita and Trinidad. When in 1739 the King extended the authority of the governor of Venezuela to the other provinces merely for a campaign against contraband, the governor himself, Zuloaga, raised
objections because of the difficulties he experienced in dealing
with the heads of the other provinces. Yet history, situation and
commercial and even family links worked toward the union of
all the provinces which came in 1777, when King Charles III
issued a royal decree unifying all under the province of Venezuela in political, economic and military affairs, and placing all
under the Audiencia of Santo Domingo for judicial matters.

The new Captaincy-general of Venezuela had its capital at
Caracas, the seat of the Captain-general, who had both civil and
military authority. The other provinces were still under governors, who were, however, subordinate to the Captain-general of
Venezuela. The seven Captains-general who ruled Venezuela
from 1777 until the Independence were all high army officers.
The new organisation was completed by the creation in 1786 of
the Audiencia of Caracas for the judicial affairs of all Venezuela, and it had been foreshadowed by the creation in 1776 of
the Intendancy of the Army and Royal Treasury of Venezuela,
dealing with the common questions of defence and finance. In
this way modern Venezuela was sketched out, since the country was already partially unified by the time of the revolution
against Spain. In 1803 a Papal Bull made Caracas the seat of an
archbishop with authority over the subordinate bishops of Guayana and Mérida.

The towns were governed by their councils, the *cabildos*, the first of which were appointed by the conquering founders from among their soldiers. The councillors elected two mayors, one of whom was the senior (*alcalde de primer voto*) and acted as magistrate. Every January 1st the citizens elected new councillors, and the latter chose the mayors. In Caracas from 1594 the councillorships were sold and became family property, although the King granted life-long membership to two men, Garci-González de Silva and Simón de Bolívar. In the eighteenth century this town council had twelve bought seats, and four free ones for Spanish residents, one town clerk and two annually-elected mayors, and besides other officials, a standard-bearer who had special privileges in the council. Other towns usually had only six councillors and two mayors.

The town council saw to the administration of the town and its large surrounding country district; the senior mayor was the executive and had police powers; officers heard minor law cases and others looked after the hygiene and the markets of the town, and other such local affairs. Gradually in the colonial period these powers were whittled down; yet in Venezuela the town councils at times had great autonomy and were centres of what political activity there was. The early councils naturally possessed wide powers throughout immense districts, and they attempted to assert political power, resisting the appointment of governors, for example, in 1533 and 1547. Again, in 1560 the town councils of Venezuela obtained from Philip II a decree that in the case of the death of a governor the mayors of the towns should govern pending the appointment by the King of a new governor. In spite of this decision, the councils accepted interim governors appointed by the Audiencia of Santo Domingo in 1561 and 1656. But in 1674, at the death of the governor of Caracas, the mayors took over the administration of the province and refused to accept an interim governor appointed by the Audiencia of Santo Domingo. An appeal to the King brought a royal decree of 1676 confirming that of 1560, and the right won by Caracas eventually became one of the Laws of the Indies until 1736, when Philip V decreed that in such cases a lieutenant-governor should take over until a new governor was appointed.

The important part played by the dominant creole class in the town councils has already been stressed. Their power on the whole worked against any higher arbitrary power, exercised either by the government or by the clergy. But the town council not only represented the interests of this dominant class, it was sensitive to the voices of the other people of the town. The "open council", where all citizens might meet on special occasions, was a sort of public debate, followed by a vote, on important questions. It was not merely an aristocratic club, but a centre for work and agitation on behalf of the whole town and even the region. The oligarchies certainly swayed the councils, but it was the oligarchies who had to lead society. In other provinces of America the town councils had less importance in history than had those of Venezuela, because they were in many cases hamstrung by the presence of viceroys and audiencias. It should be remembered that the creoles who dominated the town councils in Venezuela were the class who brought forth the emancipation movement. The councils gave some training in participation in government, through the open council meetings. The material and moral progress of the towns was inspired by the town councils, which were indeed local governments.

4.   ECONOMIC AND FISCAL POLICY

Mercantilism and the bullionist theory underlay Spain's economic policies in her empire: that is, the state intervened in all aspects of trade and production both in order to bend the economy to certain ends and in order to retain the "wealth" of the empire inside the empire, and as far as possible for the benefit of Spain herself. In this, Spain did not differ appreciably from other expanding nations of the time. Spain tried to regulate prices, routes, and types of production. Precious stones and metals were sought to the exclusion of productive industry, and America became one great mine, the private property of the King. In the sixteenth century the production of gold was 8,000 kilogrammes a year, and that of silver 400,000. The influx of this into Spain and Europe caused inflation and upheavals, and indeed America became a burden too great for Spain. The Spanish authorities understood no more than anyone else the significance of bullion, and the world witnessed the paradox of a nation swimming in gold and silver yet which was one of the poorest in Europe; and none realised that gold is only valuable according to the amount of the fruits of labour which it can buy. Instead of concentrating on production, the Spaniards tried to stop their own impoverishment by keeping as much as possible of the bullion in their own hands, which was fatal.

In Venezuela the earliest settlers had begun to cultivate crops on small plots, and friars and soldiers had planted orchards of trees brought from Spain. At the foundation of the towns, such as El Tocuyo and Barquisimeto, plots for houses and for farms were distributed to the colonists. These were worked in conjunction with the *encomienda*. Further afield, and especially in the seventeenth century, arose the large estate, which was the beginning of the wealthy oligarchy. Stock-raisers established ranches in appropriate places, especially in the *llanos*.

Agriculture began with native maize grown for the urgent need of bread. Indians worked at this while some survived, but the Spaniards themselves quickly learned how to grow maize, and many of the common soldiers became small farmers. Spanish fruit trees filled the interior yards of houses, as at La Grita, where the figs, pomegranates and quinces became famous. In the Andes there was soon wheat, and elsewhere bananas and roots and other vegetables. This household agriculture, though enough to help the Spaniards take root, was not enough for a real economy. Shortly there arose an export trade in certain products which became the basis of a flourishing colonial agriculture, such as cotton, from which was made the famous cloth of El Tocuyo. It was also spun and woven in Trujillo, Mérida, Barquisimeto, Maracaibo, Araure and Acarigua, in quantities sufficient to clothe Indians, negroes and whites, and also to provide for export. In the seventeenth century cotton growing was abandoned until half way through the next century. The most important crop, though, was cacao, with 150,000 quintals a year, and this formed the basis of the wealth of the coast, the valleys, and parts of the Andes. Tobacco was grown, especially in Barinas, and indigo reached great prosperity after 1770; while other crops included sugar and coffee. The authorities interested themselves in the progress of agriculture.

These examples are worth attention: in 1761 the province of Cumaná was supported by the farming of maize, bananas, roots, cacao and sugar cane, although the two last were not widely grown. Around Cumaná itself there were 157 small estates, in Cumanacoa twenty-six; Barcelona had fifty, some of them growing cacao. By 1785 the province of Caracas had 1,444 cacao estates, 220 growing indigo, 436 growing sugar, two to-

bacco plantations and thirty mixed estates. Maracaibo had large
cacao estates in the valleys of San Pedro, near the mountains towards Gibraltar. Barinas produced about 150,000 pounds of tobacco and 39,000 bushels of cacao.

The conquerors also brought the first domesticated animals to
Venezuela, either from the Antilles or direct from Spain. Stock-
raising quickly became important, and New Granada was being
supplied from Venezuela already in the sixteenth century; it is
known that one Pedro de Villarroel was herding cattle from Trujillo via Mérida and San Cristóbal to Pamplona in 1570. Soon
leather became an important commercial product—about
170,000 pounds in 1720 in the province of Caracas. Carora became celebrated for its cordovan leather, and produced with it
pack-saddles, whips, plaited thongs, wine-skins and pouches,
which were exchanged for the cacao and tobacco of Barquisimeto, the sugar of El Tocuyo and Trujillo, and indispensable
European articles in Caracas. Guanare, Barquisimeto, El Tocuyo
and Coro had quantities of mules, some of which were sold to
the nearby Dutch settlers.

Intensive stock-raising began at El Tocuyo, where in the
1540s Pérez de Tolosa found 300 cattle, 500 sheep, and large
numbers of pigs, horses and mares. In 1548 the industry began
to spread to the llanos from here, and by the end of the century
the llanos and other grasslands supported an enormous population of cattle, some of them ownerless. Often these wild cattle
were hunted simply for their hides. The trade in hides attained
first place in the Venezuelan economy between 1620 and 1665,
and played an important part throughout the whole colonial
period. The missions made a great contribution to the development of cattle-ranching, and the trade in dried meat and cattle
on the hoof was the great mainstay of Guayana as well as the
llanos. In the llanos the majority of estates were cattle ranches.
El Pao, for example, had thirty estates, of which nineteen were
ranches, with 4,151 head of cattle; Barcelona, with seventy-two
ranches, had 43,000 cattle—enough to make a country rich, it
was said. By 1789 Guayana was believed to possess 220,000
head, and shortly afterwards the cattle in the provinces of Caracas, Barcelona, Guayana and Maracaibo were estimated to be
over a million. The Venezuelan of the llanos was a rancher and
cowhand, the legendary llanero, a kind of centaur similar to the
gaucho of the River Plate. Carora was known for breeding

goats, Táchira for its sheep, Trujillo for its pigs, and everywhere domestic fowl were kept in the yards of the houses.

The Venezuelan provinces were never so rich in mines of gold and silver as were some other parts of America, but there were some mines, mainly of gold and copper, and there was a wealth of pearls. Pearl fisheries were established at Cubagua and Cabo de la Vela, as well as other points on the coast; and pearls were the first real riches which Spain drew from the country, in the first half of the sixteenth century. Later pearls became less prized, but served as money in Venezuela in the seventeenth century. The only gold at first was that taken from the Indians, and the earliest mines were those of Borburata, discovered by Juan de Villegas. From 1551 mines were exploited at San Pedro, and gave rise to the growth of towns at Barquisimeto and Valencia. Here occurred the slave rising led by Miguel, and Indians too attacked the mines. Other mines were discovered at Los Teques, San Sebastián, and Apa and Carapa in the Tuy valley, but production was never great, and the mines were abandoned at the beginning of the seventeenth century. Two copper mines were opened; one in La Grita was soon abandoned, but the other, at Cocorote, was fairly successfully worked from 1625 by black slaves under a government administrator.

Taxation was based mainly on production and income, although the Indians had a special tribute to pay, and for some time in the seventeenth century free negroes and mulattoes paid a poll tax. Treasury inspectors went to Venezuela with the early expeditions in order to collect the King's fifth or some other fixed proportion from the gold, slaves and other riches found. In New Cadiz a treasury branch was set up, and others continued to be established during the whole period until the creation of the Intendancy in 1776. A branch consisted of a Treasurer, an inspector and an accountant, who worked in the capital of each province, and their main equipment was a chest with three locks in which the revenue was stored. The officers each had one key, and the chest was opened only in the presence of them all. In 1560 inspectors ceased to be appointed throughout the Indies, and the local governor took their place, thus bringing the fiscal system more closely under the political authority.

The treasury officers collected taxes and paid all the administrative expenses of their area, appointing lieutenants to work in subordinate towns. The actual taxes grew in number as time went on, and their rate was frequently varied, or at times individuals and even provinces might be exempted. The main taxes were the *almojarifazgo*, the *alcabala*, the *avería* and the *media anata;* although there was too the Royal fifth, levied on pearls and gold, and in the early times on slaves. The first was an export and import tax, applied to Venezuela in 1563, when 10% was levied on wines and 5% on dry goods coming from Spain, and 2½% was levied on all exports to Spain; later this became a 10% duty. The *alcabala* was a sales tax of 2%, not applied to transactions by Indians, churches or clergy dealing for the Church, nor to things needed for labour or sustenance if bought retail. *Avería* was levied at varying rates on articles carried by sea, and its product was applied to pay the costs of the escort ships needed to defend the trading fleets. The last tax, established in Venezuela by a royal decree of 1631, consisted of the payment of a half-year's salary by all officers appointed by the King or in his name.

The Intendancy established in 1776 was expected to unify all economic effort in the Venezuelan provinces, fiscal as well as productive. The intendant was independent of the governors, and his powers were carefully fixed by an ordinance. He appointed administrators for each branch of revenue, set up an Accountancy-general and a Treasury-general, and was permitted to use the provincial governors as his delegates within their provinces. The first intendant, José de Abalos (1776-1783), was a true reformer who opened Venezuela to some foreign trade, encouraged agriculture, opposed the monopoly of the Guipúzcoa Company, and as early at 1780 foretold the loss by Spain of her American empire.

5. TRADE

From 1503 to 1790, first in Seville and later at Cadiz, the *Casa de Contratación* (House of Trade) worked as the government organ regulating all questions connected with the trade between Spain and the Indies. The basis of the empire's commerce was monopoly, as in the case of the Welser régime, but even though the Crown wanted the wealth of Venezuela for Spain alone, trade quickly arose with Spain, with the Antilles and Veracruz in Mexico, and within the various provinces of Tierra Firme and from them to New Granada. A large clandestine trade also grew up with Dutch, French and English smugglers, for contraband formed an important encouragement for colonial production and growth even though the law forbade trade with foreigners. Spain tried, sometimes without enough knowledge, to increase economic development; for example the establishment of the Guipúzcoa Company was such an attempt, which conveniently splits Venezuelan colonial economic history into two periods.

In the earlier period, at first trade was merely barter with the natives for their pearls, gold, slaves or foodstuffs, but later in the sixteenth century the establishment of towns and the growth of agriculture and stock-raising made for a more advanced system of commerce. Cattle were driven along the trails of the *llanos* and over into the neighbouring Kingdom of New Granada; the ports sent products to Santo Domingo and other islands, and received European articles in return. The mules of Tunja, the salt of Chita, the cotton of the Andes, were exchanged for tobacco from San Cristóbal and Barinas, flour from Mérida and wild honey from Guayana. In 1599 exports from La Guaira included sarsaparilla, lignum vitae, biscuit, flour, cheese, cord made from agave fibre, tallow, hides, cotton cloth, lard, horse reins and saddles; and in 1609 also valuable quantities of these articles were exported, together with a large amount of tobacco, sugar and cacao, all to the total value of 83,949 reals. The variety of products is notable, and also the fact that some were manufactured. Exports also went from Cumaná, and Mérida and Trujillo exported via Cartagena, the main port of a wide area, such products as hams, biscuit, garlic, cordovan leather, tanned sheepskins, cotton clothing, sugar and cacao.

The main products of the colonial economy in the first two hundred years were cotton cloth, hides and cattle on the hoof, tobacco and cacao. The cotton was produced from native plants and with native labour, whereas the cattle had been imported. Stock-raising was important in all the provinces, and at one time in the seventeenth century hides made up 75% of the exports of the country. Almost all the raw hides went to Spain, but the tanned hides of Carora were exported to other colonies. Tobacco growing became highly developed after the end of the sixteenth century, when Maracaibo exported about 25,000 pounds a year. Its cultivation was so widespread that it was at one time forbidden because it attracted so many smugglers; but it had to be permitted again soon because so much revenue in legitimate taxation was otherwise lost. Cacao had originally been a native crop of the Andes, but it spread into the central and eastern valleys as a commercial crop, and it was responsible for the rise of a creole aristocracy, the *grandes cacaos*, who became wealthy through its cultivation on their large estates. Cacao was also largely responsible for the opening of trade between Venezuela and Mexico, a trade which in the seventeenth century grew so important that between 1638 and 1653 no Venezuelan cacao went anywhere save to Mexico.

The most common internal currencies were pearls and nuggets of gold, but barter was for long a common practice. Even the merchants of Seville and the Royal Treasury were willing to accept payment of dues in cacao, which they could sell in Spain for a profit. Communication with Spain was frequent, even in the sixteenth century, when ships came to the main Venezuelan ports from Seville. When these did not come, the country was supplied from the Canaries, Santo Domingo, Puerto Rico and Cartagena. Before the end of the sixteenth century the provinces were given the right to have one special ship, a register ship, each year bringing goods from Seville at a reduced rate of taxation; and this system worked well until about 1600, when Spain's wars with England cut off the traffic until peace in 1604 brought more normal conditions.

At the beginning of the eighteenth century Venezuela's economy and commerce, like those of all Spanish America, were at a low ebb owing to the War of the Spanish Succession following the death of Charles II in 1700. Philip V, the first of the Bourbon dynasty, introduced monopolistic trading companies after the French model, and the French Royal Guinea Company obtained the contract to supply Spanish America with negro slaves for six years and eight months. In 1713 as a preliminary to the Treaty of Utrecht the English South Sea Company was granted the slave *asiento*, or contract, for a period of thirty years. These monopolies doubtless prepared the way for that of the Guipúzcoa Company in Venezuela, whose trade had suffered considerably for years owing to the depredations of pirates and corsairs and the uncertainties of European wars. Contraband partly satisfied the needs of the colonists, but at the same time Venezuela's agricultural production was dropping. It was hoped that the new Company would remedy the situation.

Therefore in 1728 the Royal Guipúzcoa Company was set up on royal orders to monopolise the commerce of the province of Venezuela. The King's close interest ensured both monopoly for the Company and the co-operation of the colonial authorities. The Company's shareholders included merchants of Guipúzcoa who had already become specialists in the cacao trade, the Spanish province of Guipúzcoa itself, the King, and some of the richest landowners of Caracas. Its offices were in San Sebastián until 1751, and from then till the Company's extinction they were in Madrid. The Company was assured of complete monopoly, since the King in 1742 even waived his right to make concessions in Venezuela to others; but the contract was rescinded in 1781, and in 1785 the Company was liquidated and its remains became the basis of the new Philippine Company.

The Guipúzcoa Company contracted to send two armed ships each year to Venezuela, clear the coasts of smugglers and the seas of pirates, and stop contraband inside the country. It was exempted from many taxes, and its ships were allowed to sail direct from San Sebastián to Venezuela, whereas all other ships for America had to call at Cadiz to be officially licensed. The governor of Caracas himself was judge conservator of the Company in Venezuela. In general, the Company's main duty was to supply the Province of Venezuela and carry its products to Spain, although surpluses could be sold in Margarita, Trinidad and Cumaná.

The Company's activities opened with the despatch in 1730 of two ships and a galley from Pasajes, near San Sebastián, bearing 561 men and cargoes of iron in bars and plates, spades and axes, nails, lead, and also hams, cinnamon, pepper, wax, paper, books, medicines, brandy, flour, tin-plate, olives, oil, thread, cloth and silver ribbon. La Guaira was the port of arrival, as it was to be normally in the future. At once the Company set up its trading base and its coast-guard service. Its first stroke of business was to buy a large quantity of cacao and sell it in Spain at a profit of 450%. Within three years the Company was declaring dividends of 20%. The English *asiento* company, suspected with reason of smuggling, received close vigilance from the Guipúzcoa Company's officers.

The Company proceeded to assert its hold over Venezuela's trade. First it forbade the Caracas farmers to exercise in its ships an old privilege of using a third of the capacity of any ship for export on their own account. Certainly, no law granted this privilege, and the Company were able to put pressure on the local people to sell their produce to its officers since there was no other means of export. But the farmers bought their own ship in order to continue their trade in cacao with Mexico. This brought in the governor on the side of the Company, and when an enquiry brought to light the fact that only a quarter of the exported cacao went through the Company in 1733, he ordered that about two fifths of the cacao were to be reserved for the Company. The Company even tried to take over the whole trade with Veracruz, but was unable to conquer the tough resistance of the Venezuelan landowners who were interested in it.

Indeed, the Company in the decade 1740 to 1749 still only exported just over a half of the quantity of cacao exported by the Venezuelans themselves; but since the Company was the only legal importer of European goods it could force up the price of these and force down the price of cacao used as exchange by the locals, so that between 1730 and 1749 this fell by more than a half. The Company was the most powerful capitalist in the country, with agents in every town and armed guards everywhere. The large landowners were able to resist better than the small farmers the relentless pressure to drive down the prices of local products, since the former had the money to put up for the ship to Mexico. But in sum, the Company quickly became very unpopular, and the local people were brought to employ armed rising and ambush against it. The Company did nothing to increase commerce, but it did import many books—although these had entered by other means, and there were educated men in Caracas before the Company came. New and active men of business brought by the Company certainly vivified the economy since they knew how to plan: for example, the wheat supply in Venezuela was assured by the establishment of a route from New Granada, where a great deal was grown.

The Company was bound to cause resentment, since it was too powerful in its hold over the economy and even over the government of Venezuela. The town council of Caracas, dominated by the landowners whose interests were involved, led the opposition which arose among rich creoles and small farmers and whose first manifestations have been mentioned. The small shopkeepers joined in the opposition since they tended to be displaced in business by agents of the Company, who penetrated even retail trade, opening stores and shops. The Company's men were regarded as foreigners who were enjoying rights which should belong to the creoles alone. In 1749 the Company attempted to justify itself in a manifesto, but in fact it had not kept the colony supplied—for example, flour had to be imported from foreign colonies in 1733: it had tended to use its monopoly entirely in its own interest, and its agents were too often domineering and tactless men.

There were two main uprisings in opposition to the Company, the first led by the *zambo* Andresote between 1730 and 1733. This was at the beginning of the Company period, when the governor and the local director of the Company were still establishing the new system. Andresote, who until 1730 was the slave of a Portuguese established near Valencia, was uneducated but intelligent, and he succeeded in making himself the chief of a band of smugglers operating in the western region of the country in league with the local farmers. Local produce was collected and sold to the Dutch in Curaçao in exchange for such things as flour, lead and tools, with the connivance of the local Venezuelan authorities who were not content to accept the Company monopoly. Andresote's power grew as he became the chief of a small army of escaped slaves and others, all armed by the Dutch. The local landowners, who had at first used him as a cat's paw, soon found that he was their equal and became alarmed as he was able to visit villages and towns openly without fear of the authorities. In 1731 Andresote was outlawed on the accusation of being a rebel, an armed brigand, a murderer, traitor and smuggler. Only the last charge is certainly true. Forces sent against him were defeated in July 1732, and greater efforts were made by the government, culminating in an expedition of January 1733 which pursued Andresote's men into the hills, where it met defeat. The governor himself took a hand for a short time, and soon the "rebels" were hunted down, their houses burned, and Andresote himself forced to seek refuge in Curaçao. Those landowners who were compromised were able to shirk responsibility, but many poor coloureds were executed for their part in this attempt to assert local rights against the pretensions of the Company.

The other rising, led by Juan Francisco de León, was longer in preparation, but, like that of Andresote, it was not a movement against the King and his officers, but only against the Company.

The Company's armed police force roamed the country ostensibly to suppress contraband, but in fact committing all sorts of violent wrongs. Complaints brought no alleviation, and quickly all classes became angry and fearful, with the result that León's rebellion won much sympathy and support. León was a popular local official whom the governor dismissed and tried to replace by a nominee of the Company. In 1749 the new official appeared, but the local people refused to admit him to his office and supported León, who begged the governor to appoint instead some man who had no connection with the Company. When this request was refused, the settlers set out on a march to Caracas with León at their head, and as they went they were joined by sympathisers until they numbered about 800 angry men. León publicised their intention to break the Company's power and send the Guipuzcoans back home. Entering Caracas, León gained the pretended consent of the governor, then addressed the town council and persuaded them of the justice of the general case against the Company. The council seemed to agree to take action, and León retired. But the governor secretly denounced the movement to the King as a seditious rebellion and did nothing about the Company. Accordingly León marched again in August, this time with 8,000 men, and reached the same agreement with the governor.

In September a judge arrived from Santo Domingo to hear León's plea, and in November a new governor arrived from Spain with fresh troops. The affair looked serious for León. The new governor, however, wisely offered a general amnesty since almost the whole province was implicated, and León accepted, though once again insisting on the need to extinguish the Company for the good of the country. Yet another governor came in 1751, however, and he, a close ally of the Company, harshly repressed the opposition. At this León took up arms with the support of some towns and attempted to seize Caracas and depose the governor, but was defeated by regular troops. Eventually he surrendered to the governor, who promised to pardon him but instead sent him together with his son to Spain to be tried. The Leóns were sent from there to the wars in Africa, where they distinguished themselves, and returned at last to Venezuela to find their home razed and their possessions seized. The governor imposed a reign of terror on the local people, poor and rich, but nothing could end the resistance to the Company.

6. LAW, RELIGION AND CULTURE

Law, religion and culture played their part in making Venezuelan colonial life civilised. The Spanish legal tradition is one of the richest of Europe, and the new legal problems set by the government of the American empire were immediately grappled with. The Peninsular precedent was followed in legislation: laws were passed by means of royal decrees each aimed at a particular case, and these laws became common law by force of circumstances and in the light of experience. This may appear chaotic, but in fact the system was in accord with the Spanish character, personalist, individualist, difficult to fit into categories, which was the basis of the Spanish-American and therefore Venezuelan outlook.

Various Ordinances established the relationships between the classes and colours in Spanish America: the Laws of Burgos of 1512-13, the Ordinances of Zaragoza of 1518, the Instructions of 1523 and 1526, the Ordinances of Toledo of 1528, and the New Laws of the Indies of 1542-43. A body of what was called Indies Law thus grew up, with major additions in 1571 and 1636, and this was codified in 1681 and published as the *Recopilación de las Leyes de Indias*, the famous Laws of the Indies. The first main law court in America, which applied these laws, was the Audiencia of Santo Domingo, under whose authority Venezuela remained for many years. The efficacy of Spanish-American law is proved by the balance maintained in the colonial period, and also by the need to return to its principles which is felt in some instances in these days; there is no doubt that the Laws of the Indies rank with the greatest legal monuments of the world.

It was not until July 1786 that Charles III created the Audiencia of Caracas, with jurisdiction over the whole Captaincy-general. It was a court of appeal and also, for certain special cases, it was the lowest court; the Council of the Indies judged appeals against its decisions. The occasion of its creation was a petition from Maracaibo asking for that district to be included in the jurisdiction of the Audiencia of Bogotá, instead of in that of distant Santo Domingo as were originally most of the Venezuelan provinces. The King decided that the establishment of a new audiencia for the benefit of the whole Captaincy-general

would be the best answer, and but for this decision it is possible
that what are now the States of Zulia, Mérida, Trujillo and Táchira, surrounding Lake Maracaibo, would have belonged to
New Granada and later to its successor state, Colombia, and not
to Venezuela. Military, clergy and Treasury officers possessed
special *fueros*, that is, they were subject to their own special
tribunals.

Another judicial body was the *Real Consulado de Caracas*,
or official merchants' guild, created in 1793 at the instance of
the intendant and the merchants and landowners of the district. It had a tribunal with judicial powers in connection with
mercantile cases, the idea being that this could speed the settlement of such affairs and therefore accelerate business in general; and it had a *junta* or council whose task was to encourage
commerce and production by such means as opening and maintaining road and water communications, and looking after the
port works at La Guaira. The members of the governing body
of the Consulado, naturally, were men involved in the big business of the country, members of the dominant creole oligarchy.
Its tribunal of three met every Tuesday, Thursday and Satur-
day mornings to hear cases between merchants, without the intervention of lawyers. Its judgment was given on the spot, and
the only appeal was to the Council of the Indies itself, and the
result was that business conflicts were indeed resolved quickly
and efficiently.

In the Spanish colonies Church and State were kept separate
by policy. The Church was allowed no more than its normal
spiritual power, and in Venezuela there was a series of small
conflicts between administrators and ecclesiastics, in which the
civil authorities set some limit to the Church's activities. The
first bishop was Rodrigo de Bastidas, who was given the see of
Coro in 1531. In 1638 the see was transferred to Caracas, and at
this time the religious government of Venezuela was divided,
with Margarita, Trinidad, Cumaná and Guayana dependent on
the see of Puerto Rico, while the Andes belonged still to the
Archdiocese of Bogotá. In 1777 Mérida was made a bishopric,
suffragan to Bogotá, including in its area Maracaibo, Coro and
Trujillo. In 1790 Guayana became a diocese, under the Archdiocese of Santo Domingo like Caracas. But in 1796 the whole
of the island of Santo Domingo passed under French rule, with
the result that in 1803 Caracas was made the seat of an arch-

3 Aerial view of the stadium at University City

View of part of the city of Caracas, capital of Venezuela

4   Part of a petrol Refinery in Venezuela

Oil field landscape in Venezuela

bishop, with the bishops of Guayana and Mérida under his authority.

The Spanish Crown possessed the patronage of Spanish America; that is, the King had the right to organise the Church as an institution inside his dominions, and in practice he presented clergymen for benefices and had the right of registering papal decrees circulated there. The patronage of America, which had been in the hands of the King since the first discovery, was specifically granted by Pope Julian II in 1508, and certainly from the first the sovereigns had encouraged the activities of the Church. By the grant of patronage, then, the Church was placed under the tutelage of the State. The Church's income came from the normal tithes, and from these and other gifts of the faithful the Venezuelan clergy lived in colonial times. Bastidas, for example, collected tithes in pearls and spices, and he farmed and finally died rich as Archbishop of Santo Domingo. Cathedrals, monasteries, hospitals and other charities possessed land for their maintenance. Lay societies of the devout possessed great wealth, and acted sometimes as banks. The tribunal of the Inquisition was set up in 1610 in Cartagena, with jurisdiction over Venezuela; but this body seems to have been singularly inactive, and very little can be discovered about it. In Venezuela the clergy were respected, but had little power.

Spanish culture, in the wider sense of the total way of life, passed with the conquerors to America, where it took root and, subject to the modifying influences of the environment, developed. In the sixteenth century a characteristic of the Spaniard of that great period was in evidence in Venezuela: the zeal for setting up towns, forming nuclei of men who would dominate the new land and impose a life upon it. The Catholic faith moulded Spain, and exactly at the time when Spaniards spilled into America that faith was at one of its peaks, active, purged of many long-standing vices. The conqueror was Catholic, profoundly Catholic, though not necessarily pious—even if he hardly knew enough about religion to blaspheme, the soldier's whole life was Catholic. Hence, colonial culture was Catholic. Liberty of spirit was cultivated through the town council and the pursuit of enough wealth to maintain a society, and at the same time minds were tempered by interest in the arts and in letters.

National systems of education are very modern. No country

in Europe had compulsory primary education in the Spanish American colonial period, and Venezuela followed the Spanish norm: primary schools existed from early times, as part of the services of the Church, and it was regarded as one of the duties of a family to care for the education of its children at least as far as reading and writing were concerned. The rich employed tutors, who might be university students or clergymen, but the working man was usually illiterate. It is still one of the struggles of the Hispanic nations to try to teach their poorer people both in town and country to read and write, and this was until quite recently in general the case of the whole of Europe. Education was the prerogative of the economically privileged, as was to be expected under the prevailing conditions of society. In Caracas and possibly in all the main towns there existed primary schools run at the expense of the local town councils and sometimes of the King, but the sons of the rich generally received their education at home. The most important schools, however, were those attached to monasteries. Education was for boys, not for girls, for the usual Hispanic view prevailed: woman's place was in the home.

It is known that an elementary school was opened in Caracas in 1567, paid for by the town council and citizens. Another was opened as a private venture in 1594, and the town council welcomed and supported it. Higher education was provided by Chairs of Grammar, one of which was founded by Philip II in Caracas in 1593, and Bishop Alceaga founded one in 1608. These Chairs existed from then in Caracas and possibly in some other towns, generally receiving support from the Crown. The education consisted of Latin, rhetoric, arithmetic, history, geography, divinity, and language and literature. Also, in all the big towns monasteries supported schools giving this type of secondary education as well as the primary. In the eighteenth century schools were organised using text-books current in Madrid, and there was a movement towards making the various public schools supplant the private ones.

The convent schools, with their teaching of Latin and divinity, for many years trained the priests. Philip II ordered the foundation of a real seminary in 1592, but it was 1673 before he was obeyed and the Seminary of Santa Rosa was set up by Bishop Fray Antonio González de Acuña, a native of Lima. The Seminary flourished, staffed largely by Venezuelans, and in

1721 received permission from the King to become a University. The Pope gave his blessing in 1722, so that the University of Caracas became Royal and Pontifical, with a curriculum consisting of theology, philosophy, canon law, civil law and "cases of conscience". This religious bias was destined to change, as the University became a centre of learning in modern science and philosophy, where the ideas of advanced European thinkers were discussed: Descartes, Malebranche, Spinoza, Leibnitz, Wolf, Berkeley, Locke, Condillac, and so on to Galileo, Gassendi and Newton. Some freely attacked Aristotle, as did Valverde. From this University came the leaders of the generation which revolted against Spanish rule. The teachers were most of them local creoles, locally educated. In 1788, because the University had progressed so well, a College of Lawyers was founded in Caracas, and in its turn it established an Academy of Law.

Mérida and Cumaná also had higher institutions of learning. The Seminary of Mérida was founded in 1785, and there a bishop, Manuel Cándido Torrijos, established in 1794 the first laboratory of experimental physics. In 1806 this seminary was given the faculty to grant degrees. From the early eighteenth century in Cumaná advanced Latin was taught, complemented by the introduction of philosophy in 1769.

Musical theory was taught in connection with the cathedral choir, but in 1696 the Caracas Seminary was endowed with a Chair of plainsong. Other churches and the monasteries naturally maintained the development of music. Music, indeed, developed so well that in the later eighteenth century a real school arose in Caracas, producing composers who gained wide renown. Dedicated teachers, from about 1770 onwards, worked so well to renovate the study of music that an Academy was founded, from which came a crop of composers, such as José Ángel Lamas, known for his religious work, and Juan Landaeta, famous for his music for the Venezuelan National Anthem as well as for his religious compositions.

Architecture was interesting, though of a colonial type and not so rich as in Mexico and Peru. Literature had some cultivators, such as the historian Oviedo y Baños and the philosopher Briceño. There were some literary circles, in which the Venezuelan poet and thinker Andrés Bello, who became a Chilean by adoption, read his early works. Painting, too, was practised, although in the eighteenth century Venezuelan people of artistic talent mostly cultivated music, and it is said that even the best painting of the period is more suggestive of music than of visual art, as is the case with the portrait of the Marquesa del Toro painted by a slave.

The press was brought to the centres of Spanish America very early: Mexico 1539, Guatemala 1560, Lima 1584; but only in the eighteenth century did it become generalised. Books continued to be printed in Spain, even books written, as some were, in Venezuela. Trinidad had a press in 1789, and on it were printed some revolutionary papers for circulation in Venezuela, but Caracas had no press until the nineteenth century in spite of some earlier attempts to introduce one. In 1808 the printers Matthew Gallagher and James Lamb brought the first press from Trinidad, a British possession since 1797. The first periodical to appear was the *Gaceta de Caracas*, whose first issue came off this press on October 24, 1808. It continued until 1821, passing through a succession of periods according to the events of the times. One of its most important editors was Andrés Bello, who printed some of his early work in it. He used the same press to print his first book, which was in fact the first ever printed in Venezuela, the *Calendario manual y guía universal de forasteros en Caracas para 1810*, a kind of local guide book for the use of strangers, in which appeared a summary of the history of Venezuela. The press quickly developed in importance in the country, with notable publishing firms such as that of Valentín Espinel (1803-1866).

7. FORESHADOWINGS OF INDEPENDENCE

The eighteenth century was a period of revolution in Europe and America. Both the independence of the United States of America and the French Revolution were born of similar ideas, and the Spanish Americans could not remain aloof from such a widespread movement. Venezuela was only unified in law in 1777, but for over a century before society there had been aware of a feeling of unity, owing to the preponderance of the old Province of Venezuela over the others in the region. The conquerors had become Americans, with common vital interests. On September 27, 1780, the intendant José de Abalos wrote a letter to the Universal Secretary of the Indies, José de Gálvez, analising the effect on Venezuela of the monopoly of the Guipúzcoa Company, and drawing attention to the state of social maturity reached by the country, perfectly prepared by this time to try any method of withdrawing itself from Spanish dominion if the Mother Country continued her policy towards Venezuela. His words are worth quoting: 'The name of the King, of his ministers and of all Spaniards is heard by the leaders of this country with the greatest disgust, aversion and dislike simply on account of the Company, which seems to them to be the original sin which gives rise to their wrongs. And truly this error seems at times excusable; in a sense it is true that they suffer a kind of slavery, enjoying no benefit from the operations of the Company, and oppressed by the necessity to put through its miserly hands those few products which they are able to cultivate, after seeing lifeless and buried the multitude of other products which ought to flourish in the province to the great gain of the Royal Treasury, the outstanding good of the State and the immense profit of both continents. The woeful and rancorous tone of their laments increases daily, and unless His Majesty grants them the open trade for which they sigh he can no longer count on the fidelity of these vassals, since they will lend their ears and hearts to any hint and help offered them by the Crown's enemies, and it will be impossible or very difficult to cure this ill. This is not an empty prophecy, but the forecast of one who knows the country well; and if this part of America is lost it will be the most lamentable misfortune for the monarchy, not only on account of the immense riches which these lands contain, but also because with this gate in his power he who possesses it will easily be able to absorb the rest of the continent. He who dominates the provinces of Caracas and Cumaná and the island of Trinidad will be the master of this whole western region, and with it he will have easy access to the rest."

The prevalent economic system, then, was one cause of the growth of a feeling in favour of independence among the rich, who desired freedom in which to conduct their own business, which was trade in the fruits of their agriculture. Secondly, advanced European ideas found an echo in the creoles, who translated and circulated papers containing the new doctrine. An example was a book entitled *Derechos del hombre y del ciudadano (Rights of man and of the citizen)*, which was read in the Antilles and in Venezuela, and was prohibited in the Captaincy-general by the Audiencia of Caracas in 1797. This type of foreign subversive influence was blamed on the French in Santo Domingo and on the English in Trinidad. But it is clear that neither could have had any great effect in the colonies but for the existence already of a state of preparation among the creoles.

In the lower sectors of society the new ideas also found receptive minds, such as that of the free *zambo* José Leonardo Chirino, who led a revolt of slaves in Coro in 1795 which aimed to 'implant the law of the French' and free all slaves. Chirino was defeated by the authorities supported by local creoles, who were naturally perturbed by such extremism, and in punishment many of the rebels were beheaded, while Chirino was hanged and quartered in Caracas.

Whereas Chirino's revolt only attracted slaves and some free negroes and mulattoes who desired their own advancement and embraced confused doctrines of liberty which were in the colonial air, the revolt headed in La Guaira in 1797 by Manuel Gual and José María España was more serious: it was thought out and planned well ahead, and possessed a clearer ideology. Gual was a retired army captain and España was the justice of Macuto. They were supported by creoles, some coloureds, and even by some Spaniards, Picornell, Andrés and Campomanes, who were serving a prison sentence at La Guaira for their part in the conspiracy of San Blas, which in 1796 had attempted to establish a republic in Spain. These three, while still in prison, conspired with Gual and España, and in July 1797 broke out, Picornell and Cortés fleeing to Curaçao, while Andrés went to Caracas, where he was recaptured. On July 12 the conspiracy was revealed "through the imprudence of a fool", as Gual said. The two leaders fled, Gual to Curaçao and then to Trinidad, where he died in 1800. España returned to La Guaira in 1799, was captured, tried and executed. Various men implicated were imprisoned and some were executed.

But the conspirators had had an ideal. They had meant to set up a government and make the country a republic. The revolution was to be in the name of the people; provisional juntas of government would be established as a first step; the Rights of Man were to be proclaimed; a flag was designed to symbolise the union of the four provinces which were to form the state: Caracas, Maracaibo, Cumaná, and Guayana. The revolutionaries printed various pamphlets, such as a proclamation 'to the free inhabitants of Spanish America' and an 'American song and American *Carmagnole*', and also the book on the Rights of Man mentioned above. In these writings were expressed the aspirations of the group implicated with Gual and España.[1]

The 'Great Precursor' of the Spanish-American revolution, Francisco de Miranda, was born in Caracas on March 28, 1750, and died in prison in Cadiz on July 14, 1816. He had an outstanding career of conspiracy against Spanish rule in Venezuela and in all the Indies—'the first creole of note in world history', as he has been called. He studied in Caracas University, but went to Spain without graduating. His parents were Canary Islanders, despised as low tradespeople by the *mantuanos*, and they thought they would better their son's life by sending him to join the Spanish army. Young Miranda became a captain, served against the Moors in Morocco and against the pirates of Algiers, and then was sent to the Antilles, where he gained some note in various affairs, including co-operation with the British North American colonies then fighting for their independence. He got into trouble with the Spanish authorities over a trip to Jamaica, and in 1783 travelled in the United States of America and then went to England. His life of international adventure had begun. Between 1785 and 1789 he travelled extensively in Europe, full of curiosity about the peoples and their ideas, customs and politics. In 1787 he got to know the Empress Catherine of Russia, and in 1790 he had conversations in London with the Prime Minister, Pitt. In 1791 he left England for France, where he joined the revolutionary army as a general and fought under Dumouriez in the northern campaign. He was then tried by orders of the Convention, escaped to London in 1798, returned to France and was arrested there in 1801, went back to London and received protection from the British Government. Finally in 1806 he undertook a long-projected invasion of Venezuela.

Miranda's constant preoccupation in studying, in learning from his travels, his observations and his books, and in gaining the ear of some of the outstanding people of the time, was to prepare the way for the emancipation of Spanish America. He fought for liberty in France and helped the United States, and

[1] See Pedro Grases, *La conspiración de Gual y España*, Caracas, 1949.

he set up centres of Spanish-American conspirators in Paris and London, in which such future leaders of the independence movement as the Chilean O'Higgins found encouragement. In 1790, introduced by influential friends, he presented to Pitt a plan for the emancipation of Spanish America, giving detailed information about the conditions of the Spanish possessions and including a project of the organisation of a future state. The new state would embrace all Spanish-speaking America except some of the islands, would be ruled by a hereditary Inca and would have a legislature consisting of a higher house composed of members appointed for life by the executive and of a House of Commons elected by popular vote. There were distinct reflections of the British system of government at this time, although Miranda modified his ideas in later plans which he submitted, such as the so-called Act of Paris of 1798.

In April 1806 Miranda sailed from New York for Venezuela in the Leander, eighteen guns, accompanied by two schooners. He had 200 soldiers—Americans, English, French and Irish— and some arms. On April 27, in a fight before Ocumare he lost the schooners and escaped in the Leander, leaving many prisoners behind, of whom ten were hanged at Puerto Cabello. But Miranda reorganised his expedition in Port of Spain, Trinidad, which he left on July 27th with a squadron of eight boats and 400 soldiers. They reached Coro on August 1st and disembarked on the 3rd, occupying the town on the 4th. The inhabitants fled without resistance. None of Miranda's attempts to win the people's confidence had any effect, so he was forced to leave his country, especially since forces were being brought up against him. In 1808 he was again in England, once more waiting for help in his struggle.

Miranda put all his strength into his battle for the liberty of the Spanish-American peoples. His project for a state ruled by an Inca developed into a more precise plan for a Republic of Colombia, an idea which possibly had some influence on Bolívar's creation of Great Colombia. Miranda failed, yet his actions had great repercussions. Thinking men in Europe were made to pay attention to the problem of Spanish America, and even more important, his labour as a revolutionary propagandist found an echo in the minds of the leaders of the independence movement in America, and particularly in Venezuela. His name was frequently in the English press, and he maintained a wide correspondence throughout all America. From April 1810 he used a newspaper, *El colombiano*, for his propaganda. In 1807 and 1808 the English publicist William Burke produced two books on the need to emancipate Spanish America, and there is no doubt that it was Miranda who stimulated him to write them. Miranda inspired the whole great movement which preceded the declaration of independence, and he was looked up to by such men as Gual as the mentor and protector of the liberty of Spanish America.

In a proclamation at Coro, Miranda wrote that America would 'recover' her sovereign independence, in a phrase which contained the already current idea that all peoples are free. The same idea occurs in the Venezuelan constitution of 1811 as well as in other documents. He also wrote: 'The recovery of our rights as citizens and of our national glory as Colombians will perhaps be the least of the benefits we shall draw from this conclusion, which is as just as it is necessary.' Miranda was the inspirer, in large measure, of that revolution which brought forth a handful of republics which now form a world.

CHAPTER FIVE

Independence

I. INTRODUCTION

THE history of the independence period has been written in several different ways since the birth of the consciousness of a Venezuelan State. But the literature has concentrated on two topics: the first truly revolutionary events, and the wars. Too little attention, perhaps, has been paid to the human side and to thought: to the intellectual formation of that generation and to the manner in which the man who worked with his hands reacted when he was not carried away by heroic action. The whole scene is becoming clearer with the publication of new material—newspapers and private writings.[1]

Certain things have become clear; for example the nature of the war, civil sociologically speaking, but international in law. The tones of the various historians have been different, especially when dealing with such matters as the 'war to the death' of 1813 and 1814. It is no longer possible to write of Spanish cruelty when justifying separation from Spain, as did the writers of the old *Gaceta de Caracas*. The undercurrent of cruelty present in the Spanish race spreads to all its branches. Even Juan Vicente González, in his writings, could equate the ferocity of Boves the royalist with that of Arismendi the patriot. The later history of Venezuela, up to the most recent times, has shown, without any war to the death, that cruelty is one of those deep seated characteristics which lend their nature to those moments of failure in a country's history, the revolutions and dictatorships. Venezuela's history as a republic numbers more days of dictatorship and revolution than of democracy. Social democracy is one thing, and political demo-

---

1 See facsimile editions of the *Gaceta de Caracas* and the *Correo del Orinoco* published under the auspices of the Academia Nacional de la Historia, and the *Obras* of Juan Germán Roscio (3 vols., Caracas, 1953) and of Simón Rodríguez (3 vols., Caracas, 1954).

cracy is another, and to this day in Venezuela there has never been any example of both coinciding. I mention political democracy in contrast with dictatorship. Social democracy began to develop in Venezuela in 1813.

It must also be realised that the Independence was not a popular movement; the people—those social classes which, according to the views of the period, formed the mass of the population—had no interest in independence. The Independence was organised and carried through, in both its phases, by élites, by certain classes. In fact, the Independence was the child of the intelligence and feelings of a few dozen men—nobles, writers, officers, men with a certain family tradition who wished to lead the Republic, or thinkers converted to the new philosophy. If the First Republic slipped from Miranda's grasp in the campaign of 1812, the Second escaped Bolívar's in spite of the campaign of 1813. The people, the Venezuelans, did not understand or desire Independence. It had to be imposed on them.

What did the people do? If by people we mean the masses, then it can be said that the people followed the local leaders, the *caudillos*, at first the royalist *caudillos* and later the patriot ones too. The people gave their blood, as in any revolutionary movement. If by people we understand those who were sensitive to politics—the notables, as was the word used at that time—then of course the Independence was made by the people. But the documents establish a radical difference: those concerning the events of 1810, for example, speak of the people as respectful lookers-on at what was happening, at what the ruling classes were doing.

The ideas behind the Independence can be sketched in few words. Fermín Toro mentioned them afterwards when writing of the authors who were read by the members of the generation who made the Independence: 'Rousseau, then, Voltaire, Helvétius, Diderot, Destutt de Tracy, were their favourite authors.' Incidentally, the ideals proclaimed and implanted by the French Revolution were known in Spain, where they gained some distinguished converts and spread to the people, in spite of official difficulties and the fact that the old régime, represented in 1792 by the Count of Floridablanca, was trying to keep the new ideas in check.

This contagion explains not only the somewhat curious entry of men such as Francisco Antonio Zea into Hispanic Ameri-

can politics, but also the position of the Captain-general of Venezuela, Emparan. Zea, a native of Antioquía in New Granada,
was Director-general of the Ministry of the Interior in the Bonapartist Spain of 1808 to 1812, appointed by Napoleon, and yet
in 1819 he became Vice-president of the Venezuelan Republic
created by Bolívar. Emparan was always considered a franco-
phile, and he owed his position in Venezuela to the recommen-
dation of Napoleon. He was brought up in Guipúzcoa at a time
when the new ideas were spreading there with particular success, and when, it is said, Guipúzcoa had more subscribers to
the *Encyclopédie* than all the rest of Spain.

The revolutionaries present a contradictory spectacle: fran-
cophile in their philosophy, yet they struggled at the start
against French power and remained faithful to the Spanish
nation. The interpretation often given to this phenomenon is
not correct: it was not merely a piece of political hypocrisy
meant to camouflage the creoles' movements of April and July
1810. Those who then wished to set up a representative government in the name of Ferdinand VII did not decide for a republic: this was imposed by the revolutionary extremists. No doubt
the intellectual who wrote the editorial in the *Gaceta de Caracas* of May 4th thought exactly as he wrote: 'No-one believes
that the resolution we have taken had any other object than to
assure our existence and happiness, without taking away one
jot from the loyalty which characterises us, of which we gave
the first example in America on July 15, 1808, and whose quality we would never change, not even for all the advantages
which our present state offers to us. We well knew that we
were free; we well knew that our generous conduct could only
lead us to the dignity of freedom, and make us sharers in the
glory of the nation to which we belong and whose salvation we
attempt as an integral part of it.' And this point of view was
equally sincere later, although put forward by other pens.

The more radical attitude took flesh in Simón Bolívar, converted by the wars into the supreme hero. But not only did he
direct the wars, he also stimulated the creation of the State. A
real Venezuelan State hardly existed before 1830, but the idea
of statehood certainly did exist. Great Colombia—a purely historical name—is precisely Bolívar's most happy conception in
the field of law. Perhaps this conception was not based on what
was practical, on the necessary conditions for building a State.

The political formula for uniting Spanish America was not the same as might serve to unite the Venezuelan provinces.

The Venezuelan Republic began its independent existence in 1830. For twenty years the country had been under the radical experiment of revolutionary change: the breaking of one set of moulds of life so as to create another. The breaking took place: the new creation is still in process.

2. THE FIRST REPUBLIC

Venezuela possessed independence, that is political freedom from Spain, from July 5, 1811 when the declaration was made by the first national Congress, meeting in Caracas. But the period known as the Independence is more complex: it includes the political and military events up to 1830 and the moral and ideological consequences of those movements. 1830 is especially significant for the building of the Republic of Venezuela, for at that date it separated from Great Colombia as a result of a movement which bore a stronger feeling of nationalism than was apparent during the First Republic. The latter name is given to the government which sprang from the declaration of independence, and which came to an end with Miranda's capitulation to the royalists. This First Republic was for the liberators an ideal, disputed, but defended resolutely and at times desperately.

The political situation in Spain was one cause of the Venezuelan revolution. From October 24, 1808 when it began publication, the *Gaceta de Caracas* printed news and documents on the invasion of Spain by the Emperor of the French, Napoleon, and of the changes brought about as a consequence of the resistance of the Spaniards. This struggle, called the War of Independence in Spanish history, coincided in part with the Venezuelan revolution: it began with the rising of the people of Madrid on May 2, 1808 and ended on June 4, 1814, when the last French garrison evacuated the town of Figueras, in the Province of Gerona. In political matters, the most important result in Spain of the French invasion was the forced abdication of Charles IV and of his son Ferdinand VII in favour of Napoleon. There was, then, no Spanish government with clear title, and the American possessions were led to consider how to govern themselves in the name of Ferdinand VII and to maintain themselves free from French domination.

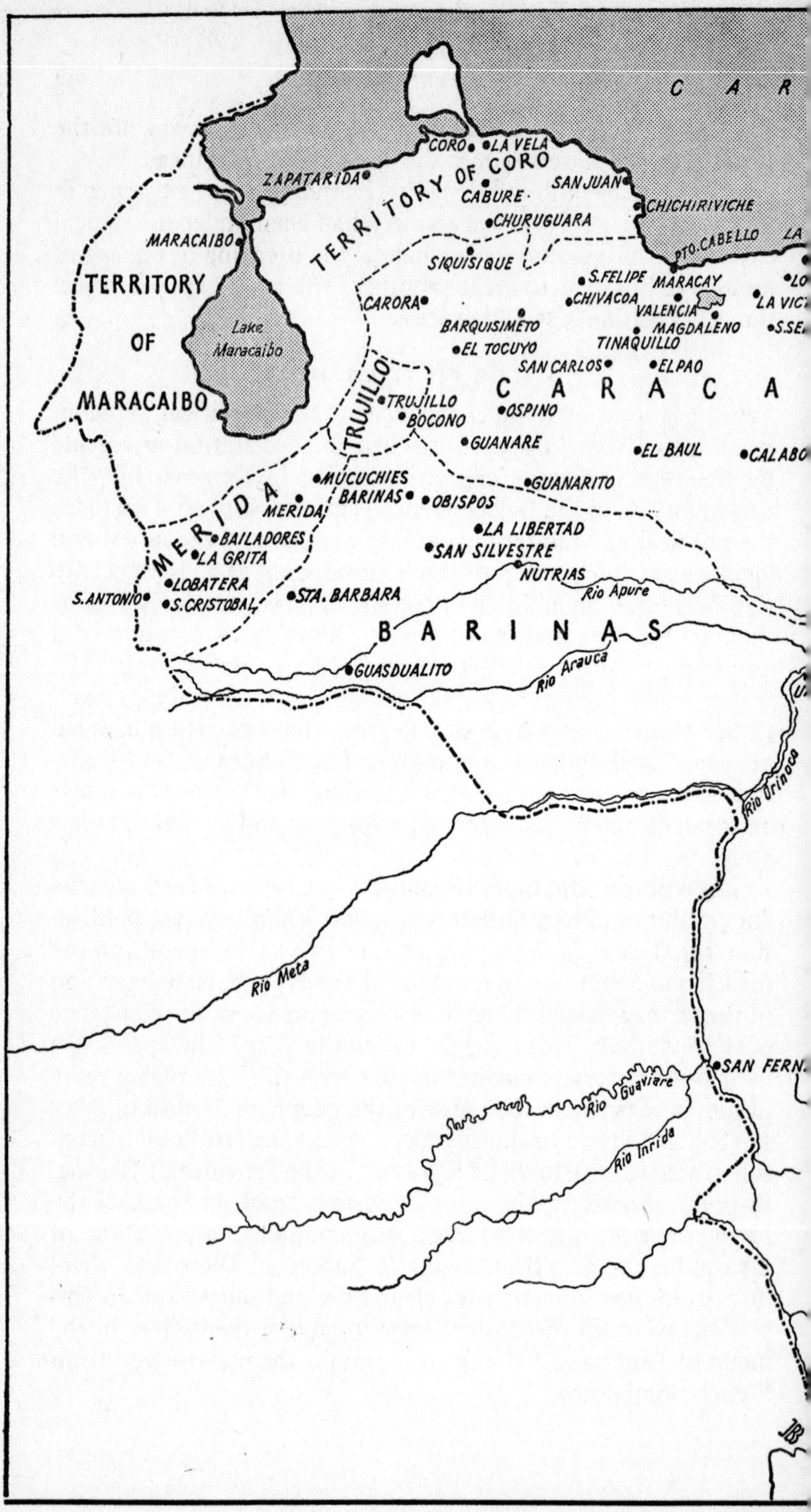

C A R
CORO
LA VELA
TERRITORY OF CORO
ZAPATARIDA
CABURE
SAN JUAN
CHICHIRIVICHE
CHURUGUARA
PTO. CABELLO
LA
MARACAIBO
SIQUISIQUE
TERRITORY
OF
MARACAIBO
Lake Maracaibo
S. FELIPE
MARACAY
LO
CHIVACOA
VALENCIA
LA VIC
CARORA
BARQUISIMETO
MAGDALENO
S. SE
EL TOCUYO
TINAQUILLO
SAN CARLOS
EL PAO
TRUJILLO
C A R A C A
TRUJILLO
OSPINO
BOCONO
GUANARE
EL BAUL
CALABO
MUCUCHIES
GUANARITO
MERIDA
BARINAS
OBISPOS
MERIDA
LA LIBERTAD
BAILADORES
SAN SILVESTRE
LA GRITA
NUTRIAS
LOBATERA
Rio Apure
S. ANTONIO
S. CRISTOBAL
STA. BARBARA
B A R I N A S
GUASDUALITO
Rio Arauca
Rio Orinoco
Rio Meta
SAN FERN
Rio Guaviare
Rio Inrida

CARIBBEAN SEA

MARGARITA
ASUNCION

RIO CARIBE
CARUPANO
CUMANA CARIACO   Gulf of   TRINIDAD
BARCELONA   Paria
GR. DE ORITUCO PIRITU

MATURIN

CHAGUARAMAS   C U M A N A
CANTAURA
LE DE LA
PASCUA   TABASCA
                                URACOA
PARIAGUAN
EL PAO

B A R C E L O N A   Rio Orinoco
SOLEDAD   Rio Caroni
AICARA   MOITACO   ANGOSTURA   UPATA
        Rio   EL PALMAR
        Orinoco   EL MANO

Rio   GUASIPATI
Coura   EL CALLAO
                                                    Rio
                                                    Cuyuni
Rio
Caura   Rio Paragua

                                         G U I A N A
G U A Y A N A

                    Rio Caroni

                                   SIERRA PACARAIMA
TABAPO

quiare

VENEZUELA
IN 1811
Shewing provinces and main towns

0 _____ 100
          Miles

AZIL

The troubles of Spain for years past were also reflected in the colonies. In Venezuela, for example, there had been an economic crisis since the last years of the eighteenth century, as there was a shortage of labour for harvesting the main crop, cacao, owing to the recruitment of many men to defend the coasts against both English and French attacks. Despite this, Trinidad was in fact lost. Again, taxation imposed because of the needs of Spain perturbed rich Venezuelans. This uneasy atmosphere provided the background for the troubles of 1808. To the economic stress were added the ideas released by the revolutions of the British North American colonies and of France on to a world tired of colonial rule, and where there was already a current of feeling for self-government. The creole felt capable of ruling himself, and struggled for full mastership of the State to complement his mastership of the land and the slaves. Thus two sets of causes worked towards independence: one material, economic; and the other spiritual, intellectual—the revolutionary ideas.

Other causes which can be cited have connections with those mentioned. For example, when Esteban Fernández de León says in his memorandum of February 27, 1796 that 'since the fatal revolution in France, in the whole province and in Caracas we have only seen one subversive notice, fixed in November 1794 on the reverend bishop's house, and this notice complained about the injustices of the civil and ecclesiastical officials, calling on them to mend their ways and warning them that if they did not, France would mend them for them', this reflects on the one hand social upheaval and on the other hand French influence. But the real point is the presence of the revolutionary surge. When Miguel José Sanz remarks that inequality between the classes is incompatible with the idea of liberty, he is stressing the economic problem.

It should be remembered that the material cause tended to predispose men's minds towards a change, especially among the middle classes composed of small farmers and merchants; whereas the theories and principles of independence penetrated deeply among the creole nobility and the intellectuals. This should make it evident that the Independence was not to begin with a popular movement. The revolution came from above. Bolívar, the greatest of the political and military leaders, was not a man of the people, in the sense of social class. Andrés

Bello, who was a man of the people, was not a revolutionary. The intervention of the people, as a mass, was brought about by the will of the leaders or through the action of demagogy. It should also be noted that the material and the spiritual causes coalesced, and the predominance of one or the other was purely momentary.

In Venezuela the last two Captains-general were Juan de Casas (October 9, 1807 to May 17, 1809) and Vicente Emparan (May 17, 1809 to April 19, 1810). The period of their governments was one of instability, enthusiasm and revolutionary ferment. In Spain there were grave events—the conspiracy of the Escurial, the fall of Godoy, the proclamation of Ferdinand VII, the abdication of Bayonne, the exaltation of Joseph Bonaparte to the Spanish throne, the rising of the Spanish people, the creation of Juntas of government by them; and in Caracas there were various riots and disturbances. On July 14, 1808 the French brigantine *Serpent* arrived at La Guaira under the command of Lieutenant Paul de Lamanon who had been ordered by the military commander and imperial commissioner in French Guiana, Victor Hugues, to inform the authorities in Caracas of the events in Spain. On the 15th Lamanon went to Caracas and had an interview with Casas, whom he urged to recognise Joseph Bonaparte as King of Spain. He failed in his mission, and was escorted back to La Guaira, where he re-embarked only to fall into the hands of the English. As it happened, the British frigate *Acasta*, commanded by Captain Beaver, arrived at La Guaira on July 15th, having been sent by the commander of the British Leeward Islands squadron, Cochrane, in order to inform the people of Caracas and Cumaná that the Spanish people had risen against the French, that the French government in the Peninsula was illegitimate, that a Junta of government had been set up in Seville, and that Britain was now Spain's ally in the fight against France, the "common enemy". Casas received the English commissioner coolly, since he was more in sympathy with the French.

Casas had known about events in Spain since the 5th, thanks to pamphlets and papers sent to him by the British governor of Trinidad and to the zeal of Manuel de Cajigal, governor of Cumaná, who had sent him by express some copies of the London *Times* which announced the fall of the Bourbons and the exaltation of Joseph Bonaparte. The Captain-general at first

G

kept this news from his people, but when it eventually and gradually became known in Caracas, two main points interested the creoles especially. The first was that Americans had some say in the Bonapartist government, since a Spanish National Assembly was called, including deputies of the Spanish provinces and, at Napoleon's own request, some in the name of the American colonies too. José Hipólito Odoardo was the deputy for Caracas, and Francisco Antonio Zea for Guatemala. The latter showed anti-Spanish feeling, for when welcoming Joseph he congratulated him on 'the first solemn act of appreciation and justice which America has been given in the metropolis'. The second point of interest was the existence of a new free Spanish government. On September 25, 1808 the Supreme Central Junta of Government was set up at Aranjuez, with two deputies for each province except those of America. This Junta was to govern in the name of the captive King and lead the Spanish nation in its opposition to Bonaparte. The news was published in the *Gaceta de Caracas* in November, and from then the *Gaceta* took a strong anti-French tone, in spite of the pro-French feelings of Casas and Emparan. Loyalty to Ferdinand VII was the cry of the patriots in Spain, and it was taken up in Venezuela, even by the revolutionaries of 1810.

On July 27, 1808 the Captain-general, Casas, called a meeting at his house of the principal Spanish officials of justice, administration and defence to decide what should be done to calm Caracas, still in a state of upheaval from the visits of the French and English commissioners and the riot of July 15th caused by the presence of the Frenchman in the capital. Casas ordered the arrest of the three men who had been the ringleaders of the rioting and also suggested to the town council that the authorities of Caracas should establish 'a junta of government on the example of that of Seville'. The arrests merely caused some personal inconvenience and ill-feeling, but the governmental proposal was the seed of a revolution behind doors. The council accepted the idea, but it was not followed up at this time.

The riot of July 15th was caused by distinguished citizens of Caracas, who were irritated by the Frenchman's visit and put themselves at the head of a mob which shouted for his expulsion and for the proclamation of loyalty to Ferdinand VII. The French mission was escorted down to the port of La Guaira, and Casas had Ferdinand's picture paraded through the streets to the accompaniment of cries from the mob. In fact, this movement was caused by revolutionary feeling harboured by some of the creoles of the highest class, such as the Bolívars, on whose farm meetings took place. The leaders of the mob were clearly Manuel de Matos y Monserrate, a retired army captain, Diego de Melo y Muñoz, a lieutenant, and the Captain of Nobles Ignacio Suárez Manrique de Lara. They were imprisoned on the 27th, since it was believed that another riot was due to break out against the authorities, and they were released only after some months. Loyalty to Ferdinand was proclaimed, and on May 9th the Caracas town council swore to recognise him as sovereign; the noble creoles declared their loyalty too, although they were restless.

In November took place a movement which gives further evidence of the state of feeling which had existed since July. Certain Caracas notables petitioned Casas for the establishment of a junta independent of that of Seville, to decide the political fate of Venezuela and to preserve internal peace. The document, signed by forty-five of the most distinguished creoles, was delivered on November 24th. But the government made a show of force and acted against the peitioners, imprisoning some and exiling others. Antonio Fernández de León, as the ringleader, was sent a prisoner to Spain. The movement was a creole attempt to take the political reins, and the government saved itself by persuading the coloureds and other lower classes that their interests would be harmed if the creoles won power. This attitude of the people persisted despite later attemps of some revolutionary leaders to win over the lower classes.

The petitioners were reprieved on February 18, 1809; but, although on the surface things returned to their normal tranquillity, throughout 1809 there was seething unrest. Emparan, who became Captain-general in May, ruled despotically and was disliked by older men and by the Church, though some younger men approved of him. Underground, *coups* were prepared to bring him down, but nothing serious happened; yet all the time the revolution was maturing.

In 1810 modern Venezuelan history opened, with the appearance at the head of affairs of men steeped in the creole traditions. The generation which took into its hands the winning of independence was organising itself, intellectually and socially, to move forward to those events which Venezuelans consider to be the most important in their history. From 1808 the young men of Caracas, with the mature men too, began to follow the revolutionary road. Already on December 14, 1809 and April 2, 1810 attempts had been made to depose the Captain-general and set up a junta, and this was finally achieved on April 19th, Maundy Thursday.

On the 18th the revolutionaries met at the house of Manuel Díaz Casado, and in the early morning of the 19th at that of Doctor José Ángel de Álamo. During this morning the town council was called to an urgent meeting by its vice-president, the Mayor José de las Llamozas, while young revolutionaries rushed about urging people to form a large crowd in the public square in front of the town hall. The council's meeting was illegal, since only the Captain-general himself, as its president, was empowered to call one. Once met, the council invited the Captain-general to attend. It was eight o'clock in the morning. Llamozas told the assembly of the plan to set up an autonomous junta presided over by the Captain-general, but the latter rejected the proposal and stood up to go to the cathedral. The revolutionaries shouted and got all the crowd to shout that he should go back into the meeting. One of the leaders, Francisco Salias, dared to approach him and request him to do so, and he acceded. At this point the meeting was joined by Juan Germán Roscio and José Félix Sosa in the name of the people, José Cortés Madariaga in the name of the clergy and the people, and Francisco José Ribas for the clergy. Finally the meeting decided to make the town council the government, and depose Emparan and all his staff. Thus the revolution began with a change of government, but it was done still in the name of King Ferdinand and still with a salute to Spain as the mother country. Emparan and his closest collaborators were deported, and Venezuelans at last ruled in Venezuela.

By the act of April 19, 1810, then, the town council of Caracas was transformed into the government of the Venezuelan provinces. It took the name of Supreme Junta for the Conservation of the Rights of Ferdinand VII, and received the title of Highness. This act is important for the rest of Venezuela's history, since from that moment every government brought in by a *coup d'état* has justified itself by a constitutive act such as this. The written constitution has in fact not acted as the final code of rules for the politics of Venezuela, and this phenomenon deserves a study which it has not yet received, since it reflects something deeply ingrained in the Spanish American character. However, the Junta acted in the name of Ferdinand VII yet claimed, paradoxically, to represent the sovereign will of the people. It consisted of twenty-three members, four secretaries of state, a chancellor and two secretaries 'with the exercise of decrees'; a superior court of appeals with nine members, to replace the deported *audiencia;* a police tribunal for minor cases; and various civil servants and military advisers. The members, whose names were published on May 4th in the *Gaceta de Caracas,* were from the creole ruling class, such men as Llamozas and Roscio, who was Secretary of State for Foreign Affairs.

Besides proceding with its own internal organisation and taking the police measures necessary for security, the Junta reorganised the militia, replacing the former commanding officers, and made other military changes. It ordered double pay for the troops who had helped on April 19th. Its administration began with an order opening trade with 'our common mother country' and with friendly, allied and neutral countries (May 3rd). It suppressed export duties and abolished the *alcabala* on articles of sustenance and 'objects of necessary consumption'. It freed the Indians from tribute 'so that the primitive owners of our soil shall be the first to enjoy the benefits of our civil regeneration'. It forbade the slave trade. It liberated many men held prisoner on pretext of being vagabonds, and hoped thereby to help the agricultural labour problem. Also there were created an Academy of Mathematics, and a Patriotic Society (as in eighteenth-century Spain) to encourage agriculture and industry.

The Junta began its political activities by sending a mission to the provinces to invite them to join the movement of Caracas, and on April 20th it launched a proclamation to say that the people of Caracas had 'decided to constitute a *provisional Sovereignty* in this Capital for it and for the other towns of this Province which may unite with it with their accustomed loyalty to Don Ferdinand the Seventh: and the people proclaimed this Sovereignty publicly and everywhere on the nineteenth of this month, reposing the supreme authority in the Most Illustrious Town Council of this capital and certain deputies whom the people appointed to be associated with it, with the special task that all of them shall make the plan of administration and government which is most conformable to the general will of these peoples.'

On May 3rd the Junta wrote to the Spanish Regency government giving notice of the withdrawal of Venezuela from its dominion. In reply the Regency declared the Venezuelans rebels and appointed as Captain-general Fernando Miyares, former governor of Maracaibo, and sent Antonio Cortabarría, minister of the Spanish Supreme Council in the Indies, to Puerto Rico to encompass the defeat of Venezuela with a naval squadron.

As a result of the appeal to the other towns of Venezuela, most of the rest of the old Captaincy-general joined the movement: Barcelona on April 27th, Cumaná on the 30th, Margarita on May 4th, Barinas on the 5th, Guayana on the 11th, Mérida on September 16th and Trujillo on October 6th. Coro and Maracaibo stood out. Finally, the Caracas Junta informed the other main cities of the continent and opened direct contact with the Antilles. Two diplomatic missions were sent, one to London, with Simón Bolívar and Luis López Méndez as agents and Andrés Bello as secretary, and the other to the United States, with Juan Vicente Bolívar and Telesforo Orea as agents and Rafael Revenga as secretary. The Bolívars had been unable to take part in the events of April 19th in Caracas since they were confined to their estates for their parts in the frustrated movement of April 1st.

On June 11th, scarcely two months after its creation, the Junta called for elections in all the towns under its rule. Juan Germán Roscio wrote both the preamble to the regulations and the regulations for the elections, and in the first he explained the Junta's motives, admitting that the Junta did not truly represent all of free Venezuela, and therefore its actions were only provisional, whereas a permanent government required the presence of deputies from all the towns. The regulations were intended to avoid 'the perils of tumultuous assemblies'. The elections were to be in two stages: the election by parishes of their Electors in the proportion of one Elector for 500 inhabitants and one other for every 250 more inhabitants; and secondly these Electors were to elect a main deputy and vice-deputy in the proportion of one for 20,000 inhabitants and one more for every 10,000 over that figure in the electoral district. The deputies were given powers to constitute a Congress named 'for the Conservation of the Rights of Ferdinand VII'. Voters had to be twenty-four years of age or else married and with their own establishment. If they lived with and worked for someone else, they must possess at least two thousand pesos worth of property. In other words, voting was restricted to the free classes, which assured the hegemony of the creole oligarchy. The number of deputies came to forty-two for the seven provinces in which there were elections, and their names were those of the great creole families.

The National Congress, as the revolutionaries called it, met on March 2, 1811 first of all in the house of the Count of San Javier, and then in the Monastery of San Francisco. Its first president was Doctor Felipe Fermín Paúl; the vice-president was Doctor Mariano de la Cova, and the secretaries the Licentiates Miguel José Sanz and Antonio Nicolás Briceño. The oath which the deputies swore mentioned independence of the Spanish government and the 'representation which resides in the General Congress of Venezuela'.

The Junta resigned its power, and the Congress elected a new executive, composed of three members who exchanged their duties on a weekly rotation. On March 28th the triumvirate chosen was Cristóbal Mendoza, Juan de Escalona and Baltasar Padrón, with Manuel Moreno de Mendoza, Mauricio Ayala and Doctor Andrés Narvarte as their substitutes. A Council was appointed to advise the government, a High Court of Justice was created, and various other measures were taken. Commissions were set up to 'compose the constitution and the civil and penal codes of law', and to establish the law of freedom of the press and the law dealing with ecclesiastical preferment.

The activities of the Patriotic Society for Agriculture and Economy were set in motion by the Junta's decree of August 14, 1810, the object being, as in the case of the Academy of Mathematics, the encouragement of the general economic development of the country. But the Patriotic Society became in fact a political club about December 1810, when Bolívar joined it on his return from London, bringing Miranda the Precursor, who also became a member. The Society contained a numerous group of young revolutionaries, not only from the creole nobility but also from among other classes, and it tended to be extreme in its views. Whereas the Congress debated problems of government with lofty serenity, the Society feverishly supported the one great idea of absolute independence.

Francisco de Miranda was welcomed home by the Junta and by many people in Caracas. Bolívar had him to stay in his home. Soon Miranda began to take part in public affairs, in the Congress, and the Junta made him a Lieutenant-general. Some politicians and men of influence, such as Roscio, opposed him, but the young men regarded him as a leader, a man of adventure and experience, with universal fame as a revolutionary. He soon found support in the Patriotic Society; and what with Miranda, Bolívar, Espejo and others, the Society became a centre of political agitation, putting pressure on the Congress to persuade it to declare the complete independence of the country. So the revolutionary movement passed from the Congress to the fevered evenings of the Society, where met men who were making history in those very days and who were to make it in the future, like Paúl, García de Sena, Ribas, Salias, Soublette, Sanz, and so on. When, on April 19, 1811, the anniversary of the first revolution was celebrated with cavalcades, festivities and public speeches, the loudest support for a declaration of complete independence came from the members of the Patriotic Society. The newspapers began to adopt political programmes. *El patriota venezolano* was the organ of the Society, and in it and in *El publicista venezolano, El semanario de Caracas* and *El Mercurio venezolano* writers of articles, essays and lampoons pleaded the cause of liberty.

On July 1, 1811 the Congress proclaimed the rights of the people: popular sovereignty, indispensable, inalienable and indivisible, and also liberty, security, enjoyment of property, equality before the law, non-perpetuity of public office, and the happiness of all as the aim of society. This was the model of what for the directors of Venezuela a State and a society ought to be: it implied division into classes, since only property owners had the right to vote, and it envisaged harmony and order.

The move towards independence gained momentum when despatches arrived from one of the agents in the United States, Telesforo Orea. They were heard in Congress on July 2nd, and the favourable attitude which they said reigned in the United States encouraged the seekers of real independence and even warmed the hesitant; so that on the 3rd the debate on independence was opened by José Luis Cabrera. The discussion became heated, but most opinions favoured a declaration, although certain objections were put forward, some tactical and others questions of scruple. Still, no ideological reason stood against the conversion of the Captaincy-general into a sovereign State. One objection, for example, was that Britain seemed to think that the new government was not incompatible with fidelity to Ferdinand VII, and that therefore it would be wise to consult her and also the United States before making a change which might lose for Venezuela valuable foreign sympathy. Again, Roscio, who was not a keen revolutionary, held that it would be wrong for a declaration of independence to be made while the provinces of Coro, Maracaibo and Guayana remained outside the movement.

But in fact by July the Congress had taken measures which were incompatible with acceptance of the authority of Ferdinand or any Spanish government, since they had even recommended the setting up of a commission to draft a constitution. Yet opinions differed: one member refused to have any truck with anything opposed to the conservation of the rights of Ferdinand VII, and in legal terms he was right. Tempers rose, especially when the priest Ramón Ignacio Méndez, deputy for Guasdualito, an opponent of the declaration of independence, tried to attack Miranda with his fists. The members of the Patriotic Society stopped at nothing and caused constant tumult. They had met in the club on the night of the 3rd and had heard Bolívar's first political speech in which he asked the Congress to hear the views of the Society, and persuaded the Society to send a deputation to the Congress on the 4th to present its ideas. This was done, and the Congress, after hearing the leader Miguel Peña, consulted the Executive, who replied recommending independence. Although the debate continued on the 5th, the most powerful bodies of opinion were in agreement, and finally it was decided to declare the end of Venezuela's relationship with Spain and the creation of the new State. It was argued that the oath of loyalty to Ferdinand VII had been annulled by the King himself when he abdicated at Bayonne.

The Act of Independence, written by Roscio and Iznardi, was approved by Congress on July 7th, published on the 14th and printed in the *Gaceta de Caracas* on the 16th. The new country took the name American Confederation of Venezuela, and comprised the united provinces of Caracas, Cumaná, Barinas, Mar-

garita, Barcelona, Mérida and Trujillo. A 'Manifesto to the
World', published on July 30th, gave the reasons for the declaration of independence. Already on the 5th a commission had
been appointed to choose a national flag, and the one they
chose for the new Venezuela was the flag which Miranda had
flown on his fruitless expedition of 1806. In October Valencia
became the federal capital, and there the Congress sat from
February to April 1812.

The most serious problem which the Congress dealt with was
that of the constitution for the new State. It was under discussion from July 20th to December 21, 1811, and the men who
were mainly responsible for it were Gabriel Ponte, Roscio, Francisco Javier Ustáriz and Iznardi. Pending the approval of the
constitution by all the provinces, a new provisional government was elected in March 1812, and in it served Fernando
Toro, Ustáriz and Francisco Espejo, with Roscio, Mendoza and
Briceño as their substitutes. The constitution itself was radically revolutionary, not only because it substituted republic for
monarchy, but because it changed the tradition of the people
and so changed the course of Venezuela's history. From the
start the constitution laid down that the new state was federal:
the Confederation of the States of Venezuela. Each province
(now called State) was independent in its internal government,
and its link with the Confederation was expressed constitutionally. As the preliminary statement on the bases of the federal
agreement held: 'To make effective the mutual guarantee and
security which the States offer to each other so as to preserve
their civil liberty, their political independence and their religion, is the first and most sacred of the powers of the Confederation, in which alone resides the representation of the nation.
Because of this power the Confederation is placed in charge of
foreign relations, the common and general defence of the con-
federated States, the conservation of the public peace in face of
internal commotion or external attack, the arrangement of external commerce and that of the States with each other, the
raising and maintaining of Armies whenever they are necessary
for the maintenance of the liberty, integrity and independence
of the nation, the building and equipping of ships of war, the
celebration and conclusion of treaties and alliances with other
nations, the declaration of war and the making of peace, the
imposition of the taxes indispensable for these objects or others

convenient for the common security, tranquillity and happiness, with full and absolute authority for the establishment of the laws general to the whole Union and the power to judge and put into effect whatever is resolved and determined by such laws.'

It is held that this Constitution of 1811 was inspired by the United States Constitution of 1787 and the French Rights of Man, but a traditional source must be added to these: Spanish ideas. Specific examples of these influences are, of course, the classic separation of the three powers and the humanitarian language, which are of French origin; the general structure—the defensive pact—and the formulas used are of North American origin; while the retention of Catholicism as the state religion (the sole theme of chapter I) is of Spanish derivation. But besides mixing these influences, the Venezuelan legislators attempted to approach the reality of life in Venezuela, as can be seen in the classification of the citizens and also in the respect for the old provinces which had made up the Captaincy-general.

The main provisions of this constitution may be mentioned as an illustration of the nature of the change from the colonial régime. Chapter II established as the Legislature a Congress composed of a House of Representatives and a Senate, with Representatives elected for terms of four years and Senators for terms of six years, both in two-stage elections. In chapter III the Executive Power was described as 'three individuals elected by the people' for terms of four years. The Judicial Power, as laid down by chapter IV, was 'deposited in a Superior Court of Justice residing in the federal capital' and other inferior courts. Chapter V dealt with the States, and determined that these should not interfere in any of the powers granted to the Congress and the Executive Powers. It was declared in chapter VIII that the Rights of Man would be recognised and respected throughout the whole country.

The establishment of self-government in 1810, converted into complete sovereignty by the declaration of independence of 1811 and the consequent creation of a State, was caused by generous impulses, ideas of freedom and revolutionary feelings; but it was also in part based on the ambition for power of the directing creole class. Those who forged the Independence were educated men, able to rule a country in time of peace, but completely unprepared for the violent reaction of Spain, of Spaniards living in Venezuela, and of those Venezuelans who were opposed to independence. The experiment, the fine ideal of the First Republic, was to end in 1812 with the capitulation of Miranda, general and dictator of the Venezuelan State, to Monteverde, the fortunate caudillo who served the Spanish Regency.

The opposition of the Spaniards and Venezuelans who supported Ferdinand VII on the one hand and, on the other, the Regency which governed the Spanish dominions in his name, began immediately after April 19th, when the town of Coro refused to join the movement of Caracas. José Ceballos, the military commander, arrested the two delegates from Caracas and sent them to Maracaibo, whose governer and intendant, Fernando Miyares, also opposed the capital. In both Coro and Maracaibo the town councils held open meetings and gave their support to their respective chiefs. Thus the first military action of the patriots, as the fighters for independence are called, was undertaken to suppress the Coro reaction; and the Junta in Caracas appointed the Marqués del Toro general in chief of the Army of the West. About the end of November 1810 he reached Coro with his army, which included battalions of coloureds together with other groups, all still under the organisation of the traditional militia; but Toro was defeated and Coro remained royalist. Various parts of the country witnessed risings against the new system. In Cumaná the Catalan residents had to be put down by force, while in Caracas the Canary Islanders rose, and in Valencia the coloureds not only rose but started a small war, since Toro was sent against them, was defeated again, and had to be succeeded by Miranda himself, who made the town capitulate. In this campaign Bolívar came to the fore, serving under Toro, who accompanied Miranda.

This uprising, although defeated, was in fact not punished since the Congress granted amnesty to almost all of the rebels, and was so exceedingly lenient that the chief rebel, Fray Pedro Hernández, was only condemned to remain enclosed in a monastery until he should abjure his errors, when he could be released to preach 'the sacred system of Venezuela and all America'. Congress tried another ten men, and sentenced some to prison and others to exile or service in the army. But such magnanimity was weakness, since it allowed the opponents of the new régime to operate easily in republican territory while Coro, Maracaibo and Guayana prepared attacks. In March a patriot ex-

pedition sent against Guayana was defeated, and at the same
time incursions came from Coro into patriot territory. Yet the
patriots were stronger at this stage than the royalists, at least
for defence, although their resistance was to be broken in a few
months, mainly because of two things: an earthquake and the
presence of Monteverde.

On March 26, 1812 an earthquake ravaged large stretches of
Venezuela along the Andes and the coast. In Caracas many
were killed that day, which happened to be Good Friday, and
much of the city was destroyed. The clergy used this event as
anti-patriot propaganda, preaching that it was God's punishment for the declaration of independence. In February, too,
Coro was reinforced by the arrival of two Spanish naval ships.
Two more arrived in June from Puerto Rico, which was Cortabarría's headquarters. From them landed the naval captain
Domingo Monteverde with three officers and 120 marines. Already Eusebio Antoñanzas, sent by Ceballos, had advanced towards San Felipe. In March, at the orders of Ceballos, Monteverde began his offensive from Coro. At Siquisique the patriot
commander went over with his troops and joined Monteverde,
and little by little the people of the state of Lara were brought
to join the royalist cause, willingly or by force, with the result
that Monteverde gathered an army. The whole west fell easily
into the fortunate captain's hands, with scarcely even a skirmish.

The earthquake, the position in Guayana and Monteverde's
unresisted advance, combined to convince the Executive Power
that it should appoint Miranda commander-in-chief with full
powers to arrange anything required for the country's safety;
and on April 23rd Miranda became, in effect, dictator. Operations were concentrated on Valencia, which Monteverde was
approaching. Miranda placed Colonel Ustáriz in charge of the
defence of Valencia, and Colonel Bolívar with a similar task in
Puerto Cabello, but Ustáriz evacuated the federal capital as
Monteverde came on and as most of the population joined the
royalists. Monteverde entered the town to the acclamations of
the people on May 3rd. Miranda tried to recapture the capital,
but his officers proved to be inept and his troops went over to
the enemy in hundreds; and at the same time the aristocratic
creoles of Caracas undermined his position.

About May 20th Antoñanzas captured Calabozo, releasing

some prisoners held there by the patriots, among them the fearsome José Tomás Boves, who joined the royalist forces and led a campaign into the *llanos*, defeating Ustáriz. So the *llanos* fell into royalist hands. Between June 30th and the first few days of July Bolívar lost Puerto Cabello, one of the mainstays of the defence of the country, and retreated to La Guaira. This situation, together with discouragement and other social, moral and economic causes, brought Miranda's capitulation to Monteverde after negotiations which ended on July 25th. Monteverde accepted the complete surrender of the patriots and promised to respect their lives, possessions and honour. The royalists entered Caracas on the 30th, and Miranda himself went to La Guaira where Bolívar and other patriots arrested him on the 31st, since they believed that the capitulation had been an act contrary to the general will and was therefore an act of treachery. Monteverde, the successful royalist *caudillo*, made himself the effective governor of the country and in what was in fact a revolutionary manner ignored the authority of Miyares, the Captain-general. Once in Caracas, Monteverde forgot the terms of the capitulation and behaved as the conqueror, imprisoning former opponents and even shipping some of them to Spain.

The short duration of this First Republic was not due to Miranda's capitulation, but to other causes. The political situation became more and more complicated until the point was reached where the Executive Power could only govern dictatorially, and its authority came into conflict with the general indiscipline and the personality of Miranda himself; and at the same time the federal nature of the constitution contributed to the lack of cohesion of the government. The causes of defeat, then, included the structure itself of the Confederation, the fatal weakness of the government, the lack of military training of the patriots, the lack of enthusiasm of the people, shown by continual desertion, administrative chaos which brought economic ruin, and the fact that the people did not understand the change of régime, since they were incapable of conceiving of any other government but one in the King's name.

3. THE SECOND REPUBLIC

Monteverde re-established the Spanish organs of government and began a personal dictatorship, while the patriot leaders fled to the Antilles or to New Granada, or remained in hiding. The

revolutionary upsurge soon reappeared, in the form of a recon-
quering expedition, once the patriot chiefs had attained maturity and learned how to win and how to lose battles. A devastating two-year war began at the two extreme points of the country, and here at last was the true War of Independence. In the
east the most outstanding leader of the patriots was Santiago
Mariño, and in the west it was Simón Bolívar.

On August 27, 1812 Bolívar embarked at La Guaira for Curaçao using the passport granted him by Monteverde through
the good offices of his friend Francisco Iturbe. From Curaçao he
went to Cartagena at the end of October, and from that port he
wrote to the Congress of New Granada (the revolutionary government of Venezuela's neighbouring state) asking for support
for Venezuela. Together with Vicente Tejera and Miguel Cara-
baño he published official papers of Monteverde's in order to
prove the failure of the royalist chief to respect the terms of the
capitulation of the Venezuelan army. On December 21st Bolívar was put in command of the river post of Barrancas by the
New Granadan government, and he showed his worth in several successful actions which freed the Magdalena valley of royalist forces and re-established communications between Cartagena and the interior. In January 1813 he liberated Ocaña and,
with the government's permission, invaded Venezuela, occupying San Antonio de Táchira on March 1st. Bolívar's chief victory in New Granada was his defeat of Ramón Correa at Cúcuta
on February 28th.

Several Venezuelan officers had accompanied Bolívar to New
Granada and fought with him in these campaigns. They were
favourably received by the governor of Cartagena, partly because he needed officers, and the men who arrived were among
the most distinguished of the Venezuelan forces: José Félix
Ribas, the Spaniard Cortés Campomanes, who fought for the
patriots, Nicolás Briceño, and several more, some of whom
were given important posts. Some civilians had gone with Bolívar too and escaped Monteverde's fierce repressions. These included Tejera and Díaz Casado, followed by others such as
Yanes, Gual and Méndez.

In Caracas and throughout Venezuela half way through
August 1812 Monteverde had arrested many of the civilians in-
volved in the revolution, and had punished some with cruelty.
In Caracas many were exposed in the pillory, where they suf-

fered the insults and worse of the brutal soldiery and the mob. Roscio was one of them, and later he was shipped off to Spain together with other civil leaders such as Cortés Madariaga, Juan Pablo Ayala, Manuel Ruiz and Francisco de Iznardi. Some of the former patriots, as was natural, changed coat. Antonio Fernández de León, the Marqués de Casa León, served the royalists; and José Manuel Oropeza, of Carora, worked for Monteverde as a bitter enemy of the Republic.

Bolívar's first activity on arrival at Cartagena was intellectual. Besides publishing his accusation of Monteverde, he wrote for the Congress of New Granada a long document exposing the reasons for the fall of the Venezuelan Confederation and imploring help. But the most important document he wrote was that signed on December 15, 1812 and known as the Manifesto of Cartagena, since here Bolívar summed up his political ideas, until this time only found scattered in other writings. This, then, is the first real expression of Bolívar's thought—thought which developed during the course of the wars and during his subsequent political career. The Manifesto can be divided into two sections, in the first of which he once again exposed the reasons for Venezuela's failure in order, as he wrote, that the example might teach America to mend her ways and give the necessary unity, solidity and energy to her governments: 'In the first place should be mentioned the nature of the Constitution which, I repeat, was as contrary to Venezuela's interests as it was favourable to those of her opponents. Secondly, the spirit of philanthropy which took possession of our governors. Thirdly, the opposition to the establishment of military forces able to save the Republic and repel the blows of the Spaniards. Fourthly, the earthquake together with religious fanaticism, which was able to gain the most important results from this phenomenon. Lastly, the internal factions, which in truth were the deadly poison which sent the country to its grave.'

The second section urged the necessity of liberating Venezuela as a base and in order to avoid the complete loss of the free parts of America. Past errors must not be repeated. Venezuela should be invaded from New Granada, and the expedition would receive support from every hand. It would be a mistake to despise Venezuela, as it was a mistake for Venezuela to despise Coro; 'Coro is to Caracas what Caracas is to America.' From Venezuela the royalists could obtain men and munitions and supplies which would be used 'under the direction of leaders experienced through their fight against the great masters of the art of war, the French.'

The Manifesto also contained ideas on government which Bolívar was later to apply, as for example his insistence on unity, on centralised power. One of his most fruitful notions was that the government should be adapted to 'the character of the circumstances, the times and the men', so that in calamitous and turbulent times, the government should be 'terrible, and should arm itself with a firmness equal to the surrounding dangers, without any regard for laws or constitutions until peace and happiness are restored.' He saw, rightly, that until the governments of America were centralised the royalists would always have every advantage, since the new countries would 'inevitably be involved in the horrors of civil dissension.' The Spanish author Madariaga has written: 'In the Cartagena documents Bolívar is revealed in complete truth, as he was by nature and as he had been made by adversity; a man resolved not to shift from his political realism on account of any abstract idea, or from his inexorability on account of an atom of compassion; an acute and penetrating mind, yet completely the Spanish swashbuckling soldier.'[1]

Torices, chief of the State of Cartagena, and Torres, president of the Union of New Granada, were two valuable friends to Bolívar at this time. The post of commander of Barrancas, on the River Magdalena and (in March 1813) the appointment as Brigadier of the Armies of the Union, together with the Congress's grant of citizenship, all provided supports for the Venezuelan leader's activity in the near future. Although some of the officers with whom he made the campaigns preliminary to the invasion of Venezuela were Venezuelans, the men were New Granadans. Thus the moral support of the government and the material support of the army gave Bolívar his start in his liberating career. When in 1814, after the loss of the Second Republic, Bolívar came back to Cartagena, Torres gave him encouragement which helped him to return to the attempt. In the struggle for independence the efforts of the Venezuelans were united with those of New Granada.

Bolívar's plan was to conquer Venezuela with forces from

---

[1] Salvador de Madariaga, *Bolívar*, México D F 1953, vol. I, p. 384.

H

New Granada, and while he was fighting for his friends he was gathering men and matériel for the invasion, so that it is possible that his refusal to help Castillo, a patriot colonel who was operating at Pamplona, was due not only to the fact that he could not move without orders from the government of Cartagena, but also to unwillingness to divert forces from the primary objective. Once the New Granadan provinces which bordered on Venezuela were free, there was nothing more to do but act with rapidity; and Bolívar intended to make a lightning campaign which would surprise Monteverde and give him no time for reorganisation. It was true that Monteverde had the bastion of the Andes and the good base of the rich province of Caracas, but he had not a large army nor good communications. Seven hundred troops guarded the main routes into Venezuela via Maracaibo and the Apure, while 500 covered the road to Trujillo. A thousand men made themselves strong on the heights of Barquisimeto. Behind this first line, 500 men were stationed in Barinas, 1,200 in San Carlos and 900 at Guasdualito on the Apure. Lastly, Monteverde kept a reserve of 700 in Caracas. The scene of operations was immense, and Bolívar prepared to embrace it all, overcoming obstacles by dint of his talent, and perseverance, and in spite of his inexperience, with only 650 soldiers. To strike rapidly and to organise an all-embracing action was Bolívar's scheme.

Between March 1, 1813, when he occupied San Antonio de Táchira, and August 7th, when he reached Caracas, Bolívar fulfilled his promise to the Congress of New Granada: he liberated Venezuela. The route from Táchira to the capital was strewn with quick military successes, in which rapidity and energy were the characteristics of the victor, who successively freed the various towns, Mérida, Trujillo, Barquisimeto, Barinas, Valencia, and finally Caracas.

Bolívar's army was at first composed of two divisions, one under the command of the New Granadan Colonel Castillo, and the other under the Venezuelan Colonel José Félix Ribas. Castillo advanced to La Grita, attacking Correa, who was withdrawing defeated from Cúcuta, but once inside Venezuela Castillo was replaced in the command by Francisco de Paula Santander, a future president of Colombia. Castillo and Bolívar had quarrelled, and soon Santander had to return also to New Granada since he could not see eye to eye with Bolívar either. The

New Granadan officers included men of distinction in the wars, such as Girardot, D'Elhuyar, Ortega, Vélez, Ricaurte and París; and the Venezuelans had leaders such as Ribas, Urdaneta and Antonio Nicolás Briceño.

The army was reorganised in Venezuela, so that Girardot became commander of the first division, in the vanguard, with D'Elhuyar as his second-in-command; Ribas commanded the rearguard, while Tejada was put in charge of the artillery and Urdaneta became Bolívar's second-in-command. The campaign fought by these men passed into history with the name of the 'Admirable Campaign', and its main battles were at Niquitao, near Trujillo, where Ribas on July 2nd defeated the royalist Colonel José Martí, Los Horcones, near Barquisimeto, another success of the same officer, on July 22nd, and Bolívar's own great victory of July 31st at Taguanes, between San Carlos and Valencia, over Colonel Izquierdo. This victory was so complete that it gave Monteverde, who was in Valencia, scarcely time enough to flee to Puerto Cabello, leaving clear the road to Caracas.

The day after his entry into the capital Bolívar wrote (August 8th) to the commission which the New Granadan Congress had appointed to supervise his actions, saying that he had re-established the Republic of Venezuela thanks to the help of New Granada, and that pending the setting up of a legal government he himself would rule. As he went he had restored patriot government in Trujillo and Mérida: in the circumstances it was natural for him to exercise supreme authority, and his victories gave him the power to do so. Before his entry into the city a meeting of notables of Caracas had sent a mission to him to arrange for the capitulation which was signed at La Victoria on August 4th, and to try to persuade him to agree to the establishment in Venezuela of 'the Constitution of the Spains' and to the choice as governor of 'the person who shall merit the confidence of all the classes in general.' But Bolívar would not throw away the revolution, and only replied that on his arrival in Caracas he would set up 'that form of Government which shall appear most just and adapted to the circumstances'.

Although Bolívar was dictator from August 8, 1813, it was not until January 2, 1814 that the supreme power was granted him by a popular assembly which he himself had convoked on August 9th. It was clear that strong government was needed, and the notables of Caracas acceded, but the result was that there was no return to the ideals of 1811. Ustáriz produced a plan for a provisional government which gave the commander-in-chief of the army all power until the country should be free of enemies inside its territory. Bolívar became dictator, and he had already been acclaimed as Liberator at his entry into Mérida on May 23, 1813. The title was officially bestowed by the town council of Caracas in an extraordinary meeting of August 14th, at the same time as Bolívar was proclaimed Captain-general of the Armies.

The most important document of the 1813 campaign was the so-called decree of war to the death. This is the most controversial of Bolívar's writings, but it should be remembered that it was linked closely with the circumstances of that time, and was not merely the fruit of the views of the author alone. The decree was signed by Bolívar, as Commander-in-chief of the Army of the North, in his headquarters at Trujillo on June 15, 1813. It stated, first of all, that the Army had been sent by the Congress of New Granada to liberate Venezuela, and that the patriot government of the Confederation of 1811 would be restored. For complete liberation it was necessary to clear the country of Peninsulars: 'Any Spaniard who does not conspire against the tyranny and for the just cause, by the most active and efficacious means, shall be considered an enemy and punished as a traitor to the country, and in consequence shall without exception be shot.' Any who joined the patriot forces were to be granted complete amnesty. As for native Americans: 'And you Americans who have been led astray from the paths of justice by error and perfidy, know that your brothers forgive you and sincerely lament your straying, convinced that you cannot be guilty and that only the blindness and ignorance in which up to the present the authors of your crimes have kept you can have induced you to commit those crimes. Do not fear the sword which comes to avenge you and to cut the ignominious links with which your executioners bind you to themselves. You will have complete immunity for your honour, your lives and your property: the simple title of American will be your guarantee and safeguard. Our arms have come to protect you and will never be employed against a single one of our brothers.'

Towards the end of May 1813 Bolívar, in a speech to the

town council of Mérida, just re-established in its authority, had already said that his aim in returning to Venezuela was only to succour the Americans and exterminate the Spaniards. The tone had hardened in a proclamation of June 21st to the people of Mérida: 'Our vengeance will be equal to the ferocity of the Spaniards. Our kindness is ended, and since our oppressors force us to war to the death, they shall disappear from America and our land will be purged of the monsters who infest it. Our hate will be implacable and the war shall be to the death.'

So much for Bolívar himself. As for the country as a whole, apart from the fact that in practice war to the death had prevailed since 1812, there were two official documents before the proclamation. Firstly, there was the penal decree of April 16, 1812, promulgated in Valencia by the Executive Power of the time, and which threatened all the enemies of the Venezuelan Confederation with death and actually established the punishment of death for conspiracy against the régime and for 'all who by word or deed oppose the fulfillment' of the decree. This decree was applied against those who shirked conscription into the army under the military law of June 19, 1812. Secondly, on January 16, 1813. Antonio Nicolás Briceño had signed in Cartagena, with the French officers who accompanied him, an agreement by which all European Spaniards, whether guilty or not, were to be shot. Bolívar accepted this agreement, with some modifications, in Cúcuta.[1]

The complete separation established by the Trujillo proclamation between Americans and Spaniards points out the main aim of the war to the death: it was to distinguish clearly who were the royalists and to put the war on an international plane. The war was to be between Spain and America, even though from the social viewpoint it could not be considered so, since the people involved were almost all Americans. Propaganda in the *Gaceta de Caracas* described the barbarities practised by the royalists, and thus attempted to justify the war to the death: 'Moderate Spaniards of the other hemisphere: your compatriots in America are not men. They exceed in cruelty the most atrocious cannibals.' But this war was not the product of one man's ideas; however reprehensible, it represented the will of many people.

[1] V. Dávila, *La guerra a muerte*, in *Investigaciones históricas*, Caracas 1953, pp. 5-46.

In the eastern parts of Venezuela, when the news of Miranda's capitulation to Monteverde arrived, the people had peacefully submitted to the royalist emissaries, but Monteverde's cruelty, and that of his subordinates such as Antonio Zuazola, quickly exasperated the locals. Some patriots had taken refuge in Trinidad, and from there a few officers led a liberating invasion of the oppressed eastern territory. At the same time as Bolívar was advancing on Caracas, Santiago Mariño was leading the liberation of Cumaná and the east. Margarita was freed, and Piar defeated local royalist troops on the mainland, and then Monteverde himself. Another man who later became an important leader of the liberation, Antonio José de Sucre, took part in this campaign.

By the middle of 1813 most of Venezuela was in patriot hands. The provinces of Guayana and Maracaibo remained to the royalists, and also the fortress of Yaguaraparo, in Cumaná, protected by the Spanish navy, and Puerto Cabello, where Monteverde had taken refuge. Bolívar laid siege to this port in August, but with no success, for in September reinforcements reached there from Spain, and Monteverde was able to go over to the offensive. The whole country was soon alight again, as towns and villages declared for the royalists and the Spanish leaders settled into strong positions. Yet Bolívar won a battle at Bárbula on September 30th, and beat Monteverde decisively at Las Trincheras on October 3rd. Monteverde was forced to retreat again to Puerto Cabello, and there his own officers obliged him to embark early in 1814. There were other successes for Bolívar, in command of operations in the west of the country, such as at Vigirima between November 23rd and 25th, and at Araure on December 5th, even though the royalist chief of Coro, Ceballos, checked Bolívar for a short time before Barquisimeto. However, at the beginning of 1814 the Republic, under the dictatorship of Bolívar, seemed to be secure again. But at this point a new royalist leader, a *caudillo*, arose.

He was José Tomás Boves, an Asturian sailor who had settled at Calabozo and become a horse-dealer. Insulted by the patriots in 1812, he became a *caudillo* of the *llaneros*. He defeated Vicente Campo Elías at La Puerta on February 3rd, 1814.[1] Boves

---

[1] La Puerta is a defile in a hill route to the *llanos*. Two battles were fought there in 1814, and another in 1818.

next advanced towards the Valleys of Aragua, while Bolívar marched from Caracas to Valencia in order to face him. The armies clashed on the 20th, when Boves attacked Bolívar at San Mateo, and skirmishing went on for some days. They fought a battle on February 28th and another on March 24th, but Boves was forced to turn to face Mariño, coming up from Aragua de Barcelona. On March 31st these two fought at Bocachica, and Mariño won. Boves retreated towards Calabozo, pursued by Bolívar. Ceballos was obliged to lift his siege of the patriot Urdaneta in Valencia, but Cajigal arrived to reinforce him, and the two faced Bolívar at Carabobo on May 28th, when they were defeated and split: Cajigal fled towards the Apure, while Ceballos went westwards.

Meanwhile, however, Boves had licked his wounds at Calabozo and on June 15th was able to defeat the combined forces of Bolívar and Mariño at the second battle of La Puerta. The patriot leaders fled to Caracas, leaving Boves to shoot his prisoners on the field of battle before advancing. On July 10th Boves entered Valencia and had the patriot governor shot. On the 16th he was already in Caracas, where he set up a dictatorship even more severe than that of Monteverde, ignoring orders from Spain for Cajigal to become Captain-general of the country. Bolívar fled eastwards, followed by most of the people of Caracas, who had no wish to suffer Boves' rule. At Aragua de Barcelona Bolívar attempted to take up his stand against Morales, whom Boves had sent after him; but Morales wiped out Bolívar's force. Boves himself moved into the Cumaná region in October, defeating the patriots there on December 5th, but dying himself of a lance-thrust during the battle. Morales, his lieutenant, pursued the vanquished patriots and had one of their chiefs, José Félix Ribas, whom he had taken prisoner, executed. 1814 was a year of fierce battles, in one of which, on February 12th, Ribas defeated Morales, employing a force composed of Caracas school-boys and students.

The bloody fame of Boves had caused two thirds of the population of Caracas to accompany the patriot army when it evacuated Caracas in July, and with them went refugees from other towns. They took 23 days to travel about 250 miles eastwards to Barcelona and left the road strewn with dead. Some of the families managed to take ship to the West Indies or Margarita.

Bolívar himself, defeated, reached Cumaná together with

Mariño on August 25th. They had to pursue Bianchi, an Italian pirate, and come to terms with him in order to recover some of the country's treasure, but then on September 3rd, at Carúpano, they were arrested by order of Piar and Ribas, and stripped of their authority. They managed to get free and took ship, together with forty-two officers, finally reaching Cartagena in safety. The last piece of patriot territory by the end of 1814 was Margarita, under the government of Juan Bautista Arismendi, although a few leaders such as Monagas, Zaraza, Cedeño and Páez carried on guerrilla warfare in the *llanos*. The Republice, Bolívar's dictatorship in fact, had disappeared.

The success of Boves needs some explanation. This Spaniard became the first true democratic leader in Venezuela, establishing social democracy in his forces and coming close to the people. He freed slaves, and promoted mixed breeds and mulattoes to high military rank, even though in 1814 the old colonial social divisions persisted in the country—and indeed were to continue until the second half of the century. His soldiers were specially recruited from the coloureds of the *llanos* and the other lower classes; and it should also be remembered that this leader possessed a real talent for leadership.

The fall of the Second Republic was evident at the defeat of the two military leaders of the patriots, Bolívar and Mariño. The main causes of the complete débâcle reflect the difficulty of the situation. Opinion in general was hostile to the idea of independence, and remained so until 1820. The mass of the people, the so-called lower classes, followed their *caudillos*, and the republican ideal had no force with them. From 1811 the country's economy was bankrupt, and the state of war which continued drove the situation further downhill as time went on. On December 31, 1813 an official report, couched in conservative language in order to avoid giving alarm, said: 'Venezuela has never been so empty of funds, has never had greater expenses to face, and the force of circumstances has never held back the country's revenue so much as during the present war.' To these causes must be added the powerful royalist reaction of the time, accompanied by the rising of guerrilla bands throughout the whole territory and marked by the organisation of armies by very competent officers. Finally, there was the overwhelming attack of Boves. His lances and his horses overthrew and galloped over Bolívar's glory, the nascent Republic, its civilisation and its hopes.

4. THE SPANISH REACTION AND THE THIRD PERIOD OF THE REPUBLIC

In March 1814 King Ferdinand VII returned to Spain from his captivity in France, and commenced to rule. He quickly nullified the liberal Constitution of 1812 and the decrees of the Cortes. With support from the army, the absolutist party and the people he ruled in the old style, according to his own will, and led a violent reaction against the liberal elements in Spain. This absolute rule lasted from 1814 until Ferdinand's death in 1833, except for a period of liberal government, imposed by a revolution, between 1820 and 1823. In 1814 a junta of Spanish generals was set to work to study the despatch of an expedition to subdue America by force, and on February 16, 1815 the expedition sailed from Cadiz, under the command of General Pablo Morillo, who had distinguished himself in the war against the French in the Peninsula. A squadron of five warships escorted the forty-two transports, which contained 10,642 soldiers organised in six regiments and one battalion of infantry, two regiments of cavalry, one mixed regiment of artillery and a battalion of engineers, with abundant stores and supplies—the best-found expedition which had ever left a Spanish port.

Meanwhile Bolívar reached Cartagena in September 1814, and from there explained to the Congress of New Granada what had happened in Venezuela. The Congress promoted him in the army, and when he visited them at Tunja placed him in charge of a division and sent him to subject the State of Cundinamarca, which had rebelled against the union of New Granada. On December 12th Bolívar won the vital battle and as a result was made Captain-general of the Armies of the Confederation of New Granada and given the mission of freeing Santa Marta from the royalists, which would allow him to invade Maracaibo and thus re-enter Venezuela. But back in Cartagena, Bolívar once again fell foul of the governor, Castillo, his old rival of 1813, who now refused to help him to continue his march to Santa Marta. So on May 8, 1815 Bolívar resigned his command to avoid a clash with a fellow patriot, and on the 9th sailed for Jamaica.

By this time Morillo and his army were in action in Venezuela, for they had taken Pampatar in Margarita on April 9th, in spite of the explosion of their flag-ship a few days before. Antonio Herráiz was made royalist governor of the island. Morillo next established a government in Cumaná, himself replacing, as he had been ordered, Cajigal, who had only become Captain-general in April. From early June until July Morillo was in Caracas, and then on July 12th he embarked at Puerto Cabello for the invasion of New Granada, leaving Salvador Moxó as interim Captain-general of Venezuela. Moxó issued a proclamation in which he claimed that his only sentiments were 'those of a tender father whose only care is the happiness of his children.' One of Moxó's posts was that of president of a Commission for confiscating the property of patriots and raising forced loans. A Royal Order of December 9, 1814 had laid down the regulations concerning such confiscations and the sale of the property seized, and Moxó proceeded strictly, explaining that the would-be purchasers of sequestrated property would have to prove their fidelity to the Sovereign with 'positive and outstanding' proofs, and that minors would have to prove that they had no taint of infamy through a traitorous father or an unworthy family. Morillo himself had started the sales, as he had also established an Appeals Tribunal, thereby avoiding the reinstatement of the older Audiencia. He had set up a permanent Council of War, and altogether had rebuilt the royalist government of the country.

His military successes were also swift. Taking with him Morales and his Venezuelan royalist troops, he went to Santa Marta, and besieged Cartagena in September 1815. He entered the city on December 6th, and went on to recapture the rest of New Granada. Bogotá, the capital, fell in October 1816; and throughout the campaign a violent repression of the patriots was taking place, with many executions of leaders.

Ferdinand VII had given certain instructions to Morillo when he sent him with the expedition. For example, Morillo was ordered to capture Margarita first, since the island was a refuge for pirates and for the insurgents from the mainland. After submission, the islanders were to be treated with gentleness in order to pacify them, and this was done. Further, Morillo was ordered to publish a general amnesty, but also to send to Spain 'under agreeable pretexts' any persons in the parts he reconquered who seemed to have played a dubious part in the previous troubles; any troops who had fought in Venezuela were to be got out of the country (and Morillo did in fact take Morales and the Venezuelan royalists to New Granada). The Audiencia was not to be re-established for the time being, but institutions of education were to be left as they were found; and therefore the University of Caracas re-opened, after the vacation, in September 1815. The Church authorities were to be respected, and merchants and landowners were to be helped; on the other hand a loan was to be demanded. Morillo was given powers, which he used, to change his instructions where necessary; and the treatment given to the reconquered people was hardly consonant with the royal protestations of paternal affection, though they were in accordance with the actual fact of armed reconquest. On May 9, 1815 Ferdinand issued a decree in which he claimed that he was 'prepared to treat like a father those who, recognising the evils brought upon their nation by their rash and criminal behaviour, wished to become truly reconciled', and then went on to describe the sending of Morillo's expedition.

Bolívar reached Kingston, Jamaica, on May 14, 1815, and stayed on the island until December 18, thanks to the generosity of the British merchant Maxwell Hyslop. Bolívar at this time tried to stir up public opinion in favour of Spanish American independence, writing articles in the Jamaican *Royal Gazette* as well as letters to influential men. His main aim was to gain the collaboration of the British, and to this end he even offered Britain territories such as Panamá and Nicaragua in exchange for her help in the liberation. His propaganda included the *Reply of a South American to a Gentleman of this Island* (September 6, 1815), known as the *Letter from Jamaica*, which was a long exposition of the situation of Spanish America engaged in the fight for liberty, and of the political thought of the author and his prognostications for the future. He began by showing how Spain and America were split in spite of their common tradition and then described how Venezuela had suffered in the wars, ending this section with a complaint at the indifference of Europe and North America to this crusade.

The prophecies for the future of Spanish America show Bolívar's insight. He affirmed that Latin America was different from all other parts of the world, claiming that it was in fact a new world although one with old forms of society; and he foresaw the creation of seventeen new nations in Latin America, all

republics. He believed already that New Granada and Venezuela would become a federal republic, and a few years later he
wore himself out in trying to hold such a state together. He
foresaw that in the River Plate area there would be a central
government at Buenos Aires, degenerating into an oligarchy or
a monocracy, that Chile would be the most stable republic, but
that the case of Peru was difficult because of the social problems there. All the new countries, he thought, would waste
their patrimony on present or future revolutions. The political
ideas of this *Letter* sum up part of what Bolívar wrote and did
elsewhere and later. For example, when writing of the question
of the form of government to be adopted, he showed pessimis-
tic suspicion, since proved well-founded, of democracy 'since
it is too perfect, and it demands virtues and political talents
very superior to ours', and for the same reason he set aside 'the
mixed monarchy of aristocracy and democracy, which has
brought so much fortune and splendour to England.' He knew
that liberal democracy was not suited to the peoples of the new
states in the state of development they had reached by then.

On December 10th Spaniards paid by Morillo attempted to
assassinate Bolívar; partly because of this, but mainly because
he had not succeeded in obtaining effective help for a new invasion of Venezuela, the Liberator sailed for Cartagena, at the
invitation of the defenders. At sea he learned that the port had
been captured by Morillo, and changed direction to go to Haïti,
where he arrived at Aux Cayes before going to Port-au-Prince,
which he reached on December 31, 1815. Here he was welcomed by the negro ruler, Pétion, an ardent republican and an en-
thusiast for the liberty of Latin America, who offered Bolívar
help for his invasion in return for the promise that Bolívar
would free the slaves in Venezuela. Bolívar established himself
at Aux Cayes, where on February 7, 1816, political and military command of the invasion was entrusted to him by an assembly of émigrés from Venezuela and New Granada, including Brion, Mariño and Piar, and foreign revolutionary soldiers
such as the Frenchman Ducoudray-Holstein.

The expedition of 240 men sailed on March 31, 1816 for Margarita, which was still partly under the command of the patriot
Arismendi. They landed after a skirmish, on May 3rd, then
passed over to the mainland, taking Carúpano on June 1st. Some
troops were raised, but after a month with no real success the

expedition left for Ocumare. The small army was met by Morales, sent by Morillo from New Granada, who beat it and forced Bolívar to re-embark, leaving a few troops on land, commanded by Soublette and MacGregor. Returning to Haïti in September, Bolívar again received help from Pétion, and was urged by the guerrillas left in Venezuela, Páez, Cedeño, Monagas, Arismendi and others, to make another attempt. Brion, now in command of Venezuela's naval forces, brought new help. A second expedition left Haïti in December, landing at Barcelona on the 31st. Bolívar proclaimed his arrival and urged the *llaneros* to join him. But some of his former lieutenants, Mariño, Bermúdez and Piar, had refused to recognise his command in August, and Bolívar took his men into the Guayana interior in order to build up from a fresh base.

Bolívar fulfilled his promise to Pétion when, on June 2, 1816, the day after his landing at Carúpano, he published a decree freeing the slaves, though imposing certain conditions on the 'new Citizens' of the republic: all males (just freed) between the ages of fourteen and sixty must join the army within twenty-four hours, and if they did not do so they forefeited their new liberty and so did their children under the age of fourteen, their wives and their parents.[1] A similar decree was issued on July 6th at Ocumare, including the slogan 'from this time forth there will only be one class of men in Venezuela, all will be citizens.' But slavery continued in fact even in the Republic which was founded after the break-up of Great Colombia in 1830.

1816 saw the beginning of what Bolívar called the third period of the Republic. Margarita was the original base on Venezuelan territory, since it had been free, under Arismendi, from November 1815 onwards. Bolívar's expedition from Aux Cayes and subsequent events drew royalist attention away from this useful base, and in November 1816 Arismendi was able to invite émigré patriots to take refuge on the island, where he was governor. Arismendi's rising had given Bolívar's expeditions a useful start, for at Villa del Norte, on the island, an assembly of notables recognised Bolívar as supreme chief of the Republic on May 7, 1816, thus ratifying the act of the previous February

---

1 The cynicism of this decree seems to pass unnoticed. The fact is that Bolívar needed soldiers, and this was the easiest way of getting some. (Editor)

7th at Aux Cayes. And on May 8th Bolívar issued a proclamation to all Venezuelans announcing his appointment and calling for a national congress.

Mariño and Bermúdez recognised Bolívar's authority again at the beginning of 1817. These two were fighting in Cumaná, and Piar had invaded Guayana, while Arismendi had left Margarita and come to help in the campaign on the mainland. By the first weeks of 1817, Bolívar considered that Piar had broken the ground sufficiently in Guayana, and that it was time for him to go there himself, so he left Barcelona. Mariño then set up for himself, calling a congress at Cariaco and proclaiming a Federal Republic; but he was soon defeated and lost Cumaná and Barcelona, whereas Piar continued to win great territories in Guayana. Bolívar came up with him in April, and joined the siege of the royalists in the capital, Angostura. In July and August the royalists withdrew from the province, leaving it in Bolívar's hands. He set up a Council of State in October.

The previous June he had given Piar, with whom he was not reconciled, a free pass to retire to any part of the Republic or abroad, and Piar had chosen to come to Angostura and engage in plotting against Bolívar, attempting to put himself at the head of the coloureds. This activity not only endangered the unity of the army, but threatened to lead to a class war, and therefore Bermúdez was ordered to capture him. But Piar fled to Cumaná, where he joined Mariño and worked with him in August and September, until he was finally captured and sent to Angostura, where he was tried and, on October 16th, shot as a conspirator, rebel and deserter. Bolívar realised that he could not pardon Piar if he wished to maintain unity and discipline and ensure victory.

Morillo had returned to Venezuela, now the point of danger, in January 1817. He partly subdued Margarita while his lieutenant La Torre campaigned in Guayana, and in August he made his headquarters at Calabozo. In December Bolívar opened his campaign, counting on Páez's recognition of his authority. He took his army to the Apure region, crossing the rivers Orinoco and Arauca in boats. The combined army of Bolívar and Páez numbered 4,300, of whom 1,000 were *llanero* cavalry. Behind them were a free Guayana and a free Cumaná; but Morillo dominated the rest of the country from Calabozo. Bolívar tried to suprise Morillo, appearing before the town on February 12, 1818, and chasing the royalist army towards Caracas. Páez could not or would not bring his men to leave their chosen fighting terrain, the *llanos*, so that Bolívar, advancing in the Valleys of Aragua, was forced to retreat by Morillo, reinforced by fresh troops under his lieutenant Calzada, before being defeated in a battle at Semen on March 16th. Still retreating, Bolívar was almost wiped out in April, and in May Páez was defeated, so that soon the patriots were driven back to the south of the Orinoco, leaving the Spaniards in possession of all to the north, since they had beaten Mariño and also Bermúdez in Cumaná.

Now it was time to turn again to matters of government. In Angostura Bolívar had established the beginnings of the organisation of the Republic, with himself as *Jefe Supremo*, aided by a Council of Government consisting of Brion, Cedeño and Zea. There was a Council of State to act in place of the as yet non-existent legislature, and a High Court of Justice. The free provinces had been given governors—Cedeño for Guayana, Monagas for Barcelona, Bermúdez for Cumaná and Francisco Esteban Gómez for Margarita. There was even a newspaper, *El correo del Orinoco*. After the last campaign, Bolívar returned to Angostura on June 5th, determined to affirm the new Republic. In October he asked the Council of State to agree to call an immediate National Congress, which met on February 15, 1819 in spite of all the difficulties of the situation. Zea was elected its president, and Bolívar gave a speech presenting the projected constitution of the country. He then resigned his powers, and was immediately elected President of the Republic, with Zea as Vice-president. Palacio Fajardo was made Secretary of State and Treasury, Briceño Méndez Secretary of War and Navy, and Diego Bautista Urbaneja Secretary of Interior and Justice. In September Arismendi replaced Zea as Vice-president. The most outstanding members of the Congress were Roscio, Mariño and Urdaneta.

Bolívar's message and constitutional project were composed during a journey in the Apure region in December 1818 and January 1819. Firstly Bolívar resigned his powers since he held that frequent elections were essential for a healthy government and 'nothing is so dangerous as allowing power to remain for long in the hands of the same citizen.' Then he offered his project for consideration, beginning with an examination of Venezuela, whose people were American by birth and European by rights, and who had been deprived of their part in government by the Spaniards who alone had ruled in colonial times. The first republican Congress had established democratic government, yet the government of Venezuela must now be reformed, for 'the more I admire the excellence of the Federal Constitution of Venezuela, the more I am convinced that its application to our country is impossible'. The system was 'weak and complicated'. But the main thing was equality: 'My opinion, Legislators, is that the basic principle of our system depends directly and exclusively upon the equality established and practised in Venezuela.' Theoretically, 'the most perfect system of government is that which produces the greatest possible happiness, the greatest possible social security and the greatest possible political stability.' In practice, 'the government of Venezuela has been, is and must be republican; its bases must be the sovereignty of the people, the division of powers, civil liberty, the ending of slavery, the abolition of monarchy and of privilege'. One essential thing must be remembered, 'that the excellence of a government is not in its theory, its form or its mechanism, but in being appropriate to the nature and character of the nation to which it is applied'.

On August 15, 1819 the Congress of Angostura adopted a Constitution which retained most of Bolívar's ideas, with the most important exception of having a life Senate in place of Bolívar's proposed hereditary Senate. The Moral Power suggested by Bolívar (a sort of national conscience) was also rejected, but submitted for public discussion. In fact the new Constitution had no effect because of the prevailing state of war. It was centralist, with a President who was elected for a four-year term and was responsible to the Senate. Bolívar was sure by now that concentration of power was necessary for the new state, and his proposed president was little different in his powers from the King of England. Only the ministers were to be responsible for their actions. The legislature consisted of two Chambers, one of them a hereditary Senate like the House of Lords, and the other an elective Chamber of Representatives. The judicial power was independent, and judges could only be removed by a process of impeachment. Perhaps the most notable thing in Bolívar's project was his suggestion for the creation of a fourth power charged with the supervision of the morals of the citizens, discouraging ingratitude, selfishness and indifference in matters of public moment, and idleness, and eradicating corruption and bad examples. Bolívar asked for trial by jury, freedom of the press, the most explicit guarantees of civil liberty and the abolition of slavery. And, as his aide O'Leary wrote: 'He carefully avoided any mention of religion, since he sensibly refused to go against what he considered to be the prejudices of a people educated in the crassest superstition.' His errors were those of a great man, trying to improve men and to overthrow vice.

Still Bolívar pressed on the campaigns against the royalists. In August 1818 he gave Francisco de Paula Santander the rank of Brigadier-general and sent him as governor and commandant general of the New Granadan province of Casanare, which he had taken temporarily under the Venezuelan wing. Santander was ordered to make contact with the patriots of New Granada and urge them to rebellion. Bolívar sent a proclamation telling them that Venezuela was marching to their aid, and 'the sun shall not complete its present period without seeing altars to liberty raised throughout your territory.' Skirmishing went on. Páez kept Morillo in constant activity in the Apure region. Soldiers were brought from Europe to swell the patriot armies, especially British, who formed by themselves an army of 1,500 men who were to play an important part in future battles.

In April and May the opposing armies took up their positions, Morillo's towards the north, and Bolívar's at Mantecal, in Upper Apure. On May 27th Bolívar began to advance on the first stage of his invasion of New Granada. Zea took over the government of the free part of the country, and Bermúdez, Urdaneta, Mariño and Brion were to advance into the Apure from Margarita, passing through Cumaná, Barcelona and Guayana. Bolívar's plan of campaign was to effect a junction with Santander and then cross the Andes, while Páez was to penetrate the valleys of Cúcuta.

The Arauca was crossed and Casanare was entered in the period of the hardest rains, when the troops marched for a week in water up to the waist. Bolívar met Santander at Tame, so that the army then consisted of 1,300 infantry, including the British Legion, and 800 cavalry. A squadron of Hussars deserted. The main leaders were, under Bolívar, Soublette, Santander, Anzoátegui and the Englishman Rook. They crossed the Andes by the

I

little-used and difficult route over the Páramo de Pisba, and by July 5th the troops, decimated by the rigours of the march, began to reach the other side of the mountains, at the village of Socha. From then the advance was a triumph for Bolívar, who won decisive battles at Gámeza (July 11th) and Pantano de Vargas (July 25th). Tunja was occupied on August 5th, and on the 7th the army had a great victory at Boyocá, where the royalist chief, Barreiro, and the remnants of his army were taken prisoner. On the 10th Bolívar entered Bogotá, from which capital the viceroy, Sámano, and his government had fled. So by this stage New Granada was liberated and almost empty of royalist forces.

Throughout the latter half of 1819 and all of 1820 Venezuela remained in much the same situation as when Bolívar left for the invasion of New Granada, with Morillo in command of Caracas and the west, while Guayana and much of the east was in patriot hands. Páez remained in the *llanos* instead of invading Cúcuta; and in Guayana the political situation became tangled since Bolívar's rivals placed Arismendi in the vice-presidential chair instead of Zea. But Bolívar's successes disconcerted the trouble-makers, and when he returned to Venezuela he encountered no opposition of importance. The war had changed its nature, and was now one between nations, as Morillo and the other Spanish leaders recognised. Fighting went on throughout New Granada and Venezuela, now organised as a single Republic, called Colombia.

A fresh expedition prepared in Spain could not leave for America because of the Spanish liberal revolution of 1820 led by Colonels Riego and Quiroga, who forced Ferdinand VII to accept a constitutional government. Morillo was sent orders to enter into negotiations with the patriots on the basis of recognition of the central Spanish government and of the liberal Constitution of Cadiz; but although representatives of Morillo and of Bolívar met at San Cristóbal no agreement was reached. Bolívar himself wrote on September 21, 1820 offering to continue negotiations with Morillo and to accept the armistice which the latter had proposed, and the correspondence continued while Bolívar advanced and occupied towns evacuated by the royalists. Finally three royalist commissioners were received at Trujillo by three commissioners, led by Sucre, nominated by Bolívar, and this conference produced on November 26th a document declaring a six months' armistice and another regularising the conduct of the war.

These agreements were important for Venezuela, for although the armistice lasted only a short time, the regularisation brought to an end the war to the death. The seventh article gives the gist of the second agreement: 'Since this war springs from a difference of opinions and since the men who have fought ferociously on both sides are bound together by close links and relations, and since all desire to spare as much bloodshed as possible, it is laid down that any soldiers or officials who, having at one time served either of the two Governments, have deserted and are captured while serving the other, shall not be punished by death. The same shall hold for conspirators and rebels of either side.' But the armistice did allow time for the reorganisation of the armies, the other agreement made the war less cruel, and by both agreements Spain officially recognised the existence of the new nation, Colombia.

On November 27th Morillo and Bolívar met in the village of Santa Ana, and Bolívar's aide O'Leary has left a classic description of the event: 'Soon afterwards the Liberator's party was descried on the hill which overlooks the village of Santa Ana. Morillo, La Torre and the chief officers went forward to meet him. The Spanish general was in full uniform, wearing his military orders and other decorations received from the hand of the sovereign for his services. As the two parties drew close together, Morillo enquired which was Bolívar. When Bolívar was pointed out to him, he exclaimed: 'What, that little man dressed in the blue frock-coat and forage-cap and riding a mule?' He had scarcely finished speaking when the little man was at his side, and when the two generals saw each other they instantly dismounted and gave each other a close and cordial embrace. After this greeting they went to the principal house of the village, where General Morillo had had a simple banquet prepared in honour of his illustrious guest.'

5. THE REPUBLIC OF COLOMBIA

In his Letter from Jamaica (September 1815), Bolívar had mentioned the possibility of the unification of New Granada and Venezuela into a single republic to be called Colombia, and later he took up this thought again in order to urge the creation of a stable and powerful state. On December 14, 1819, during the course of a report he was making to the Congress of Angostura on his New Granada campaign, he proposed the setting up of such a republic: 'The union of New Granada and Venezuela is the sole aim I have entertained since I first took up arms: it is the desire of the citizens of both countries and it is the guarantee of the liberty of South America.'

Two days later the Congress sanctioned the Fundamental Law of the Republic of Colombia, on the grounds that the union would bring power and prosperity to the two countries and thus ensure respect for their independence. The new state's boundaries included the former Captaincy-general of Venezuela and the former Viceroyalty of New Granada, whose public debts were to be consolidated. The executive was to be a president, but the Departments into which the state was divided were each to have its own administration and chief officer, to be known provisionally as vice-presidents. The Departments were the former main colonial divisions: Venezuela, with its capital at Caracas; Quito (modern Ecuador), with Quito as its capital; and Cundinamarca (modern Colombia), with its capital at Bogotá. The capital of the whole country would be a new city to be called Bolívar, and the provisional flag would be that of Venezuela. A Constituent Congress would meet at Cúcuta on January 1, 1821, and the Constitution of Angostura would be submitted to it as a model. The Congress of Angostura itself would be dissolved on January 15, 1820; but meanwhile it provisionally appointed the chiefs of the new state, making Bolívar president, Roscio vice-president of Venezuela, and Santander vice-president of Cundinamarca. At this stage Quito was yet to be freed. Zea was sent to London to try to gain recognition of the new republic, to negotiate a loan, and to fund the public debt.

Cúcuta was declared the provisional capital of Colombia, and the government settled there early in 1821. Roscio had died, and Azuola, who replaced him, died too; finally Mariño was elected vice-president. The new Congress was opened on May 6, 1821 in the presence of 57 deputies, who elected Félix Restrepo their president, ratified the Fundamental Law of the Republic, and on August 30th approved the new Constitution. The seat of government was then transferred to Bogotá.

The Colombian Constitution of 1821 made the government centralised, popular and representative. The executive consisted of a president and a vice-president, elected for terms of four years by provincial assemblies, with ratification by the Congress. Presidential authority was limited: the president was responsible to Congress, and the ministers were responsible to the president. The legislature had a Senate and a Chamber of Representatives, whose members were elected by an indirect system which kept votes in the hands of men of some property. Senators had to be at least thirty years of age and possess property to the value of 4,000 pesos, and Representatives had to be at least twenty-five and possess property to the value of 2,000 pesos. A complete legal system was also set up. The Constitution elaborated the point that sovereignty resided in the nation, not in the people, whose only role was that of primary electors; on the other hand all Colombians were declared to have the right to write, print and publish their thoughts freely and without previous censorship, 'but those who abuse this precious faculty will suffer the punishments to which they are liable according to the laws.'

Early 1821 saw the decision of the war in Venezuela. On January 28th Maracaibo joined Colombia, having thrown off the Spanish yoke by means of a revolt. Urdaneta had been in contact with the rebels in Venezuela, and the royalist leader, La Torre (Morillo having returned to Spain), considered this as a rupture of the armistice. War became open on April 28th, and Bolívar planned his campaign as a general invasion of the Valleys of Aragua by his various forces from the *llanos*, the Andes and Maracaibo. Bermúdez had advanced towards Caracas from the east, and although Morales threw him back, the royalist forces were split. At Carabobo on June 24th royalists and patriots clashed. Bolívar led the latter, who were in three divisions respectively commanded by Páez, Cedeño and Ambrosio Plaza. Mariño was chief of staff. La Torre commanded the royalists, with Morales as his second-in-command. Bolívar won the battle, and La Torre, with only one battalion left, shut himself up in Puerto Cabello, while other royalists continued to resist at Maracaibo, Coro and Cumaná. However, Puerto Cabello at last surrendered on November 10th, and the whole of Venezuela, now free, became incorporated into Colombia.

The consequences of the Battle of Carabobo, at which many

British soldiers fought, were far-reaching, for not only did it result in the freedom of Venezuela and New Granada, but it allowed the Liberator to turn his attention to affairs further south in the continent. Bolívar reached Caracas on June 29th, spent some time on civil affairs, and then on August 1st left for Bogotá with his mind already on the south, leaving Soublette as vice-president of Venezuela.

The Congress invited Bolívar to join it at Cúcuta, and there offered him the presidency again under the new Constitution. He refused, but was finally persuaded to accept the post for which he believed himself to have no real vocation. He had a military temperament, and was a despot in the sense that when in power he insisted on being the ruler; he had refused the presidency before for this reason, and only accepted it when obliged by circumstances. Now, on October 3, 1821, he took office with war in mind: 'The Constitution of Colombia, together with independence, will be the sacred altar of my sacrifices. For it I will march to the limits of Colombia to break the chains of the sons of Ecuador, to invite them to join Colombia after I have freed them.' Therefore Bolívar was given dictatorial powers to prosecute the war and to administer the territory in which he was fighting, while Santander was made vice-president of the Republic and put in charge of the civil administration.

Guayaquil, the main port of Ecuador, had rebelled in 1820 against Spain and set up its own government; and now Bolívar sent Sucre there, who succeeded in 1822 in persuading the city to join Colombia. There was a historical precedent, since the old Presidency of Quito had been made part of the Viceroyalty of New Granada in 1740, but Peru also claimed the possession of the territory. In the event, Bolívar entered the Quito territory and defeated the royalist forces there, ending with the victory of Bomboná on April 7, 1822, while for his part Sucre finished his campaign against the royalists opposing him with the victory of Pichincha on May 24th. On June 15th the two victors were in Quito city, and Ecuador was declared incorporated into Colombia by means of the proclamation of the Colombian Fundamental Law.

Inside Guayaquil various parties had formed; some of the people wanted to be annexed to Peru, and others desired complete independence, but few wished to belong to Colombia. San Martín, Protector of Peru, had no wish to clash with Bolívar, who believed that Colombia had a valid claim to Ecuador. Bombiná and Pichincha gave the answer Bolívar wanted, but the Liberator and the Protector had a meeting at Guayaquil. Bolívar reached the port on July 11th, intending to bring about the definitive incorporation of Guayaquil into Colombia, and on the 25th San Martín arrived. The two leaders met but did not discuss the incorporation question, since San Martín grasped the situation. Instead, on the 26th and 27th the two had talks on the independence of Peru and other general questions, and there was some discussion of San Martín's request for a Colombian force to help the Peruvian campaign against the royalists.

San Martín, the Argentine general by whose efforts Chile had been liberated, had opened the liberation campaign in Peru using Chilean and Argentine forces. Peru, in spite of unsuccessful rebellions by the patriots in 1810, 1812, 1813 and 1814, had remained the bastion of royalist power opposed to the two great movements of liberation, that led by Bolívar starting in Venezuela, and that led by San Martín from Argentina. Peru was still ruled by a viceroy, Pezuela, when the Spanish liberal revolution of 1820 brought into effect there the Constitution of Cadiz of 1812. That same month, September, San Martín landed at Pisco, south of Callao, with his expedition from Chile. He could not come to terms with the viceroy, and would not march straight on Lima as he was urged by his naval commander, the Scottish Admiral Cochrane. But in December the coast of Peru rebelled and joined the patriots, and in January 1821 the viceroy was deposed and the Spanish royalist commander, Laserna, put in power by a local movement. Laserna and San Martín opened inconclusive negotiations, and San Martín let it be known that he believed that the future government of Peru should be an independent monarchy, not a republic. It was apparent that the war between patriots and royalists in Peru was at a stalemate.

After Guayaquil San Martín returned, disheartened, to Lima where he was unpopular with many, who thought him monarchical and possibly personally ambitious, and in any case where he was a foreigner; therefore on September 20, 1822 he resigned as Protector of Peru. On his departure on a journey which was to take him to Chile and then to a self-imposed exile in Europe, he was replaced in Peru by a weak junta, which was forced to resign and was itself replaced in February 1823 by a president, José de Riva Agüero. But the fluctuations of politics were reflected in the war, which went badly for the patriots in Peru, while at the same time both money and men became scarce.

Riva Agüero therefore sent an envoy to Bolívar at Guayaquil to ask for aid against the royalists, with the result that on March 18, 1823 a treaty between Colombia and Peru was signed whereby Colombia would send 6,000 soldiers to Peru, and Peru would pay and equip the troops and replace any casualties. Bolívar could not accompany the troops until he received the necessary permission from the Colombian Congress, so he sent Sucre instead as his plenipotentiary in Lima. After three requests from Peru Bolívar was given permission to go, and reached Lima on September 1st.

Peru was by now practically in a state of civil war, on the patriot side, with the royalists under Canterac regaining both initiative and territory in the major struggle. Sucre had not been able to beat him, nor to persuade the Peruvians to combine with himself. Accordingly on September 10th the Peruvian Congress, at logger-heads with Riva Agüero, gave Bolívar complete military command in Peru, together with all ordinary and extraordinary powers demanded by the situation. This meant that Bolívar became dictator of Peru. He quickly organised the army and made his plans, but even so there were important reverses: he himself was shut up in Pativilca in January 1824; Callao surrendered to the royalists in February; the royalist forces were reinforced to the total of 18,000 men, while at the same time some important Peruvians joined the royalists too. At this point the Congress officials made Bolívar dictator and suppressed both the presidency and itself. By June Bolívar had reorganised the army, and in two battles he and Sucre decided the issue. Junín (August 7, 1824) and Ayacucho (December 9th) shattered the royalist army. The latter battle was Sucre's great triumph, which sealed the liberty of Peru and of South America.

It is true that before Bolívar trod Peruvian soil San Martín had already won possession of its coast, and that the patriots of Peru owed much to the liberator of the south of the continent. But it was Bolívar who carried through the campaign which liberated the whole country and consolidated its independence. The Liberator saw the liberty of Colombia—Venezuela, New Granada and Ecuador—as a step towards the building of a great nation, and to him it seemed essential that by the side of that nation other nations, independent also, should be founded. San Martín began the struggle for Peru, but did not finish it, and indeed raised internal discord which allowed the royalists to become stronger. On the other hand Bolívar brought his own campaign to fruition, relying on Sucre, then he also achieved internal political peace, and thus laid the foundations of the Republic of Peru.

Ayacucho was a resounding victory for the patriots. The royalists who surrendered to Sucre included two lieutenant-generals, four marshals, ten brigadier-generals, sixteen colonels, sixty-eight lieutenant-colonels and 484 other officers, as well as the rank and file. These soldiers were well treated, being sent back to Spain by Peru. But the territory of Upper Peru, a part of the former Viceroyalty of the River Plate, remained royalist and held out under the leadership of Olañeta. On December 25, 1824 Sucre asked Bolívar for instructions concerning Upper Peru, and Bolívar sent him into this one remaining royalist redoubt with the dual mission of liberating the country and giving it a political organisation. These tasks were completed in 1825, Bolívar's year of greatest triumph, in which he received every honour from the Peruvian Congress, and, in a triumphal tour, from the main cities of the country. He also founded a new nation named after himself, Bolivia.

Sucre freed Upper Peru with comparative ease between January and April 1825, and made himself its master. But the political organisation was a more difficult matter, for some of the people desired annexation to Argentina and others wanted complete independence. Sucre called a national Assembly to discuss the question, but Bolívar himself pointed out that Upper Peru had belonged to the Viceroyalty of the River Plate and that therefore, according to what had been accepted among the patriots, it still fell within the sphere of the free country based on that Viceroyalty, which was Argentina. Sucre solved the constitutional problem by consulting the authorities in Buenos Aires, who approved the convocation of an Assembly for Upper Peru, and thereby set Bolívar's scruples at ease.

Bolívar therefore allowed Sucre to call the Assembly. It met at Chuquisaca on July 10th, refused to allow the country to become part of either Argentina or Peru, and instead proclaimed the independence of Upper Peru, with about a million in-

habitants at that time. The Assembly gave the new country the
name of Bolivia and honoured the Liberator in every way: it
made him president and begged him to give the country a political organisation, and even to write its Constitution. Accordingly Bolívar made a rapid tour of the country, decreeing reforms in the administration, and returned to Lima at the end of
1825, leaving Sucre in charge of the government of Bolivia.

From Lima Bolívar sent his proposed Constitution, which was
accepted with some modifications by the Constituent Congress
at Chuquisaca in July 1826. In the accompanying message Bolívar made the illuminating comment that voters need not have
wealth: 'Knowledge and integrity, not money, are what is needed for the exercise of the public Power.' The form of government was to be popular and representative, with sovereignty
of the people, exercised through indirect elections. There were
four branches of the supreme power: the electoral, the legislative, the executive and the judicial. The addition of the electoral power to the classic trilogy is a not very important inno-
vation. Another new thing was the division of the legislature
into three Chambers: the Tribunes, concerned with administration and making war and peace at the proposal of the government; the Senators, concerned with actual law-making and co-
dification; and the Censors, who were to supervise the whole
system. The president was to serve for life, and had only the
power of appointing officials of the treasury and those concerned with making war and peace. He also commanded the army,
but he was not responsible for the acts of the administration.

A constant preoccupation of Bolívar's was his idea of con-
voking some assembly of all the new states of America in which
all could seek mutual agreement and some form of union. From
1812, in various ways, he had put this forward, and from Lima
he issued invitations to various governments asking them to
hold a meeting. The union of South America which Bolívar desired from 1818 was not brought into being, but the Congress
of Panama was an attempt to implement it, although the matter went no further. Bolívar's over-all scheme had two stages:
firstly the creation of Colombia, and secondly the organisation
of a sort of confederation of the Hispanic American states.

Between 1822 and 1825 Colombia made treaties with Chile,
Peru, Mexico, the United Provinces of Central America, and
Buenos Aires, with the aim of reaching agreement about a de-

fensive alliance and some political connection. On December 7, 1824 invitations were issued from Lima to the governments of Colombia, Mexico, the River Plate, Chile and Guatemala inviting them to send plenipotentiaries to Panama in six months' time in order to discuss 'some fundamental basis which will perpetuate, if it is possible, these governments.' From the later part of 1825 delegates began to congregate at Panama, coming from Colombia, the Central American Republic, Peru and Mexico. Britain sent E. J. Dawkins as an observer. The Congress opened on June 22, 1826, and closed on July 15th having discussed many things and signed a treaty of union, league and confederation, and two conventions, one of which dealt with future sessions of the Congress and the other with the contingents and subsidies which each state would supply for a common armed force. Tacubaya, in Mexico, was named as the next meeting-place of the Congress, but none ever took place. None of the governments paid enough attention to the Congress, and even Bolívar ignored its conclusions, holding that nothing of any real value had been accomplished. The anarchy of the rest of the century prevented any effective union, but the Congress of Panama did lay down rules of conduct regarding war and peace, and certain liberal principles in private international law, particularly with respect to citizenship.

The brain behind the Congress was in fact Pedro Gual, one of the two delegates for Colombia, who was elected president of the Congress itself. He had been in politics since 1812, and was one of Bolívar's best advisers and one of the important civilians concerned with the creation of the Republic of Colombia. He had begun his diplomatic career in 1815 as agent of New Granada in the United States, which he got to know well and whose political organisation impressed him. In 1820 he was civil governor of Cartagena, then he took part in the Congress of Cúcuta and became Minister of the Treasury. But his best work was as Minister of Foreign Relations of Colombia, in which post he served for four years and gained for his country the recognition of the United States and Great Britain, and made treaties with the major new Spanish American countries. He it was who drew up the programme for the Congress of Panama, and it was owing to his efforts that the Congress ever met. Gual left the Colombian service in 1830 and went into a law practice in Bogotá, then years later he became Minister of Ecuador in Spain, and gained Spain's recognition for his new country. As an old man, he acted as a highly respected elder statesman in Venezuela. Since his time, his opinion concerning American unity has become a common ideal, and his principles of international law have been accepted in the western hemisphere. He was the first diplomat of Spanish America.

Bolívar's political thought envisaged the creation of free and powerful states, and then the union of these states into a federation which would bring greater possibilities of liberty, well-being and greatness. Many documents show this, but none better than the letter to O'Higgins, Supreme Director of Chile, dated January 8, 1822. In spite of the victories, he wrote, the great day of America had not yet arrived; 'we have expelled our oppressors, splintered the tablets of their tyrannical laws and founded legitimate institutions; but we still lack the basis of the Social Pact, which will make of this world a nation of Republics.' The 'nation of Republics' was what Bolívar wanted in America, and the Congress of Panama was the nearest he got to it. The Bolivian Constitution, on the other hand, was Bolívar's model for the individual nations which would form the nation of Republics. Bolívar's aspirations in the international field were later to be represented on a world-wide scale by the Assembly of the League of Nations and the General Assembly of the United Nations, and on a continental scale by the Panamerican Conferences.

The Congress of Cúcuta sanctioned its new Colombian Constitution on October 6, 1821. The country was now divided up into Departments, each under an intendant who was responsible directly to the president. In Venezuela the old provinces were grouped into three Departments: Guayana, Cumaná, Barcelona and Margarita formed the Orinoco Department; Coro, Trujillo, Mérida and Maracaibo became Zulia Department; and Caracas and Barinas were joined as Venezuela Department. A military and civil chief, Soublette, was appointed to take charge of these Departments because of the war which continued, but the intendants were also appointed. Páez was made military commander of Venezuela Department. The co-existence of the constitutional intendants and the provisional chief caused difficulties over questions of jurisdiction and administration. Páez, whose fame as a *llanero* warrior gave him great prestige, felt himself relegated to a secondary plane since not only was he

subordinate to the chief, but he was even inferior to his depart-
mental intendant. In Bogotá, Santander was acting president of
the whole republic since Bolívar was on campaign in the south.
Santander, ambitious for power himself, employed methods
which caused friction, especially with Venezuelans. So that the
Constitution of Cúcuta, in intention centralist and strengthen-
ing, was in fact the cause of the birth of suspicions and hostility
between the various parts of the Republic, and therefore the
cause of Colombia's eventual disgregation.

Parties formed in the absence of Bolívar in Peru and Bolivia.
In Bogotá there were Santanderistas opposed to the Bolivaristas,
whereas in Caracas some were Paecistas and others Bolivaristas,
but all were antisantanderistas. So from 1821, in Venezuela
there was an important group of men opposed to rule from
Bogotá, men who wanted a reform of the constitution, and who
in 1826 brought on a separatist revolution. Already in December 1821 and January 1822 the town council of Caracas, in the
act of swearing allegiance to the new Constitution, had protested against it; but the real movement began in January 1826
when the same town council accused Páez of going beyond his
powers. Santander, when informed, allowed the case to stand
and relieved Páez of his command. The latter received the news
in Valencia, where there happened to be living at that time
Miguel Peña, a leading Venezuelan politician who had also been
relieved of his post for defending Venezuelan rights. Peña joined Páez in rebellion against the central power in Bogotá, and
public opinion was stirred. The town council of Valencia hesitated at first, then under the pressure of a Paecista mob, broke
with the Congress and with Bogotá, and offered command of
the local forces to Páez, who accepted. This was revolution, the
breaking of the Constitution, and the beginning of the end of
the Republic of Colombia. Other towns, even Caracas, joined
in against Bogotá.

On receiving news of this movement Bolívar decided to return to Colombia to protect his creation. Beginning his journey
in September 1826, he passed through Bogotá in November and
reached Puerto Cabello on December 31st. Páez attempted to
turn him back by sending commissioners to argue with him,
but Bolívar imprisoned the commissioners and issued a decree
declaring that he, as national president, was taking over the
command of the Venezuelan departments, and calling also for

a convention. Seeing that the game was up, since Bolívar was welcomed home, Páez submitted. Bolívar and he entered Caracas together, and the menace of civil war was averted. Bolívar stayed for six months reorganising the territory's government, before leaving on July 4, 1827 for Bogotá, where he re-assumed the presidency in September.

The Congress of 1827 called a National Convention to meet in Ocaña in 1828. Protests against the Constitution of Cúcuta came not from Venezuela alone, but from the whole of Colombia. Revolts in various places caused Bolívar to order special precautions through the country except in Ocaña. Bolívar and Santander reached extremes of mutual suspicion: when in Caracas, Bolívar had refused to have further correspondence with his vice-presidents; and in February he reduced Santander to impotence by putting Secretaries of State in charge of the government in the president's absence.

On April 9, 1828 the Convention of Ocaña opened, with delegates from all parts of the Republic. Bolívar's message was read on the 17th, but little attention was paid to the president's opinions. He asked, in fact, for elimination of the Constitution of Cúcuta and the adoption of the Bolivian constitution, which Peru had taken up and then dropped. Bolívar wrote: 'Consider, legislators, that energy in the public power is the safeguard of individual weakness, the threat which awes the unjust and the hope of society.' The Bolivian constitution was the strong implement which Bolívar wanted.

But the Convention dissolved on June 10th without either reforming the present Constitution or adopting the Bolivian one. It had been able to accomplish nothing because of party strife. The main split was between Bolivarianos and antibolivarianos, with the latter calling themselves constitutionalists since they supported the Constitution of Cúcuta. Santander, their leader, took every opportunity of damning Bolívar, even using the official *Gaceta de Colombia* for anti-Bolivarian propaganda. His party soon became known as the Santanderistas, and they put forward on May 21st a project for a constitution in which the presidential power was almost non-existent. In reply the Bolivarianos on the 28th presented a project in which the president was given very ample powers. But there were various other factions too, for example the federalists, who were mostly Venezuelans, and who wanted a federal state as a method of regaining autonomy. There were three main tendencies among the delegates: a liberal group, which coincided with the Santanderistas and was in favour of weak central power; a centralist group, known as Bolivarianos, Goths, serviles, and so on, who were in favour of a reform leading to really strong central government; and some independents, who formed an inactive minority.

In the event, Bolívar became dictator. A popular meeting in Bogotá on June 13th rejected the Convention of Ocaña and asked Bolívar to take all necessary powers to reorganise the Republic. Constitutionally, Bolívar as president could make himself dictator in case of internal commotion or external threat to the country, and both these conditions were fulfilled at this time since there were some small rebellions taking place in the east of Venezuela, and Peru had invaded Colombian territory. On June 24th, then, Bolívar took his powers; and in the period from July to September the cities of Venezuela, with Páez's agreement, declared for this solution.

The situation was serious. On September 25th an attempt was made on the life of the Liberator by conspirators who were friends of Santander. The coup was unsuccessful, and fourteen of the conspirators were shot, although some, including Santander, were forgiven. After this, the dictatorship became severe, as town councils were suppressed, the freedom of the press was stopped, secret societies such as the Freemasons were prohibited, and even the programmes of studies were tightened up and made more dogmatic.

At the same time the Peruvians were engaged, and an army of theirs was destroyed by Sucre on February 27, 1829. The insurrection of Córdova, a former supporter of Bolívar, was put down by O'Leary, but the atmosphere of continual unrest prevented any peaceful settlement of the country. Yet Bolívar desired to bring his dictatorship to an end, and for this purpose in 1828 he called for a Constituent Congress to meet on January 2, 1830. Also, in 1829 Bolívar flirted with a project to turn the country into a monarchy, and made enquiries about the acceptability to the people of this solution, but the only result was that anarchy was unleashed, and the dissolution of the Republic was brought rapidly nearer.

Bolívar's Congress, meeting on January 20, 1830, elected Sucre its president, and accepted Bolívar's resignation. The Congress, the last one of Bolívar's Colombia, wrote a constitution and offered it to Venezuela, which had already in fact seceded from the union. Sucre and two others were sent to meet delegates of Páez in order to discuss some way of avoiding the Republic's dissolution, but nothing could be agreed. Sucre returned to Bogotá, and then started off to join his wife in Quito. On that journey, on June 4th, he was assassinated at Berruecos by murderers under the orders of José María Obando, the commandant-general of the Cauca. Santander's partisans on June 1st had published in the Santanderista newspaper *El demócrata* an article attacking Sucre, in which were printed the words: 'Perhaps Obando will do to Sucre what we have not done to Bolívar.'

As soon as he had resigned the presidency, Bolívar had retired to Cartagena with the intention of seeking exile abroad. Whilst he waited for money to reach him from Venezuela, angry voices were raised against him on all sides. Even the Congress of Venezuela made the proscription of Bolívar a condition of their agreement to enter into relations with New Granada. Bolívar left Cartagena and, passing through Soledad and Barranquilla, reached Santa Marta on December 1, 1830. On the 6th, dying of tuberculosis, he went to a country house, the Quinta de San Pedro Alejandrino; and there he made his will on the 10th and died on the 17th. His last proclamation still rings painfully in the history of his country: 'You should all labour for the inestimable benefit of union: the people, obeying the present Government, in order to break free from anarchy; ministers of religion, directing their prayers to Heaven; and soldiers, employing their swords to defend the basic guarantees of society. Colombians! My last wishes are for the happiness of our homeland. If my death helps to bring factions to an end and to consolidate the union, I shall descend in peace to the grave.'

On November 29, 1829 the governor of Carabobo had called together a popular assembly in Valencia, in which it was agreed that Venezuela should withdraw from the Republic of Colombia 'since the laws which are good for the other territories are not appropriate for ours, which is entirely different in customs, climate and products, and since laws applied over a great area lose their strength and energy.' On the 25th Páez's government called a similar meeting in Caracas, which on the 26th agreed on separation from Colombia, on the calling of a Venezuelan

National Convention, and on the assumption of the government by Páez. At about the same time the cities of Ecuador were taking similar action, and there Juan José Flores called a Congress in May.

The dissolution of the Republic of Colombia had in truth begun in 1826 with the movement in Valencia supported by Páez, as Bolívar himself said in 1828. Both in 1826 and 1829 it was obvious that Páez wanted to rule, and also that Peña's gift for intrigue was at his service. Soublette also collaborated with these two. The Colombian government saw clearly from the start what was Páez's role, and also realised that most of the important men in Venezuela would support Páez with little or no resistance, since separation from Colombia would open a vast field for the ambition of many. Bolívar knew all this, but before the end he appears to have been convinced that Venezuela would certainly leave the union, and that all that could be done was to make the dissolution peaceful; therefore he decided to take no active measures against Venezuela, but to accept the inevitable.

6. LITERATURE IN THE EMANCIPATION PERIOD

The surge of revolutionary feeling, the wars of emancipation and the passion for politics which arose successively in the period from 1810 to 1830 were no obstacle to the cultivation of literature in Venezuela. It is true that men studied in the atmosphere of tension natural in such an insecure situation, but the most sensitive spirits realised that a people cannot abandon the cultivation of the intellect, in both science and arts, even in the midst of the most threatening dangers. The generation brought up in those years began to come to the fore in the new Republic presided over by Páez. A different generation—that called of the Independence—was present through the long years of struggle and of attempts at organisation. This generation sprang from the old Captaincy-general, from the education of the latter years of the eighteenth century and the first years of the nineteenth: it was nurtured on tradition and revolution at one and the same time. The forgers of the thought which became action during the Independence were inspired by two

K

streams of ideas, that of the *Encyclopédie* and that of Spanish tradition.

Literary *genres*, as such, were thrust into the background. In place of a classical type of poetry, such as was practised in Caracas in 1808, there came a burst of warlike songs, popular melodies and attempts at epics. Only the speech full of revolutionary emotion, the political letter, the message or memorandum had any real quality, and these were the things which were heeded. Thought was put entirely at the service of politics. Newspapers, speeches, even official and private letters were all about politics. As yet the intellectual labour of this period has not been thoroughly investigated, although the main names are known. In fact only part of the actual production has so far been collected. But three important figures stand out, those of men whose influence on the events and on the atmosphere of those years is unquestionable: Simón Rodríguez, Miguel José Sanz and Juan Germán Roscio.

Rodríguez had great influence on the formation of Bolívar's mind, especially in his literary tastes and his view of political philosophy. The best proof is in the Liberator's letter to Rodríguez, written at Pativilca on January 19, 1824: 'My master, how closely you must have watched me, although you were so far away. How avidly you must have followed my steps—those steps so early directed by yourself. You formed my heart for liberty, for justice, for the great, for the beautiful. I have followed the path which you pointed out to me. You were my pilot although you remained seated on a European shore. You cannot imagine how deeply the lessons you gave are engraved on my heart. I have never been able to erase even a comma of the great axioms which you made mine. Always present before my mental eyes, I have followed them as infallible guides. In sum, you have seen my conduct; you have seen my thoughts written down, my soul painted on paper, and you must constantly have said to yourself: "All this is mine, I sowed this plant, I watered it, I staked it up when it was weak, and now it is strong, erect and fruitful; here are its fruits. They are mine, I am going to taste them in the garden which I planted; I am going to enjoy the shade of its friendly limbs, for my right is eternal and complete there".' Rodríguez was the great teacher, practical in his education of Bolívar as well as the theoretician in his book.

Sanz was a political theorist of sound ideas and moral integrity. Of his writings, three are now known; his speech on the installation of the Royal Academy of Public and Spanish Law in 1790, his essay on public education, of unknown date, and his bases for a provisional government, of 1813.

Roscio wrote treatises with the aim of providing juridical and philosophical bases for the new state and demonstrating the spiritual quality of the country's independence. His book *The triumph of liberty over despotism* was an attempt to justify before the conscience the changes which had taken place—a sort of confession of all the men who made the revolution; and in it, also, is found a political programme for the Republic.

Many others gave their intellectual help in the revolution, in the wars, and in the various attempts to make a Republic (1811, 1819, 1821), such as, for example, Francisco Espejo, Pedro Gual, Cristóbal Mendoza, Manuel Palacio Fajardo, Miguel Peña, José Rafael Revenga, Bautista Urbaneja and others. This generation of writers and thinkers dedicated themselves to the patriotic speech, the administrative memorandum, the opinion-setting article. Some wrote with poetic sensibility, others with purely erudite style, but all with intellectual vigour. There were others too, of different stamp, including José Domingo Díaz, the only historian of that generation. Andrés Bello was one of them, but his influence was only felt later, and it must be said that the revolution turned its back on this important author.

CHAPTER VI

The Republic

I. INTRODUCTION

FROM the very moment of the establishment of the Republic with the Constitution of 1830—that fine attempt at political consolidation which was brought crashing on January 24, 1848 by the forces of personalism and social anarchy—Venezuelan history has been distinguished by popular unrest and the consequent rush to revolution. The country has lived in an atmosphere of war, and whenever that atmosphere has not been present, it has been replaced by dictatorship. In 1920 one thinker wrote: 'With only slight exaggeration it has been said that in Venezuela we have lived *de facto* according to many of the ideas of the Bolivian Constitution. And this was and still is natural, since the psychology of a nation is not formed by laws established to that end, and it can only change very superficially during a single century. Politically, though not socially, we still live, with some small, external differences, just as they did in the days of the great fight for independence.'[1]

That is, political evolution has been slow, whilst social evolution has proceeded at a jog-trot. One superficial observation will corroborate this assertion. In Venezuela power belongs to the president; it is authoritarian, even though the Constitutions have always limited the powers of the president of the Republic. It is not merely a theory that there must be a sort of policeman at the top to keep everyone in order, this is the actual reality of what has happened. The strong men of Venezuela are proof: Bolívar, Páez, Monagas, Falcón, Guzmán Blanco, Castro, Gómez, Pérez Jiménez . . . But although a hundred years of presidential rule underline this idea, they do not destroy the ideal of man in society, which is to build a state in which the living

---

[1] G. Espinoza, *El vértice victorioso*, in *Cultura venezolana* no. 16, August 1920, p. 51.

together of men shall be regulated by Law, and in which Law is an application of Liberty. No dictatorship can be justified by the existence of previous dictatorships.

The strong men believed that energy was the only factor which could govern a people like the Venezuelans. All the energy expended in the last century and in the present one has not, however, been enough to create a stable political power, which shows that besides energy other virtues are needed, such as the integrity of Vargas and the human goodness of Falcón. If in the nineteenth century these three qualities had coincided in one ruler, there would not be any political dictatorship at this end of Venezuelan history.

Within the compass of the ideas which were most influential in the field of politics—setting the state on an even constitutional course—the lack of balance between 'people' and 'nation' stood out from the very start. Thus, for example, the Constitution of Cúcuta laid down that sovereignty resides in the nation and that the people 'shall not in itself exercise any other attribute of sovereignty than that of taking part in primary elections.' When, later the Constitution makes 'people' and 'nation' the same thing, Venezuela attains social democracy. In general terms, what has happened is this: political democracy has been attained in the whole of Venezuelan history only in the letter of the written Constitutions (1858, 1864); but political democracy has never worked, since revolution, war and dictatorship have held sway. On the other hand, social democracy did become a fact, with the result that at certain times the process of levelling has given rise to general chaos and the lowering of cultural standards.

Social democracy was not ushered in, as is generally believed, by the Federal War of 1859 to 1863. Those five devastating years did no more than bring to an end the process which had begun with the wars of emancipation. To the influence of the pitiless atmosphere of war which tended to promote social democracy was added the ideological influence of men who were active in the Conservative party, in those political circles which were attempting to build the framework of the Republic on traditional lines. Such is the case with Fermín Toro, who preached the necessity of equality, and this equality, as time went by, turned out to be no other than social democracy.

This last fact is illustrated by two points made by the modern thinker Augusto Mijares: 'Firstly, our democracy was not brutally imposed by certain facts (the rise of *caudillos*, poverty, miscegenation, etc.), but it was accompanied at least by a conscious spiritual element which gave it unanimity and a characteristic continuity.' This can be glossed: the writing of political democracy into the Constitutions is the 'conscious spiritual element'; the rest, the 'brutal' action, leads to social democracy as the social system of colonial times, which still existed when the Republic of 1830 was founded, has gradually disappeared. 'Secondly, by about mid-century the process of building the new society was complete. The Federal War, which came later, had not in this matter the importance which some believe it had, although, as in the case of all our civil wars, (only more strongly since it was longer) its repercussions on many aspects of the life of the nation are undeniable.' True, but the Federal War swept away the last forces opposed to social equality, since it brought to power representatives of the lowest ranks of the people, just as they exist still: unable to read and write, with no concept of citizenship, and therefore with no understanding of the exercise of government as the toil of administration and the higher direction of the social group which is the nation.[1] This form of democracy was what the first lawgivers wished to avoid when they denied the people any active sovereignty.

When we contemplate what happened to power in the nation, we find one concrete form of its exercise: dictatorship. The intervals of legitimate and law-abiding rule are so few that when one views the whole scene they are lost to sight. Dictatorship is the governmental formula used up to now. The dictatorships have been so overwhelming that even the most modest activity fell under their shadow. Intellectual effort has been enervated by the iron hand of the soldier in power, especially since Guzmán Blanco set out to found Academies and his authoritarian spirit conceived literary vanity, which received its fine flower of flattery in the volume published in 1884 by the firm of Sanz, of Caracas. The title of this book, translated, runs: *Venezuelan Academy. Inaugural discourse, a criticism and a defence. Various judgements. Homage of Spain to Guzmán*

1 A. Mijares, *Sobre la estructuración social en Venezuela*, in *Revista Shell*, December 1956, pp. 52-7.

Blanco. Homage of the Venezuelan Academy to its Director. In the days of Castro and Gómez authors were forced to dedicate their works to the presidents because, among other reasons, the state was the only patron of culture, since it alone could pay for it. Even in 1956, half of the population of Venezuela could not read, and a book had at most two thousand readers; although by 1962 the illiteracy rate had fallen to about 30%, an author still cannot live by his books alone.

Militarism was an immediate consequence of the wars of Independence, and it grew stronger during the revolutionary wars with the blank commissions in the army dealt out by Falcón and with those which every rebel granted with lavish hand. The census of 1873—the first taken with any technical preparation —gives the most curious facts about the military population. Ten years after the Federal War, the State of Carabobo alone had 449 generals, 627 colonels, 967 majors, 818 captains, 504 lieutenants and eighty-five second lieutenants—no less than 3,450 commissioned officers. The male population over twenty-one years of age was 22,952; which means that in that State over fifteen per cent of the active men were army officers. If this figure is applied to the whole country it will be easy to understand why there were revolutions.

The Federation established a disastrous administration. But the revolutionaries who tried to correct its defects had recourse to methods which in their turn brought on war. Sometimes we hear a voice which dies away without echo. For example, Francisco Mejía, a general, said: 'We have had enough of trying to set up a democracy by wading through lakes of blood, especially since we have at hand the road of elections.' That is the question—when the road of elections was at hand, as with Falcón and Medina Angarita, men preferred to use arms. Impatience for power and lack of civilisation amongst the mass of the people are two of the factors most to blame.

With the dictatorships of Castro and Gómez the epoch of the *caudillos* came to an end. Revolution led by a soldier of some degree of prestige was the simplest way of gaining power. One local chief, with his rising and his proclamation, was enough to bring the country to a state of war, and the republican ideal of alternating in office was only achieved in this way. After the long, harsh, slow-moving and cruel dictatorship of Gómez, the rising was replaced by a more agile method: the *coup d'état*

(1945, 1948, 1958), in which the highly-trained army decides
the changes without the intervention of the people, either of
country or of city, except as a very short-term and tumultuous
mob. The warrior peasant has disappeared; the modern work-
ing-man does not like revolts. He prefers to have the opportunity to throw his political weight into the ballot box, sup-
porting a trades-union organisation affiliated to some party programme.

Up to 1928 there did not exist any basis for the growth of
the discipline of good citizenship, a fact which partly hindered
the formation of political parties and the building up of some
feeling of public responsibility among the ruling classes and
those social groups who had some education. This situation began to change slightly as the growth of the oil economy transformed the social groups. From the decade 1920-1930 the state
—enjoying social democracy and rigid political dictatorship—
began to become stronger thanks to the material wealth produced by the oil royalties. About 1945, the material wealth of
the country was extraordinarily great.

Venezuela has not known how to use the great mass of money
which since 1920 has flowed into the country through the exploitation of oil, perhaps because in the administration there
is no sober, work-a-day social group, but also because the great
majority of the people have known nothing of it all. Their ignorance is not their fault, for lack of education must be fought
from above. Peculation, costly public works for the sake of
show, and political propaganda, have swallowed the money.
The country has not possessed a few clear brains able to organise from a position of power what has been called the sow-
ing of the oil: the conversion of this wealth of exploitation
money into national industries which might strike permanent
root. It is reported of Miranda that he once said that the country would be the prey of foreigners, not exactly their possession, but that they would dominate and the Venezuelans would
bear the costs as the owners, and be forced to keep the 'estate'
productive.

Although it is clear that, from the purely national point of
view, the only question is how to acquire effective political democracy in order to put the country's economy into the good
order which the times require, from the international point of
view the whole matter becomes more complicated for Miranda's

prophecy has been fulfilled. It is clear that the great problem of Spanish American politics today is this: can these young peoples wait? Are they in a position to forego today the exploitation of their natural riches in order to go forward free into the future?

In the nineteenth century, Venezuela persisted until she attained social democracy; she is still struggling today for political democracy. Venezuela is searching for a team of statesmen and for a system which together will allow her to solve her problems now and in the future.

2. THE CONSERVATIVE OLIGARCHY

In 1830 Venezuela regained territorial autonomy such as she had enjoyed under the Captaincy-general after 1777 and under the first native governments after 1811. From 1830 Venezuela's history is that of a republic, under the constitutions imposed by the successive generations, sometimes after free discussion and sometimes according to the will of a dictator. Although Santander and Páez caused the dissolution of Colombia, and Páez and his friends made the revolution of 1829-30, the people too wished for separation from Colombia, and Venezuela began a new period of her history. On January 13, 1830 Páez set up a provisional government, with himself as head and with a cabinet consisting of Peña, Urbaneja and Soublette, and also called a Constituent Congress to meet in Valencia, which now became the capital.

From 1830 to 1848 the successive governments are known as the Conservative Oligarchy. Páez's great prestige made him the central figure in whatever happened in the country, even up to the point that other presidents—Vargas and Soublette— were elected with his support and owed their stability to his strength. The governments were constitutional, and the country began a new life of apparently healthy progress. The Constituent Congress met at Valencia on May 6th, and heard a message in which Páez said: 'My sword, my lance and all my military triumphs are submitted with the most respectful obedience to the decisions of the law.' Páez was asked to remain as head of state, and everything went with decorum. The Congress contained men of real capacity, able to organise the new state, but incapable at this stage of seeing the good in Bolívar's work, so that before it closed on October 14th it had written a new Constitution and had formed Páez's government.

The Constitution, signed on September 22, and proclaimed on October 23rd, was of a conciliatory nature. Government was declared to be republican, popular, representative, responsible, and alternating, although the sovereignty of the people was still restricted to voting in the primary elections, and the status of domestic servant incapacitated a man for even this function. Electors and elected had to be males, married or over 21 years of age, literate, with a small annual income from property, or exercising a trade, profession or office producing double that income. The legislature was divided into a Senate and a House of Representatives. Every Province would elect two Senators, and Representatives at the proportion of one per 20,000 of population, plus one for an excess of 12,000 over the 20,000 or its multiple. The Executive was a president elected for one period of four years, and not eligible for immediate re-election, and a vice-president who served for a period overlapping the last two years of one president and the first two years of the next. An Electoral College chose both these magistrates. Provinces had as their government a Deputation consisting of one Deputy from each district (*cantón*), with a governor as the Executive. Finally, it was laid down, in pious hope, that 'the armed force is purely obedient, and can never take governmental decisions.'

In March 1831 the Congress met in Valencia, and proclaimed the president and vice-president who had been duly elected. They were Páez and Urbaneja, who served for the period up to February 1835. Páez was again elected, and served again as president from February 1839 for four years, with Urbaneja as a member of his cabinet. These terms of office were fairly peaceful, although Páez had to put down a revolt of the Monagas faction in 1831; but at any rate the Constitution was not violated, there were no persecutions, and the administration was honest.

Socially, the country was evolving. It was calculated in 1825 that Venezuela had about 700,000 people, and in 1830 about 800,000, of whom over a half were of mixed race, and one third white. The Constitution made only free men citizens of Venezuela, and slavery continued in spite of Bolívar, and in spite of a Law of Manumission of 1821 which was still extant. On October 2, 1830 this law was reformed to allow a longer period of years before manumission of a slave was required. The colonial nobility was fast disappearing, but not its economic style of life: great estates remained, but had passed into the hands of the warriors of the independence movement. Páez was a large landowner whose title to his land dated from only a few years back, since he had won it at the point of his lance. On the other hand, a great number of people had been displaced in the wars and they were a source of unrest in city and country districts. Something was attempted to organise and educate the people, for to this end a Direction of Public Education was set up in 1839, in which worked good and well-meaning men such as the immediate past president, Doctor José María Vargas.

Venezuela's economic situation was shaky, although the Congress of 1830 did impose a forced loan of 200,000 pesos for necessary expenses. All the administrations of the Conservative Oligarchy paid close attention to improving the country's situation, encouraging trade in all ways and economising as much as possible. In this effort they received the valuable help of the economist Santos Michelena, at one time Treasury Minister, and later envoy to Colombia.

Bolívar's Colombia had a large and growing national debt, which in 1829 required the payment annually in London of £472,000. Only in December 1834 was this debt apportioned between the component parts of the former state, when it was agreed that Colombia should be responsible for 50% of the debt, Venezuela for 28.5%, and Ecuador for 21.5%. Santos Michelena signed on behalf of Venezuela, but Ecuador sent no plenipotentiary.

From 1830 to 1844 the governments were setting up an economic system, as far as this could be done by laws and the creation of organisations. At this period customs duties, stock-raising and tobacco production brought in the biggest part of the revenue. In 1836 a Society of Friends of the Country was set up, as in eighteenth-century Spain, to channel opinion and create an informed economic public. The country's revenues were small but steady in 1830, 1831 and 1832, running at about 1,500,000 pesos annually. Exports in the fiscal year 1831-32 reached nearly 3,000,000 pesos in value, and by 1840-41 they came to over 6,000,000 pesos. That is, things were steadily growing better in spite of the complaint of the conservative Fermín Toro: 'Venezuela is essentially an agricultural country, and its products have not increased in proportion to its intellectual development and to that of its political institutions. And

at the same time the old simplicity is disappearing, because of
the division of properties and the emancipation of the slaves,
and little by little the people are being levelled down.'

It was Santos Michelena who set the tone in that period of
the new country's first efforts, up to the time when the Monagas seized power. His views were that customs duties were the
easiest and cheapest to collect of all revenue; that an *ad val-
orem* duty was the most just as well as the most convenient for
an agricultural country; that the tariff needed careful revision;
that it had often been proved that excessively high taxes reduced consumption, harmed agriculture and cut down income,
so that a system must be found which was fair to both trade
and treasury and which did not induce fraud; that the length
of Venezuela's coastline made it essential to take every precau-
tion against smuggling; and that to allow goods to remain in
bonded warehouses without paying duty before sale would encourage merchants to take on greater operations, to everyone's
eventual advantage. Following this realistic spirit, treaties of
commerce and navigation were signed, one, for example, with
the Hanseatic cities in 1837.

In 1835 the presidency was contested by such strong candidates as Soublette, Mariño, Urbaneja, Salom and Vargas, and
finally, although no candidate gained the necessary two-thirds
majority of the Electoral College, the Congress, as was its right,
chose Vargas. He did not want the post since he felt himself too
weak as a politician; whilst Páez himself tended to favour Soublette. But in the end Páez supported and helped Vargas, who
made an exemplary chief magistrate, with his spirit of liberty,
care for the moral and material advance of the country, and
republican austerity. Much was promised in education, economy, hygiene, public works, and other concerns of government,
but a militarist party led by Mariño, disappointed in the election, became impatient and arrogant. Vargas resigned, but Congress refused to accept the resignation, and a military conspiracy caused a revolt in Maracaibo in June 1835 and in Caracas a
few days later. High army officers led the movement, which
was joined by the police. When Vargas was arrested and still
refused to hand over his authority to the rebels, he was exiled
to St. Thomas on June 10th.

It was Mariño who led the so-called party of reform who acted in this unconstitutional way merely to gain power. He took

over command of the country and organised what was in fact military rule, calling a Popular Assembly which confirmed what had just taken place and recommended the calling of a National Convention. Páez was appointed provisional president, with Mariño as military commander-in-chief. Some other cities followed the lead of Caracas, and in the east José Tadeo Monagas proclaimed the existence of a federation, as he had in 1831, in order to gain autonomy for himself.

But some old independence fighters, such as Urdaneta, Arismendi, Carreño, Salom and others, declared for the Constitution. And when, in July, Vargas from exile appointed Páez as his own Chief of Operations, the old warrior accepted and showed the 'reformers' where they stood. From July 15th to 28th Páez disarmed the rebels after easy victories, and then reorganised the government, so that in August Vargas was able to return and take over the reins. After defeating Monagas, Páez proclaimed an amnesty and even allowed Monagas and his officers to keep their ranks, an act of lenience which angered the Congress of 1836, which itself summarily punished some rebels who had held out until then in Puerto Cabello. Páez, who had promised these troops their lives and honour, broke with Congress, and Vargas, caught between two friendly fires, despairingly resigned the presidency, which was held briefly by three other men in turn until the end of the disastrous term, in 1839.

Vargas had gathered about him those men who wished to bring truly civilian government to the country, believing that the state must not go in fear of the army nor live for ever under the shadow of the prestige of the old warriors. The electors of Vargas wanted civilian rule, but in his term there came the clash between the two forces which have continued in rivalry since in Venezuela. Although the other governments of the Conservative Oligarchy stood by the Constitution too, it was in fact the presence of Páez which kept the militarists in check and subdued the ambitious who craved for power.

The growth of parties in Venezuela followed on from the tumultuous days of the war of emancipation. In this war, the political question was simplified into royalists versus patriots, but in the internal affairs of the Republic of Colombia, matters became mixed with separatists in 1826 and 1828, and, in the Congresses, Bolivaristas, Santanderistas and Paecistas. In the

same way, immediately after 1830 the groups struggling to win
the government were merely improvised. Páez gathered about
him conservative constitutionalists, and by 1840 two names
came into use: Conservative and Liberal, the historic parties of
the country since then. The Liberal party was founded in 1840
by Antonio Leocadio Guzmán, who had been a Paecista and a
minister under Páez, but who had fallen out of favour because
of a personal clash with a stronger Paecista. Guzmán founded
the Liberals as the party in opposition, that is, the party wishing
to replace the reigning conservatives in power. There did not in
fact exist two opposed political ideologies, and the parties were
power-seeking groups—it is only in the present century that
parties based on ideologies have arisen in Venezuela, after the
death of the dictator Gómez in 1935. Guzmán, the Liberal founder, in fact followed a conservative philosophy; Fermín Toro,
the great Conservative figure, had a liberal outlook. Groups of
newspapers quickly formed behind each party.

There were two currents in the Liberal party. One, which represented the attempt to make the government more democratic, attracted many men of different interests who had in
common a desire to bring new blood into public life to re-invig-
orate the running of the country under the system started in
1830. Among these were many of the founders of the party,
men such as the newspaper editor Lander, and also Urbaneja
and other political figures. Then these faded out, and what was
left was another sort of men, such as Guzmán himself, who
were really only interested in power, but still called themselves
Liberals. The Monagas family joined in and brought the Liberals to power, and the party, together with the Federalists, became known as the Yellow Liberal Party. It pursued no direct
line of policy, for, as usual in Venezuelan politics, events led
the way, not policies.

The free elections of 1842 were the first opportunity for the
parties formed in 1840 to try their hand. The Conservative
party supported Soublette, and the Liberals supported both
Santos Michelena and Urbaneja. Soublette, who won, became
president in 1843, and found that the opposition respected the
decisions and the new cabinet, but objected to the continued influence behind the scenes of Páez, still the arbiter. However, the
government saw its term out to 1848, and retired with dignity
and honour since it had continued the tradition of respect for

the Constitution, for the Congress and for the courts, and had not permitted peculation. This is in fact one of the few honest governments which Venezuela has ever had.

In Soublette's term the country was faced with a deepening economic crisis which began in 1842 with a fall in the prices of coffee, cacao and cattle, Venezuela's principal export commodities. Toro noted in March 1842 that production had become stagnant, and that nothing had been done in the country to encourage the use of modern aids, such as farm machinery or new processes. The parties made the crisis a motive of heated argument, but the talk went on too long—some newspapers were even founded especially to take part in this discussion. Some landowners persuaded Congress that something must be done, but a proposal for an Institute of Land Credit was sunk by the opposition of economists such as Michelena and some Congressmen. However, the Liberals became more popular since at least it was a Conservative government, and they could be blamed for accomplishing nothing.

In 1843 the government published an amnesty for all those involved in political troubles from 1830 to 1836, with the result that the Liberal opposition gained great support from militarists and 'reformers' who took the opportunity to join in politics again. No political programme was changed, and it was admitted in the newspaper *El venezolano* (Liberal) that the only real question was that of a change in the administration. The Liberals gained more prestige when the leader Guzmán won a shady court case in 1844, and a triumphant mob rioted in the streets. But the Liberals went too far over Congressional elections in that year, which they used as a pretext in some places for making up conspiracies and in others for revolts. To the disgust of the Liberals, the government called out the army and the militia to defend the Constitution.

The campaign of the Liberals to gain power was stepped up in 1845, when the party was re-organised and a commission studied the methods to be used in order to win the presidential election of 1846. One thing which was decided was that the party must gain greater representation in Congress; it had already the year before won success in the local government of Caracas District. Páez, who was consulted, replied that he himself did not seek the presidency, would not recommend any candidate, and would respect the decision of the nation, whoever was elected.

Propaganda in the crucial year of 1846 was mainly carried on by the papers *El patriota*, which was Liberal, and *El liberal*, which was Conservative. The moderate Liberals began to be suspicious of the personalism of some leaders of the party, in particular Guzmán. Most effective in those days was the personal approach in letters, and fiery correspondence caused tension to rise throughout the country. The Liberals split into three groups, each with a candidate: Guzmán, José Félix Blanco, and Salom. In the east, always a separate issue, the candidature of José Tadeo Monagas was warmly approved and keenly supported.

The Conservatives had supported Urdaneta as their single candidate, but when he died in 1845 opinions became divided. Páez supported Monagas, who in effect swayed the whole east, and Soublette agreed. Monagas had been a separatist and conspirator in 1829, 1830, 1831 and 1835, but Páez thought that, once in power, Monagas would settle easily into the role of national leader and responsible ruler. Many other Conservatives could not forget Monagas' past, and had their doubts.

The elections were duly held, and when the votes came to be counted in January 1847 it was found that out of the 8,798 electors in the country, only 319 had voted. Even though no more than 107 votes had been cast for José Tadeo Monagas, who led the poll, Congress declared that he had won. Guzmán, who was under judicial investigation, was declared ineligible, having already been expelled from the Caracas town council. What had happened was that the Liberals had rioted in various parts of the country in 1846, and Guzmán had revolted at the request of some Liberal *caudillos*. The revolt had been quashed, the leaders were tried, and in March 1847 Guzmán was condemned to death, but the sentence was diminished to one of exile. He left the country, soon to return and become a collaborator of Monagas.

3.   THE LIBERAL OLIGARCHY

The rise to power of José Tadeo Monagas marked the opening of the period of the Liberal Oligarchy, although in fact Monagas governed for only a short time with the support of the Liberals, since these soon united with the Conservatives in opposition to the dictator. The ten years of Monagas rule, 1847-

57, was a period of dictatorship by José Tadeo and his group of henchmen. Some liberal reforms were made law, such as the abolition of slavery, but in fact this was a purely personal government.

José Tadeo Monagas began to govern in 1847 with a Conservative cabinet, but within a few months Liberals had replaced the Conservative ministers, the Liberal leader Guzmán became vice-president, and in 1850 even the Liberals deserted Monagas. In the presidential election of that year José Tadeo's brother, José Gregorio Monagas, was declared the next president, and newspapers began to talk of a Monagas dynasty. Guzmán had been a candidate, and the result of the election displeased him and the Liberals so greatly that they could not continue in alliance with the Monagas faction. José Gregorio took office in February and saw his term out, supported by his brother, with nothing more than some small risings to worry him. At the next election, in 1855, all pretence of democracy had gone: José Tadeo received 397 electoral votes, and only one other was cast, for Fermín Toro. A revolution in March 1858 brought the dynasty to an end.

During José Tadeo's first term the country was in a state of high political passion, with intransigent and very hostile parties, and the sudden adoption of personalist rule in defiance of the Constitution. Risings occurred, the laws were not respected, but some reforms reached the Statute Book, at least. The Liberals did succeed in having slavery abolished, in abolishing the death penalty for political reasons, and in bringing education more within reach of the poor; also the town councils were made autonomous and boundaries were rectified. In general, the movement was towards greater equality and more even-handed justice. The Conservative party as a government was shattered, as José Tadeo changed the whole personnel of administration, from provincial governors to civil servants, until by the end of 1847 the Conservatives were only active in one place, Congress. What was in that year spirited opposition to Monagas soon became conspiracy, however.

Monagas showed his true colours on January 24, 1848. The Conservative-led provincial Deputation of Caracas had in December made a formal protest to the Chamber of Representatives accusing the Executive Power, Monagas, of unconstitutional excesses. Conservative newspapers took up the cry, and opinions became very fiery: in Congress, the Conservatives were preparing to ged rid of Monagas by a process of impeachment, while outside Monagas dug himself in by appointing provincial governors loyal to him personally, making sure of the national militia, and attracting the Liberals to his side.

The crisis arose when, on January 23rd, Congress debated the creation of a special private guard of its own in order to ensure its safety in face of any attempt of the Executive to suppress it; and a small guard was established under the command of one Colonel Guillermo Smith. The government quickly reacted, calling this act unconstitutional—which it was not—and in effect forbidding the creation of the guard, so that when Congress met on the 24th, the members were insulted by army officers, and soon the guard and the Congress were attacked by a mob inspired by the government. Smith was shot and bayoneted as he shut the main door of the building. Monagas himself did nothing but send a cannon to the Congress, presumably to blow in the door if necessary. Meanwhile, the mob attacked the Congressional guard, with casualties on both sides. During an attempt to get Monagas to intervene, a Congressman was killed and another, Michelena, was badly wounded; and when the members tried to make a mass break-out, together with some of the spectators, several were killed by a volley. The survivors ran away, and some who were left in the building were eventually saved through the influence of a member of the government. In the end Wilson, the British Minister, persuaded Monagas to go to the building and stop further bloodshed, and several Congressmen and members of leading Caracas families took refuge in various foreign legations.

On the next day, Congress had another session, since Monagas, advised by his vice-president, Urbaneja, had decided to try to keep the appearance of constitutional continuity. Indeed by now Congress was thoroughly cowed, and he could govern exactly as he liked with its consent to everything. As he remarked: 'The Constitution is useful for any purpose.' But the Conservative statesman Fermín Toro did not return to his seat, refusing to lend himself to this farce. Although the mob did the deed, there is no doubt that Monagas was responsible for the destruction of Congress, for if he did not exactly order the murders, he did nothing to stop them. He forced the members on the 25th to grant an amnesty and vote him dictatorial powers, which resulted in what can only be described as civil war, and in the propagation of the belief that in Venezuela the Executive can always overcome Congress.

Having got rid of the Conservatives who had brought him to power, Monagas broke with Páez, whose influence became nil. These two *caudillos* soon became enemies, in spite of efforts at mediation undertaken by General Juan José Flores, ar old patriot leader who had become first president of Ecuador. After January 24th Páez realised his mistake, and decided to revolt. A first rising lasted from February to March 1848, but Páez was defeated by trickery and perfidy as much as by force of arms, and retired to New Granada. A second attempt in July 1849, in conjunction with a Conservative rising in Caracas, was badly co-ordinated and was also unsuccessful. Páez was captured and sentenced to exile to Europe or the United States, but the lives and property of his adherents were to be spared. The capitulation was dishonoured, and Páez was kept in prison for months, suffering the disillusionment of the old, despised warrior when even his dignified protest to Congress was, of course, rejected.

In May 1853 there broke out in Valencia another revolution with connections throughout the country, since Conservatives and Liberals were all united against the régime, the 'Monagato'. Monagas, however, broke the main revolt, although conspiracies continued and their members, to gain more support, made the abolition of slavery one of their aims. Many had clearly desired this since the emancipation; even Fermín Toro, in 1839, had praised the freeing of slaves as the best measure to ensure the continuance in their full vigour of republican ideals. Manumission existed in law, but in 1854 it was still not practised; the lot of slaves had not in fact improved with the coming of the Republic, and manumission was very slow. In 1853 a new minister asked for a law abolishing slavery, which Congress sanctioned on March 23, 1854. The president, José Gregorio Monagas, confirmed it the next day, and soon a total of 40,000 slaves were freed. In fact, the Congress had been divided over this question, for some members believed in emancipation, while others hesitated since it would be an attack on the rights of property, so that eventually the government had imposed abolition, not for humanitarian reasons, but purely in order to forestall the conspirators and to gain support for itself.

Monagas' next move was to reform the Constitution of 1830 in order to be able to prolong his own term of office. Accordingly, on March 2, 1857 he sent a draft Constitution to the Chamber of Representatives, and the new charter was duly promulgated on April 18th. The actual changes were comparatively unimportant—the presidential term was increased to six years, and the president was given free choice of the governors of Provinces — but the reason for the reform was expressed in the regulations governing the period of transition, which gave the Congress the power to choose the president and vice-president for the next term. One Representative, Doctor Argimiro Gabaldón, bravely spoke against giving Congress the choice of the next president, since, he argued, the nation should be asked to exercise its own choice. Only three Representatives voted against the new Constitution, and on April 20th, Congress servilely elected José Tadeo Monagas president, and his nephew and son-in-law Francisco J. Oriach as vice-president.

In 1857, the opposition of both parties to Monagas became intense, with Páez and his friends, from New York, and Manuel Felipe Tovar, in Venezuela, organising the Conservatives, while the Liberals were led by Guzmán together with Wenceslao Urrutia and Joaquín Herrera. These conspirators tried to find a common leader, but agreed that Páez would not do, since he was too deeply committed to the Conservatives, while Juan José Flores gave plausible excuses and Falcón refused; but in the end Julián Castro, governor of Carabobo, accepted the leadership and betrayed his chief Monagas. As it happened, Herrera was appointed governor of Caracas, which helped the movement in its communications.

The Congress of 1858 quickly agreed to give amnesty to all who had been political exiles since 1848, but it was too late to avert the storm. On March 3rd the military chief of Puerto Cabello set out for Caracas with urgent news that a revolution was about to break out. Castro, hearing of this journey, put forward his plans by a few days so that the revolution broke out at once, before the government could act. Valencia first 'pronounced' its revolution, and the movement spread quickly. Castro's 'pronouncement' ended: 'The cause is common to us all, and whatever may have been the opinions which have divided us, the day of union has dawned. Venezuela shall appear before the civilised world rising as one against the tyranny which degrades and besmirches her.' Monagas tried to rouse some opposition to the revolution, but the government was demoralised, and on March 15th the dictator resigned and took refuge together with his family in the French Legation. Congress elected a provisional government before dissolving, and this body handed over power to Castro on his arrival in Caracas on the 18th. He declared: 'No party has triumphed. The whole nation has triumphed. Let us all unite.'

Castro assumed power and set up his cabinet, including sound men such as Tovar, Fermín Toro and Urrutia. He changed the entire administration, and all politicians tried to work together and let bygones be bygones. But Toro almost caused trouble when he demanded a commission to inspect the Treasury accounts in order to discover who was guilty of peculation, since many who had joined the new movement were implicated, and became nervous. Urrutia, in order to get Monagas out of the country, signed an agreement with the foreign diplomatic representatives guaranteeing safe-conduct to the ex-president. This was regarded by other members of the government as a stupid action which allowed foreign powers to take part in Venezuela's internal affairs, and Urrutia was forced to resign. Toro, who was given the task of resolving this question, circularised the diplomatic corps with the information that the government accepted the signatures of the foreign representatives on the safe-conduct agreement merely as their signatures as witnesses to Urrutia's promise to Monagas, and not as those of parties to an agreement. Most of the diplomats let the matter pass, but the *chargés d'affaires* of France and Britain chose to make an issue of it, and suspended relations with Venezuela. This eventually led to a blockade in May set up by French and British warships.

With Monagas' fall the Constitution of 1830 came back into force, pending a new charter to be debated by a National Convention installed at Valencia in July 1858. The Convention contained both Conservatives and Liberals of prestige, but already the radical wing of the Liberals, led by Guzmán, Falcón and Zamora, was discontented and began to plot another revolt. However, Fermín Toro became president of the Convention, which at once took up the question of the safe-conduct for Monagas. Although it was agreed to allow Monagas to leave the country as soon as the Franco-British blockade was lifted, it was discovered that the representatives of France and Britain were encouraging the Liberal plotters in Caracas. Castro was therefore granted dictatorial powers to deal with the imminent revolt.

The two *chargés d'affaires* retired to their ships, issuing an ultimatum. The rebel Falcón rose at La Guaira, but was defeated by Soublette, and the stalemate was resolved on August 27th by an agreement between the blockaders and commissioners of the government whereby Monagas would be allowed to leave, and the three countries would return to their former friendship. All the Convention could do was accept, with some protests by radicals, and expel Monagas for life, with loss of honours.

In July the Convention had before it two rival draft Constitutions, one written by the Conservatives and the other by the Liberals. The debates were prolonged, passionate and sometimes lofty, but at last, on December 31st, the new Constitution was promulgated. This time the people were declared to exercise sovereignty directly through elections, and indirectly through the authorities of the state acting in the name of the people. A new power was invented, the Municipal Power, to add to the classic three: it was simply a carefully organised local government system allowing provinces and districts a representative body as well as an administration. Elections were direct and suffrage was universal for males, so that the whole system was closely controlled by popular opinion. The additional importance given to local government was a method of decentralisation made to appear desirable by recent experiences of dictatorship; and, it was said, it might lead gradually to a real federal system if the nation decided later to establish one. The legislators proclaimed a fundamental truth when they wrote: 'But do not forget that the Constitution is a book, inert matter, without life or efficacy, unless the spirit of the people inspires it; and that only the feeling, the will, the free action of all those associated with the Constitution in a harmonious combination of efforts and hopes make it a vital law, a law of progress, a law with the highest aims for a virtuous, active and intelligent people.'

4. THE FEDERAL REVOLUTION

For a hundred years Venezuela has been a federal republic with the name of United States of Venezuela and with a written federal Constitution. but in practice it has functioned as a centralised state, with government in the hands of the president. In the periods of tyranny—under Guzmán Blanco, Castro, and Gómez, to mention only those on which we have a historical perspective—but no less in periods of democracy, the president has exercised a centralising power. Federation is not, as the Liberal thinkers in Venezuela believed, a demagogic formula, but simply a method of bringing autonomous communities into union, without reference to the form of central government established, which may be republican, monarchical, aristocratic or democratic. A state may adopt federation as it may adopt any institution, but it may later be realised, as it came to be in Venezuela, that what was believed to be a magic formula for the solution of the country's problems merely aggravates those problems and even creates new ones. In Venezuela, the Federal Revolution (1859-63) established a federal Constitution and consolidated social democracy. The first of these effects was purely theoretical, a question of name, since the Constitution of 1858, although not called federal, adopted the spirit of federation and brought political democracy except for one thing: Senators still had to possess some capital, as a last relic of the old Conservative Oligarchy.

Federalist ideas were mooted amongst the first republicans of 1811, and federation was mentioned at the establishment of the Republic of 1830. Some revolts, such as that of the Monagas, had a federal programme. The Liberals, when they began to make themselves into a party, adopted federalism as one of the ways of bringing political democracy. Indeed Federation was put about as the panacea for all political and economic troubles, and its name was used to rally the opposition to the Monagas dictatorship and then later, once Castro had expelled Monagas, against the Conservatives.

Writers and politicians, probably in all honesty, put forward claims for federation as the best way of bringing all Venezuelans to live together in peace and concord. Some showed how federation would give so little benefit to men in the government that few would want what little power there was, and none would make a revolution for its sake (Julián Viso, in El foro, March 30, 1858). Others stressed the radical nature of the differences between the Venezuelan provinces, and pointed out that each needed to be able to look after its own interests, especially in the economic sphere.

One fundamental cause of the Federal War was simply personalism. Some ambitious *caudillos* and politicians supported and directed the revolt in order to gain power for their own use, and this type of activity has been one of the most important in causing the many revolutions of Venezuela and indeed of all Spanish America. As early as 1864, only one year after the federalist triumph, some of their former supporters were already disillusioned by the cynical immorality of the federal leaders: 'The Federation has begun its government with the same immorality that former Administrations have developed at the middle or the end of their terms', as José L. Arismendi wrote. Guzmán himself, who became a strong federalist for the sake of bringing his party to power, could say in Congress in 1867: 'I don't know where people have got the idea that Venezuelans love federation, when they don't even know what the word means. The idea of federation came from me and some others, who said to ourselves: "Since every revolution has to have a slogan . . . , let's invoke the idea of federation. For if our opponents, gentlemen, had said *federation*, we should have said *centralism*!" '

Another main cause of the Federal Revolution can be summed up as the desire of Venezuelans for equality, a desire which brought social democracy. This is connected with an economic motive, since in 1859 the distribution of wealth followed a class pattern. The rich were the landowners, old-established or risen with the emancipation, and the merchants, sometimes grown rich through the use of power; and on the other side was the mass of country and town working people, without lands or money. Federation was really a matter of form, and the true struggle was for democracy; and this issue was confused since, wrongly, federalism became associated with the Liberals and centralism with the Conservatives. In any case, observers were horrified at the amount of blood it cost to bring purely imaginary benefits. Vallenilla Lanz pointed out, in 1919, that the fire of the Revolution was the same as had been lit in 1810: the same hordes of poor men turned warriors followed a *caudillo* of prestige, who possessed the same spell, courage and background as, for example, Boves or Páez. Royalist under Boves, patriot under Páez, Liberal under Guzmán and Zamora in 1846, the same hordes were federalist under Zamora, Falcón and Sotillo in 1859. Rómulo Gallegos, novelist and for a short time president of the Republic, hit the nail on the head in *Pobre negro* (1937): 'It is democracy, born in the camps of the war for Independence, which sallies forth to conquer for itself in battle what it was promised there, and what those who should have fulfilled that promise could not or would not give. It comes like fate, but also like hope: the incendiary torch in one hand, and the other hand stretched out towards the unattained gift. It is barbarism, there's no denying it, seizing its own heritage; but there was no other way, since the civilising activity of those men who might have tried another method lost itself amid political abstractions and never reached down to the deep and positive root of the troubles. A world apart, a social class of foreign culture superimposed on to the native barbarism, which is still intact, were the civilisers, the men of government, who, full of theories, spoke a language which the people could not and cannot understand, and it is not at all surprising that they have been demolished by the wild *machete* fighter, who at all events is a genuine product of our violent earth, this Venezuela where the Liberator showed his mettle.'

From March 15, 1858 to July 24, 1863, a wave of anarchy transformed the country, and as government after government weltered, the social and political structure changed radically under the blows of war and desolation. Government was unstable even from Castro's first unsuccessful efforts to work with the Conservatives, and then with the Liberals. A cabinet emerged in February 1859, at the start of the war, but in June Castro retired and left his vice-president, Tovar, to struggle. Under Tovar, Páez was invited back to the country by Castro, but after a week Castro re-assumed power, and throwing out Tovar's men, changed the cabinet for a Liberal administration, which began negotiations with the Federalists. Páez therefore left the country, while Castro tried to come to terms with the Federalists, but on August 1st these defeated Castro and set up a provisional government. Tovar was declared president by the Conservatives, and as he had left Caracas, Gual took over, designated by Castro who was now in prison. Gual formed a cabinet, and then handed over to Tovar on the latter's return in September. Elections were held in spite of the war, and in April 1860 Tovar became constitutional president, with Gual as vice-president, and with Páez as Minister of War and Navy.

The government issued an amnesty, but tried Castro for trea-
son, and then when he was judged guilty, absolved him. Anarchy grew, as Paecistas urged the claim of their hero to be made
dictator, and Tovar resigned in May 1861, to be succeeded by
Gual. Páez tried to negotiate with the Federalists, Gual therefore asked him to resign his ministry, and the commander of
the Caracas garrison arrested Gual and proclaimed Páez as chief.
Páez became dictator on September 10, 1861, failed to concili-
ate the Federalists, and carried on the losing fight until on June
6, 1863 he ratified the Treaty of Coche, which brought to
power the Federalist leader, Falcón, and federation thus triumphed after five years of bloodshed.

These are the external facts of governmental instability, but
now we must go back and trace the politics of the Federal Revolution. In 1858 the new Constitution had accepted federalism
in all but name, and the Conservatives who surrounded Castro
seemed to believe in administrative federalism, but political
centralism. Straight away the conspirators got to work, and the
Federal War began with a revolt in Carabobo in July 1858. The
whole west of the country contained many who liked *caudillismo*, and by early 1859 the region was full of *caudillos* in arms
but with no clear aims; the necessary organisation, therefore,
was worked out in various West Indian islands, by men whom
Castro had exiled. Monagas and his henchmen were among
these, and also Juan Crisóstomo Falcón, Ezequiel Zamora, Guzmán and sixteen other citizens of the Liberal persuasion. These
formed three groups of conspirators: Falcón in St. Thomas with
Guzmán Blanco (son of the Liberal founder) and a few others;
Monagas in Trinidad with Sotillo and his henchmen; and Zamora in Curaçao with Guzmán and his friends. These met in a
Junta at St. Thomas in October and worked out their revolutionary plan and their federalist programme, which in fact differed very little from the Constitution of 1858 then in force.
Falcón was accepted as leader, as had already been decided at
meetings in Caracas.

The first stroke was dealt on February 20, 1859, when a band
of 40 revolutionaries captured Coro and sent the news to Zamora, who hurried from exile, and on the 22nd landed as chief of
operations of the Federal Army of the West. Coro proclaimed
the federation, and a provisional government for the whole

country was set up, consisting of five men, including Falcón and Guzmán. Zamora then set out to capture Puerto Cabello, leaving Coro to fall to a government force soon afterwards. The east of Venezuela was invaded by Sotillo, and was welcomed by a series of risings in sympathy, and indeed the whole country seemed ripe for federation.

Zamora's campaign in the west and in the *llanos* was a string of victories and defeats, marked by great violence when, for example, Barinas and Guanare were burned down, as well as smaller places. At Barinas on June 14th, however, Zamora was enshrined in popular favour by a grateful people who gave him the title Valiant Citizen. In the east Sotillo and other leaders opened operations, and Falcón arrived in July to take over the direction of the war. Zamora still operated on his own account in the west. But the war became general, and innumerable small actions took place in the course of a revolution in which even the bandits became Federalists. There were, however, only two major battles. Firstly on December 10, 1859, at Santa Inés, Zamora beat the Constitutional army under the commander-in-chief, Pedro Ramos. The Constitutionalists retreated to Barinas, then to Mérida, and the campaign in the west was thus decided in Zamora's favour. The government was badly shaken, and the main strong points were left defenceless. Still winning, Zamora happened to be killed by a rifle bullet on January 10, 1860 while directing a siege. Falcón, nominally commander of the Federalists, pressed the campaign on towards Valencia.

The second major battle took place early in February, Falcón collected Sotillo's forces together with his own, and turned towards the *llanos*, but on the 17th he was overtaken by Constitutional forces under Febres Cordero, from Valencia, and at Coplé he was completely smashed and lost his army in dispersal. Falcón himself fled to New Granada, and only the absolute anarchy into which the government had sunk prevented the war from ending then. Instead, the fighting went on, more barbarous than before, with Páez as dictator trying to come to an agreement with Falcón. A meeting between the two leaders in December 1861 at Carabobo gave no result, and from then it was war to the death until Falcón's hordes at last reached Caracas.

In August 1862 Falcón sent Antonio Guzmán Blanco to open a Federalist campaign in the centre of the country, Caracas,

Aragua, Carabobo and Guárico. Guzmán Blanco succeeded, but even more important was the contact he made with Páez's substitute, Pedro José Rojas, in order to negotiate a settlement. By early 1863 the Federalists were in possession of most of the country, and were fighting close to the capital; and even at times Federalists took part in riots and mutinies in the city itself. Disloyalty began to show amongst the Constitutionalists. Guzmán Blanco and Rojas, negotiating in the names of their chiefs, succeeded on April 24, 1863 in completing the so-called Treaty of Coche, named after the country house in which it was signed, and which brought peace at last. The treaty provided for a convocation of a National Assembly, half of whose Deputies would be nominated by Páez and half by Falcón, in order 'to avoid in the present circumstances the clash of parties'. This Assembly would establish a new government. Originally Falcón was to be made commander-in-chief of the whole army, then, by a later modification, he was to become dictator as soon as the Assembly met. And in fact, on June 17th the Assembly appointed Falcón provisional president of the Venezuelan Federation, and Guzmán Blanco vice-president.

The government of the Federation was far from peaceful even after this, since from 1863 to 1868 Falcón governed amid the greatest unrest, putting down risings, and constantly faced with political crises and economic troubles. He preferred private life, and retired to his lands in Coro, leaving the job of government to his nominees. In August 1863, however, in an attempt at national reconciliation, Falcón published a Decree of Guarantees, with which he tried to affirm democracy in the country and to ensure that the people should henceforth enjoy their political and human rights. Therefore he guaranteed the lives of all, even abolishing the death penalty, and also guaranteed property, inviolability of the home, secrecy of papers and correspondence, freedom of thought and expression, the right of universal suffrage (for males), the rights of free association and petition, liberty, equality before the law, and individual security (exile was therefore abolished). The Decree also abolished for ever slavery in Venezuela, and closed certain infamous places of confinement. Falcón, there is no doubt, was generous and well-intentioned.

The federal government inherited a national economy ruined by the war and the anarchy of the country, which had turned the peasants into soldiers, ruined trade and brought external credit to nil. Previous governments, including the late one under Páez, had taken loans without being able to pay them off, so that Falcón's government became responsible for the debts. Accordingly Guzmán Blanco was sent in August 1863 to negotiate in London a loan of two million pounds, mortgaging for it the customs duties, which were substantial. The loan was agreed in London with the General Credit and Finance Company, and the terms were approved by the Venezuelan Constituent Assembly on January 14, 1864. Under them Venezuela contracted for a loan of a million and a half pounds (at a rate of discount which in fact would only give her £900,000) at 6% interest and repayment of 2% per year. The customs receipts of La Guaira, Puerto Cabello, Maracaibo and Ciudad Bolívar were to pay the charges, and if the income were not enough, the money would be made up from the receipts of other customs houses. Some Deputies opposed the terms, but they were overborne by the majority and by Guzmán Blanco. The contract was signed in April 1864, but the finance company had such difficulty in persuading subscribers to part with money for such a notably insecure country that, in spite of the favourable discount, Venezuela only received a million and a half pesos instead of the four million and a half expected. Guzmán Blanco made his fortune over the deal, but the country's finances sank still lower, with the result that the total national debt that year reached 51,000,000 pesos and the circulation of money was chaotic.

Obviously a federal constitution had to be produced, and a Constituent Assembly met on December 24, 1863, with Guzmán Blanco as its president and many military members, mostly generals and colonels. The Assembly's first acts were to confirm Falcón and Guzmán Blanco as national president and vice-president respectively, decree honours to the dead hero Zamora and pensions to his mother and widow, and grant Falcón the title of Great Citizen, the rank of marshal, and the salary of president since 1859. The Constitution itself was passed on March 28, 1864 and put into effect on April 13th. It was, naturally, federal: the country was named United States of Venezuela, the States were independent and only united to form the nation. The president was elected by direct and secret ballot for a four-year term, without the possibility of immediate re-election. Twenty States were made from the old provinces, and since most of these were poor they were to receive an annual subsidy from the national income, derived mainly from the customs duties. The Municipal Power was retained and made the basis of the federation, with the result that a dual system of taxation was needed, one for the State and the other for the Municipality. The legislature was in two Chambers, the Senate and the Chamber of Deputies; the administration of justice in the States was independent of the federal judicial system; the federal government and the other States were not permitted to interfere in the affairs of any State; and finally all the guarantees decreed by Falcón, and even more, were given by the Assembly.

But Falcón could not bring peaceful government, and as early as August 1863 he was forced to undertake a campaign against Puerto Cabello, while in Zulia two generals disputed the power and, in Guayana, Dallacosta caused trouble. In 1864 there were risings in Trujillo and Táchira and political troubles in Carabobo, mutinies in Cagua and others in Guárico and Carabobo; and so it went on until 1868. Political anarchy, military despotism inside the States, national confusion and administrative chaos were what the Federation brought, but also the end of the oligarchies, and violent social democracy. There was a levelling which gave equality of opportunity in military rank and in the government, but which also put all citizens on one grade, whatever their intellectual or moral capacity; this levelling meant that an illiterate could rise to the direction of the State and the exercise of justice.

5.   THE AUTOCRACY OF GUZMÁN BLANCO

At the end of 1867 the country was again in flames. Early in December General Miguel Antonio Rojas, president of the State of Aragua, made a *pronunciamiento*, and he and his friends adopted a blue badge and called themselves the 'Reconquerers'. On January 8, 1868 they told Falcón: 'after five years of your domination, everything was and still is arbitrariness in your government, poverty and discontent among the people.' Aragua, Carabobo and Guárico rose in violent revolt. An attempt to gain the support of Monagas and the easterners for the revolution failed, but unrest spread in the west throughout the Andes, and some members of Congress declared themselves sympathisers in February. The East became infected when José Tadeo Monagas, after declaring that 'only peace is legal, only peace is legitimate,' put himself at the head of the whole revolution.

In March Rojas allowed himself to be pacified and accepted the post of commander-in-chief of the army in the States where the revolution had taken place; but in May Monagas opened his own campaign against Caracas, and early in June Falcón left the country. Fighting continued, in spite of negotiations, until Monagas won by occupying Caracas on June 25th after street battles. So ended the Blue Revolution, with Monagas in Caracas, not ruling in person but nominating a government. The Constitution of 1864 was declared to be in force, and a Congress was called for the next year. The government of the Blues was a short-lived union of Conservatives and Liberals, who soon split, mainly because José Tadeo Monagas died towards the end of 1868, leaving his son José Ruperto and his nephew Domingo Monagas disputing the power.

José Ruperto was made his father's successor by the Congress of 1869, and he took over power on March 8th, soon to face a ministerial crisis and the outbreak of factionalism. Antonio Guzmán Blanco led one of the factions, but he took no armed action until provoked in August, when a government-inspired mob stoned his house in Caracas when he was holding a ball to gain converts to his side. Then Guzmán Blanco put himself at the head of the Liberals in conspiracy against the régime, and, the better to make his plans, first took refuge in the American Legation and then went to Curaçao, followed by his father the old Liberal leader.

While other Liberal leaders revolted in various parts of Venezuela, Guzmán Blanco prepared an invasion, and landed on February 14, 1870, to be recognised as leader of the Yellow Liberals by those already in the field. He marched on Caracas from Barquisimeto, joined by the contingents of Matías Salazar and José Ignacio Pulido, and entered the city in triumph on April 27th. After assuming power he at once called for a Congress of plenipotentiaries of the States, to meet at Valencia in June in order to arrange for elections as laid down in the Constitution of 1864, and to elect the provisional president of the Republic. In the event Guzmán Blanco remained dictatorially in command for seven years.

Not all the country accepted the change at once, and *caudillos* kept the war going in both east and west until, after two years, Guzmán Blanco imposed peace. But before this, his former comrade Matías Salazar revolted against him, only to be defeated and shot on May 17, 1872. Meanwhile the plenipotentiaries in Valencia, under the presidency of Guzmán senior, had duly made Guzmán Blanco provisional president in July 1870.

As dictator, Guzmán Blanco worked hard for the material progress of Venezuela. He was the 'Civiliser' as well as the 'Autocrat', and under him order brought bigger crops, railways and roads were built, and an aqueduct was constructed to supply Caracas with water. The government had a modern outlook, since the dictator realised the need to make his rustic, agricultural country more enterprising. From 1870 onwards politics became the labour of organisation, building not merely for ornamentation, but to solve problems of national importance. For example, the University of Caracas was reformed in 1870, with a plan of studies which placed emphasis on science, and foreign professors were brought in. In the same year the Institute of Fine Arts and the Museum of Natural History were founded. A Venezuelan Academy of Literature, opened in 1874, organised literary contests. Public works were organised on a national scale and present an impressive list: roads, aqueducts, squares, the Capitol, bridges, university buildings, the National Pantheon, streets, markets, and port works at Barcelona, La Guaira and Puerto Cabello.

Guzmán Blanco had the gift of choosing competent men to help him in his task. Economists and financiers worked, for example, on a scheme for the gradual extinction of the national debt and on other necessary adjuncts of a modern commercial country. These included a national credit company, an agricultural council for the encouragement of the cultivation of wheat, a national statistical institute, the establishment of a stable currency, and the lightening of some internal taxes on trade. In 1873 a census gave the number of Venezuelans as 1,784,194.

At the same time, Guzmán Blanco engaged in a struggle with the Church in order to secularise and liberalise the country, and reorganised the legal codes concerned with all branches of justice, including the military. In his anticlericalism, Guzmán Blanco expelled the archbishop of Caracas and exiled the bishop of Mérida (who died before he could leave the country). Then in 1872 he seized the funds of religious houses, before dissolving them altogether in 1874. Among other measures was the establishment of civil marriage in 1873, which he defended as being the practice of almost all civilised peoples and a method, together with freedom of religion, of attracting foreign immigration 'which will rapidly accelerate our growth'. All this led to a break with the Vatican—it is no coincidence that among Guzmán Blanco's public works was the Masonic Temple in Caracas.

Public education was one of the dictator's first cares, for on June 27, 1870 he decreed free obligatory primary education for all children, to be organised by the State through a National Directorate of Primary Education and a series of Juntas for education in all the local government areas. The school system was to be financed by a special national tax. The National Directorate was installed on August 14th, encouraged by the dictator's words: 'Wherever ten children can be gathered together, there must be a schoolmaster teaching them to read and write and the first four rules of arithmetic; if there is no school-house, the school must function even in the shade of some tree, in order that there shall be no Venezuelan who cannot read the Constitution of the Republic.' Schools, primary and secondary, began to be built throughout the country.

Guzmán Blanco governed dictatorially for two years, as the plenipotentiaries had arranged in 1870, but he insisted on holding elections for the presidential term 1873-77, with the foreseeable result that Guzmán won with 239,691 votes. His nearest rival was Pulido, with eight votes, and the total number of votes cast for the other four candidates was nine. Then, in 1874, the dictator asked Congress to discuss certain reforms for the Constitution: public and signed ballots, responsibility of public servants for their actions, no presidentially-appointed substitutes in case of the president's absence, and the reduction of the presidential term to two years. Congress added to the list no re-election of the president and no election of his relatives, increased subsidies for the States, and direct election of members of the Federal High Court. Guzmán Blanco also declared that he wished to retire in 1875. But all this was propaganda by means of which the dictator hoped to calm the growing discontent of some politicians, including some of his own lieutenants, at the

M

continuance of his rule. Indeed in 1874 and 1875 Guzmán Blanco was forced to fight a rising of his own former supporters, including Pulido. He succeeded in beating them and exiling the leaders. The first five reforms were added to the Constitution, but it was declared that Guzmán Blanco would in fact continue in office until 1877, thus completing the four-year term for which he had been elected.

Long before the term was up, in May 1875 in fact, Guzmán Blanco began to prepare for the presidential succession by inviting various loyal generals to become candidates for the term 1877-79. Electoral excitement spread in the towns, but all the candidates were loyal supporters of Guzmán Blanco, and all were concentrating their efforts on gaining the vote of their boss, the 'Illustrious American, the Regenerator of Venezuela.' Guzmán Blanco was the sole elector who mattered.

6.   FROM AUTOCRACY TO THE RESTORATION

From 1877, when Guzmán Blanco left power in the hands of a chosen successor, to 1899, when Cipriano Castro came down from the Andes, Venezuela had governments of very varied political hues. The personal power of the Regenerator, the Civilising Autocrat, the Illustrious American, met violent opposition and although he reigned again, his power in the end waned and left a short breathing-space for rulers who made a last effort to avoid perpetual personalism and military dictatorship.

General Francisco Linares Alcántara, one of the Guzmancista candidates for the presidency in 1877, somehow became the Autocrat's favourite, gained his vote, and occupied the presidential chair. As early as 1875 he had published a manifesto praising Guzmán in the most servile manner and offering to rule in order to preserve his great work: 'I should be the sentinel of the immortal glory which he has conquered.' Before he died, in November 1878, Linares had shown that he intended to govern on his own account—that Guzmán Blanco could be opposed. He gathered Conservatives and Liberals round him in an attempt to have the presidential term extended to four years in order to break Guzmán Blanco's hold on the country, and for this he was given the title 'Great Democrat'. On the other hand, the Autocrat left the country with the honorific exile of the post of Minister Plenipotentiary to Germany, Italy, the Holy See, Spain and Switzerland—a post which he soon resigned. Linares called back the exiles, such as the archbishop of Caracas, and tried to build up the anti-Guzmán feeling. Guzmán senior and other loyal Guzmancistas such as Joaquín Crespo and Rojas Paúl tried to defend the absent Illustrious American.

Linares' death was a blow, but it did not stop the movement. which was now headed by Jacinto Gutiérrez, president of the Federal High Court. A Constituent Assembly called by Linares in order to reform the ruling Constitution did meet in December 1878, but Gregorio Cedeño, the president of Carabobo, denied its authority and rose in revolt in the name of Guzmán Blanco. Soon Crespo and others joined him, calling their movement the Revindicating Revolution. After a bloody battle at La Victoria, both armies united under Cedeño, who entered Caracas in triumph in a few days. Guzmán Blanco was proclaimed Supreme Director of the Republic, and returned to govern dictatorially as before on February 25, 1879. A rapidly convened Congress of Plenipotentiaries legalised the régime and declared the Constitution of 1864, as modified by Guzmán Blanco in 1874, to be in force, except for the public and signed vote. Guzmán Blanco was so sure of himself that he could return to unfinished business in Paris from June to November, leaving his underling Diego Bautista Urbaneja in charge.

In 1880 Guzmán Blanco was elected president—as in all elections since those of Monagas, there was no doubt about the victor before the polling took place. He ruled for his two-year term according to the letter of the Constitution, although he tampered again with the latter in 1881 when he reduced the number of States from twenty to nine, and created a Federal Council (consisting of one Senator and one Deputy from each State) whose sole task was in effect to elect the president of the Republic from amongst themselves. Once again Guzmán Blanco, despite his protests, was elected president for the term 1882-84, and legalised the matter by having himself made a member of the Federal Council. Thus, the governments of Guzmán Blanco, though legal in appearance, were tyrannous in fact. From 1884 to 1886 he took a holiday in Paris, returning as president for the term 1886-88 amidst a stirring popular acclamation organised by his friends. Guzmán Blanco was kept a short time in Paris by the business of marrying his daughters to French nobles, and at the end of the term went off early back to Paris, leaving General Hermógenes López as his proxy.

In total, the Autocrat ruled for nineteen years, either directly or as the director behind the scenes, copying Páez's best years between 1830 and 1848. He was dictator from 1870 to 1877, 1879 to 1884 and 1886 to 1888. He was cleverer than Monagas, better educated than Páez, and more energetic than Falcón, and was able to keep down the militarism which threatened the country after the Federal Revolution and the troubles of the years 1864 to 1870. Under him there was peace, good administration, external credit, prosperity, although he brooked no denial or criticism of his own power. He has some Liberal reforms to his credit—education, and separation of the Church from all affairs of State. He called himself a Liberal always, but his rule was always personal and was exercised with the aid of a purely personalist party.

The term 1884-86 was given, at Guzmán Blanco's direction, to his loyal friend General Joaquín Crespo, the young but hardened *llanero* warrior. The government posts were all filled by other loyal Guzmancistas in case Crespo showed personal ambitions, but this was not necessary for the general was proud of his loyalty and of the title granted to him in 1879—'Hero of Duty Done'. There was at one moment a hint that he was being tempted by a friend into joining a new party of truly Liberal ideas, but he was kept straight by the Guzmancistas and by Guzmán Blanco himself—so straight that he imprisoned the tempter's catspaw, a journalist.

Crespo's term was notable for an economic slump, manifested in a drop in coffee production and therefore in revenue. It is true that there had been a plague of locusts, but the administration under Crespo was inept, and in any case the personalist rule of Guzmán Blanco was producing a reaction of weariness and even desperation in many people. It is a curious fact that just when Crespo came to power the country was economically in a good state, and when he left power it was climbing out of the slump, as the figures for exports and imports indicate. In the economic year 1885-86, imports were worth forty-seven and a half million bolívares and exports eighty-two and a half million, or almost double. In 1887-88 imports had risen to nearly seventy-nine million bolívares and exports were still higher, at just over eighty-six million. Between 1886 and 1888 the population grew from 2,198,320 inhabitants to 2,238,922. Almost all of the increase was due to the excess of births over deaths, for immigration was extremely small at that time—only 4,537 immigrants entered the country between May 1, 1881 and January 1, 1888.

Again at Guzmán Blanco's behest, the presidential term 1888-90 went to Pablo Rojas Paúl, a supporter of the Autocracy, but a civilian who had some administrative capacity. Since Vargas, elected in 1835, there had been no civilian president, except during the brief interim periods of Tovar and Gual during the anarchy of 1859-61. Rojas Paúl saw his term out, even though he had not been elected by the will of the people, and, on the other hand, even though he tried to establish a civilian régime despite the will of the Great Elector, Guzmán Blanco. The latter, in fact, faded out during this term, and in 1890 Rojas Paúl was able to hand over to another civilian government for the next term.

In 1890, political parties arose again. In May was founded the Democratic Union, with a programme including proportional representation and the jury system of trial. The members of this movement refused to form a true party, since they would not pledge themselves to party discipline. In any case, although Rojas Paúl allowed civilians to aspire to real civilian government, this advance was not to go on for long, since new dictatorships soon crushed it.

Doctor Raimundo Andueza Palacio, another civilian, was elected president for the 1890-92 term, with the support of Rojas Paúl and without opposition. Andueza wanted to reform the Constitution in order to allow a longer presidential term, which would make the work of each successive government more cohesive and less fragmented. Also, he wanted the people to play a direct part in the election of the presidents. But what really interested him was what has been called 'continuism', that is, the reform of the Constitution in order to keep himself in office. In 1892 both the opposition and the president's supporters were less than happy about the jettisoning of the principle of no re-election, which was believed to be one of the mainstays of the attempt to perpetuate civilian rule. Rojas Paúl had been expelled in 1891 as a revolutionary, and in June 1892 a successful revolution forced Andueza to resign, leaving behind him a state of war and an economic crisis. The historian Gil Fortoul, writing from Liverpool, observed sadly: 'What an English thinker called "legal fibre" is a part of our body politic which has become atrophied, and we shall need many years of normality for the working of the body to reinvigorate the fibre.'

General Joaquín Crespo had risen against Andueza with the cry of legalism. Opposition in Congress and in the street to Andueza's continuism brought many partisans to Crespo's side. The thinker Lisandro Alvarado arrived from Europe to join him. Fighting went on until October 1892, when Crespo reached Caracas and called a Constituent Assembly, which lengthened the presidential term to four years. From 1894 to 1898 the legalist general ruled as president with some examples of liberalness. In his provisional rule, he allowed, in 1893, the formation of a Republican Liberal Party; and in July 1894 was formed a group whose aim was to rebuild the Liberal Party, and who elected Crespo himself their leader. In opposition to this party stood another, led by José Manuel Hernández. And in 1897 these new formations were faced with the presidential elections for 1898-1902.

These elections were controlled by Crespo's government—and were naturally won by the official candidate, General Ignacio Andrade. He occupied the presidential chair from February 1898 to October 22, 1899, when a new revolutionary and dictator, General Cipriano Castro, entered Caracas victorious. Crespo's political opponent, Hernández, had revolted at the electoral victory of Andrade. He defeated Crespo—who died in the fight—but was himself defeated by General Ramón Guerra. Crespo's successor as commander of the government army. Guerra then revolted himself, but was defeated. Now the country was back in revolutionary chaos, the civilian attempt at government had itself failed in the person of Andueza, and dictatorship would soon settle the political question for a long time to come.

7. FROM THE RESTORATION TO THE REHABILITATION

For almost half a century, from 1899 to 1935, Venezuela was dominated by two men who came to power through one revolution. The dictatorships of Cipriano Castro (1899 to 1908) and of Juan Vicente Gómez (1908 to 1935) transformed Venezuelan history, modifying political, moral and economic habits.

Castro's rule was called the Restoration, and Gómez's the Rehabilitation.

The campaign which brought Castro to power began with his invasion of Táchira on May 23, 1899 and ended on October 22nd, with his reception in Caracas by a government and by the people *en fête*. Only sixty men opened the campaign, including Gómez, who was also the financial backer of the movement. Crossing the River Táchira they took Capacho, and grew to 180 men, then, in operations in the district, they were joined by local farmers, small traders and students, and soon became an army of 2,000. From May to August they had a series of victories in the Andes, and then fought their way towards Valencia. The government in Caracas became so nervous that the president himself fled, leaving the president of the Council of Government, General Víctor Rodríguez, to hand over to Castro on his arrival by rail on October 22nd.

Castro claimed to bring new men, new ideals and new methods. But he was surrounded in fact by old politicians such as Andueza, Castillo and Pulido, and by a group of diehard localist Valencian politicians. He took Hernández out of prison, since this general, the former opponent of Andrade and Crespo, was acknowledged as the chief of the nationalists and might therefore be useful to the new régime in helping to unify the people behind Castro. The first cabinet consisted entirely of men from these groups, and the 'new men' claim went by the board. From the start government was a dictatorship, in which Castro gave his henchmen posts in the public service, imprisoned hostile journalists, and imposed forced loans. Hernández revolted, was defeated, and was imprisoned again. In March 1901 restless students who opposed the militarism of the government were expelled, and on the 11th the University of Caracas was closed. No new methods, no new ideals, became apparent.[1]

The causes of the Restoration movement can be traced to the whole history of Venezuelan *caudillismo* since 1830, for since the beginning of the Republic *caudillos* disturbed the country and broke up society with their constant wars and revolts, which gave no period of quiet for rebuilding. Castro had the same motive for his pronouncement as had previous *caudillos* from the *llanos*, or the east, or the centre: ambition for power.

[1] M. Picón Salas, *Los días de Cipriano Castro*, Caracas 1953.

'War in Venezuela seemed to follow a natural cycle, like earth-quakes and floods. It was still an exodus of rural tribes through a rural land: old-fashioned Venezuela, with its rope-soled sandals, short jacket and poncho, its gourd of rough spirits, its scapularies and childish prayers.' Everything was backward, and this allowed *caudillismo* to flourish: illiteracy in Venezuela has not yet been overcome, as is true of all the Hispanic countries. The sparse population in a vast rural country encouraged revolts, since illiterate and tough peasants flocked to join the bands of marauders. Those of the Andes quickly followed Castro.

The lack of any constitutional tradition and therefore of any political consciousness also aided Castro's movement. All the people were ignorant; every political notion needed explaining from the start, even to the supposedly educated. The only salvation for the countries of Spanish America seemed to Gil Fortoul to be 'the increase of the population with men from some superior race, and the importation of foreign capital.' On the other hand, Castro's excuse for his movement was the fear that Andrade sought to perpetuate himself in power. In April 1899, under Andrade's domination, Congress had voted to preserve the 'historic autonomy' of the States; and this had been regarded as a perpetuist manoeuvre, which gave Castro his chance to march. Hernández, the nationalist chief, was imprisoned by Andrade after he had revolted but the imprisonment caused a wave of hatred for Andrade. Crespo was dead, so Andrade had no forces. Government was in anarchy, and Castro had really no opposition.

After his victory opposition soon arose, firstly from Hernández, who, only a few days after taking his oath of loyalty, pronounced and raised an army with support in various parts of the country. He was beaten after six months. Then from 1901 to 1903 there was a civil war, called the Liberating Revolution, which spread throughout Venezuela. The dictator dictated a new Constitution in 1901 to give the semblance of legality to his rule, at the very time that Rolando was preparing an invasion in the West Indies, others were rising in Guárico, Cumaná and Margarita, and Garbiras invaded the country from Colombia using Colombian troops. Venezuela and Colombia were almost brought to war over this incident.

The Liberating Revolution was led by the general and businessman Manuel Antonio Matos, who gained support from the United States and Europe and from many provincial *caudillos*. He bought a ship in England and sent it with Colombian papers to Martinique carrying a cargo of rifles and munitions. There Matos met his supporters and their 400 men, while at the same time Castro's War Minister, Guerra, and some capitalist in Caracas joined the movement. The arms were landed at various points on the coast of Venezuela, the rebels captured a government warship, and several generals rose in support of Matos. Yet the government managed to win the three main battles of La Puerta (December 1901), La Victoria (October-November 1901), and El Guapo (April 1903), and Gómez, who had been most successful in the war, ended the pacification of the country with his capture of Ciudad Bolívar in July 1903. The Liberating Revolution was in fact the last of the *caudillo* wars in Venezuela, for Castro now affirmed his complete power, which was inherited by Gómez, and which made impossible the risings so typical of the nineteenth century.

Castro was unlucky enough to reach power in 1899 when the country was having one of the economic upheavals common in the nineteenth century. Certainly capricious government was one cause of these, but also there were causes which were out of the control of any rulers, such as the international market and declines in production. Figures available show economic irregularity: the national revenue in 1896-97 was over 48 million bolívares; in 1897-98 it was only 33 million and a half; in 1898-99 it rose to 40 million; and in 1899-1900 it slumped to 27 million and a quarter. By 1900 the national debt stood at nearly 190 million bolívares. Foreign claims became urgent after this year, and Castro's efforts against the rebels in the years 1901 to 1903 were sabotaged by foreign firms such as the German-owned railway and the French-owned telegraphs. On March 1, 1902 Castro was obliged to suspend all service of the debts, internal and external, and this naturally brought strong protests from foreign creditors. The dislocation brought on a conflict with the North American directed Bermúdez asphalt company, which led to interventions by the United States government. Castro stood firm, even though leading figures in that government were financially involved.

But there was a serious repercussion of the default on foreign debts. Germany in 1901 began to claim payment on a loan made in 1896 and asked for damages for German residents whose interests had been injured. In 1902 the diplomatic agents of Germany, France, Britain and Italy presented demands for payment, and in November the British Minister in Caracas, Haggard, threatened measures to protect British interests.[1] The Venezuelans replied that they might claim against Britain for having allowed the Liberating rebels to buy a British boat and for having permitted Trinidad to be used as a rebel base. In the capitals of all the countries involved complaints and accusations were published. Castro haughtily declared: 'It is inconceivable that civilised nations which cultivate cordial and friendly relations with Venezuela should prize the power of their material strength more than the powerful attraction of their proclaimed civilisation.'

On December 7, 1902 the German and British Ministers delivered an ultimatum to the Venezuelan Foreign Minister, López Baralt, then went to La Guaira to take up quarters aboard warships of their respective countries. The Venezuelan navy in La Guaira was captured at the orders of Douglas, admiral of the joint Anglo-German fleet, and so four 'little boats, smelling of rust, bananas, stew and *mestizo* sweat' became prizes. Castro threw German and British subjects into prison, but released them at the instance of the United States Minister, Bowen, who hoped that his country would mediate and bring peace. Castro invoked the Monroe Doctrine, as did the students who thronged the streets and squares of Caracas. In Puerto Cabello a mob seeking revenge invaded the British vessel Topaze, and two British cruisers bombarded the forts and sacked the fortress, bringing panic to the locals. Italy joined the action on December 11th, sending two warships to join the blockade. In spite of the Venezuelan government's protests circulated to foreign governments, the only Spanish American country which reacted was Argentina, whose Foreign Minister, Luis M. Drago, protested against the use of force to collect debts.

Bowen was commissioned by the Venezuelan government to represent it in claiming a quick solution to the situation, and the American went in January 1903 to inform the Secretary of

---

1 See D. C. M. Platt, *The Allied coercion of Venezuela, 1902-3—a reassessment* (in *Inter-American Economic affairs*, Washington, D.C., vol. XV, spring 1962, pp. 3-28) for a modern British view of this episode. (Editor's note)

State, Hay, about the case and to have talks with representatives of the blockading powers. From the countries involved came in more claims for payments by Venezuela, until the list of debts, according to Castro himself, reached a total of 490 million bolívares, which would mean that the whole national income for ten years would be needed to pay off the claims. Even with the utmost economy the country could only extinguish the debts at the rate of four million bolívares per annum. But on February 13th were signed the Washington Protocols, which put forward a solution on the basis of dividing the claims into two categories: those caused by civil wars previous to Castro's rise to power, and which would be settled within a few months; and those caused by Castro's government and civil wars. These would be scrutinised by a mixed commission consisting of one member designated by Venezuela and one by the creditor country, with appeal to a nominee of the president of the United States in case of disagreement. Those claims justified would be paid out of the customs duties collected at La Guaira and Puerto Cabello. In return, all Venezuelan ships which had been captured would be returned to Venezuela and the blockade would be lifted. Venezuela rejected the Protocols and the case was referred to the international court at The Hague, which in 1904 gave a verdict favourable to the claimant nations.

All Castro's actions prove his ardent nationalism, as for example his release of Hernández in 1899 and again in the time of the blockade, since Hernández was a nationalist symbol. The Liberating Revolution, with greater forces than Castro's, was not victorious since public opinion was whipped up by the dictator against Matos, whose actions were shown as unpatriotic. This nationalism was at its most acute over the question of the foreign claims and the blockade. Castro was against nations which abused their power, and also against the German merchants who monopolised the trade in coffee and other products, against the German railway and the French cable. But on the other hand he was an incompetent administrator, and he implanted despotic rule, to be continued by his successor. Still, Castro's nationalism acquires some importance since it symbolises the defence of the small Latin American country against the monopolistic invasion of the foreigner. Although the other Latin American countries were too frightened to do anything about the Venezuelan case in 1902—their strongest word was 'deplore'—the peoples, and especially the youth, showed their sympathy with Venezuela. This was the time just after the Uruguayan José Enrique Rodó, in *Ariel*, had called Latin America to union, and Manuel Ugarte, one of the early Argentine socialists, had passionately decried imperialism. In Mexico they compared Castro's situation with that of Juárez, faced forty years before with a French invasion and the imposition of the Empire of Maximilian.

On November 24, 1908 Castro went to Europe to have an operation, leaving in charge his vice-president, Gómez, who on December 19th imprisoned the leading Castristas and began to govern on his own account. Gómez was clever enough to ask the United States to support his move, and on December 27th American cruisers reached La Guaira. The people welcomed the change of government, for it was hoped that Gómez would bring constitutional rule at last, in spite of the treachery and violence which had brought him to power. Rómulo Gallegos, who was twenty-five at the time, lived through this hour of hope, short-lived and decisive.[1] The situation favoured Gómez, for Castro had quarrelled with the United States in June and July 1908, and in December relations with Holland were strained, while at home Gómez's friends made public demonstrations against the Restorer. Castro, when informed, telegraphed his friend General Cárdenas telling him to kill Gómez, who used this as the pretext for his revolt on December 19th.

The actual *coup d'état* was smartly carried out, beginning on the 18th with Gómez's orders to General Galavís to have the presidential guard of 300 men ready and to General Jaimes to warn the friends who were to form the first cabinet to be with him at eight o'clock the next morning. On the 19th they all went to the Mamey barracks, where Gómez paraded the troops and then took the growing army to the Yellow House, the seat of the government in Caracas. Meanwhile, other troops and the police were called out by loyal friends of Gómez. At the Yellow House, Gómez led his intimates into the room of General Cárdenas, whom he accused of plotting his murder and then had arrested with the words 'Arrest that c . . . '

At once the prisons were thrown open and political exiles

---

[1] R. Gallegos, *Una posición en la vida*, México D F 1954, p. 5.

were allowed to return. Thirty thousand exiles came back, whose leaders, opponents of Castro, with one accord put themselves at the service of Gómez, and many of them, including General Hernández, were given high posts. Gómez took as the slogan of his régime 'Peace, Union and Work', and the name given to his period was 'The Rehabilitation'. It lasted, in reality the most absolute despotism, until 1935. The dictator kept up constitutional appearances, for those periods in which he himself was not in office he gave to friends to rule, such as Victoriano Márquez Bustillo (1914), and Juan Bautista Pérez (1929-31). He himself was provisional president from 1908 to 1910, and constitutional president in 1910-14, 1915-21, 1922-29 and 1931-35. In the brief intervals, he was still commander-in-chief of the army.

The economic results of Gómez's régime are interesting, for in 1908 Venezuela was still an agricultural country, whose fortunes were based on large herds of cattle in the *llanos* or on large coffee and cacao plantations in the Andes and near the coast. The national revenue came from customs duties, and through the customs went, especially, coffee, which was largely monopolised as an export by a few German firms. Gómez's economic policies were very different from those of previous dictatorships, since he was able to come easily to an understanding with the more powerful commercial countries, with the result that large foreign investments were attracted, and these changed the whole aspect of the country. Foreign capital was kept safe, without too much notice being taken of the true interests of Venezuela.

There were two main periods, one from 1908 to 1920, when conflicts with foreign companies were resolved and when agriculture and stock-raising were still of great importance; and the second from 1920, when the income from oil royalties initiated a complete change for Venezuela, which reached its highest point about 1945.

Gómez himself had a peasant outlook, which is why he preferred to isolate himself at Maracay, seizing the lands round about in order to turn them into what were called model farms. As the theoretician of the régime, Laureano Vallenilla Lanz, explained in an article in the Gómez newspaper *El nuevo diario*, the General stopped the depredations of bandits in the cattle lands, giving every support to the landowners. Stock-raising

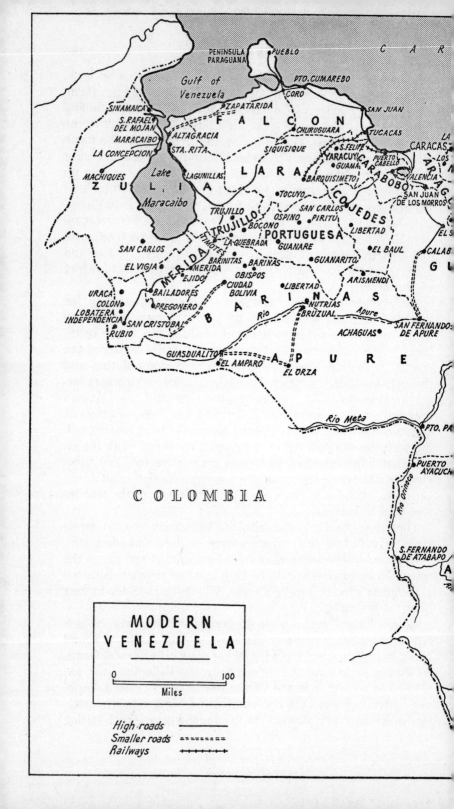

MODERN
VENEZUELA

0   100
Miles

High roads
Smaller roads
Railways

CARI B B E A N S E A

TORTUGA

TOBAGO

LA ASUNCION
NUEVA ESPARTA

RIO CARIBE

CARENERO

RIO CHICO

N D A

BARCELONA CUMANA SUCRE

EL PILAR

TRINIDAD

Gulf of
Paria

PAGRACIA
RITUCO

Pto. PIRITU
CLARINES

CARIPE

SAN ANTONIO

ONOTO

S. MATEO

CAICARA

MATURIN

ARAGUA

ZARAZA

MONAGAS

VALLE DE LA
PASCUA

CANTAURA

URACOA

TUCURITA

DELTA

ICO

ANZOATEGUI

PARIAGUAN

BARRANCAS

ZUATA

SOLEDAD

Orinoco

S. FELIX

AMACURO

Caroni

TERRITORY

MAPIRE

RIO

CIUDAD
BOLIVAR

UPATA

AICARA

MARIPA

EL MANTECO

GUASIPATI

EL CALLAO

TUMEREMO

BOLIVAR

BRITISH
GUIANA

Rio Paragua

GRAN SABANA

LUEPA

BANAS

Ventuari

STA. ELENA

Z O N A S

MESETA DEL
CERRO DUIDO

B R A Z I L

Rio Casiquare

E. G. MORTON

meant landowners, and it is certain that the dictator gave stock-raising every encouragement if by that is meant becoming himself the owner of enormous estates.

The régime's positive contributions can be seen in the paying of the national debt and in the construction of roads. For example, in 1916 a conflict with the foreign-owned Puerto Cabello to Valencia Railway Company was settled when Gómez paid a cheque to the Company for £190,000 (the debt was in fact £405,000). As the official newspaper pointed out, this was the first time that the government of the country had ever paid out such a large sum; and it argued that this proved that the country was in a sound financial situation thanks to the modern scientific methods applied to the Treasury and mainly to the new political system. In reality, modern methods had been applied since the Autocracy of Guzmán Blanco, and had been somewhat toned down under Gómez, whose idea of the function of the Treasury was rigid.

The prosperity was due not only to the peace imposed by Gómez, for the economy was treated as a private estate and the country drew little real benefit, but also to the appearance of oil. This drew in the foreign capital which Gil Fortoul thought essential for the country's progress. Venezuela's advances, economic and political, are due to the prosperity brought by oil; at all events, that is the economic basis. Since Gómez protected the foreign investors and in effect alienated the national sovereignty, the world economic powers and their firms helped him to pay the debts, build some public works and stay in power. But strangely enough, fiscal prosperity produced economic deformation and plunged the nation into poverty. This is still the real situation: while the state has great wealth, the nation—the people—lives in poverty. Gómez and his advisers had not the perception to ensure that the wealth of the state should be turned into the prosperity of the people. And yet in 1928 the oil boom reached its first spectacular stage, when exports jumped to a hundred million barrels.

Gómez ruled for twenty-seven years before he died, on December 17, 1935, to be buried with lavish honours. His period produced social loosening and moral deformation in the generations who had to live it through. The ideas of political liberty and civic integrity lacked all meaning since public feeling was blunted. Any voice which made a criticism was silenced; the

RAIMUNDO ANDUEZA PALACIO

JOAQUÍN CRESPO

PRIANO CASTRO

JUAN VICENTE GÓMEZ

6 Harvesting cocao beans

Coffee bushes in flower

gaol or exile were Gómez's 'peace'. In the Libertador castle of
Puerto Cabello, the castle of San Carlos in Maracaibo and La
Rotunda in Caracas about 38,000 political prisoners were kept
—men who had committed no crime, but were opposed to the
iron régime which lasted so long. These prisoners were made to
work on the new roads, in chains and under close guard. The
Venezuelan roads made under Gómez cost little precisely for
this reason; and also because of the law of 1916 which obliged
country workmen to perform a certain amount of service without pay for the state in exchange for being excused military
service.

Vallenilla Lanz in July 1916 wrote an article in *El nuevo
diario* in which he claimed that there was social peace in the
country and economic solidarity, and therefore there was now
political peace. Certainly, there was social peace in the sense
that the old party struggles and the *caudillismo* had disappeared.
Castro had begun to tame the *caudillos*, and perhaps even broke
their real power with his defeat of the Liberating Revolution;
but Gómez annihilated that power completely, and *coups d'état*
since his time have been entirely different from the risings before it.

In 1919 Vallenilla Lanz published a book called *Cesarismo democrático* (Democratic Caesarism), whose subtitle ran: 'A study
of the sociological bases of the effective constitution of Venezuela'. The author, a reputable scholar, was rigorously scientific
in his method of interpretation of historical and social phenom-
ena. One chapter was on the concept of the 'necessary policeman', the need for power to emanate from some one strong
man, who would be the representative and defender of national
unity. Vallenilla Lanz was able to support the theory by reference to Venezuelan history: Bolívar, Páez, Monagas, and Guzmán Blanco. And from that moment, Gómez's régime was
wrapped in a social theory developed by a respected and serious
thinker: it was accepted that the strong man was essential,
though only at certain stages of a people's evolution. Still, he
was necessary 'to protect society, to re-establish order, to defend the home and the motherland against demagogues, Jaco-
bins, anarchists, Bolsheviks, against all those who set themselves
up, batten, tyrannise, rob and murder under cover of anarchy
and in the name of liberty and humanity.' Vallenilla had been
editor of Gómez's newspaper since 1915, yet he was sincere.

N

The trouble was that his sincerity was misplaced, since battening, tyranny, robbery and murder became a state enterprise under his patron.

But underground there was a current of opinion in favour of overthrowing the dictatorship and bringing political freedom. Subjugated peoples always produce such a reaction, and in Venezuela although most of the soldiers were loyal to the régime—65% of the army leaders came from Gómez's home State—some soldiers made unsuccessful attempts at revolution. The most important revolts were those of Emilio Arévalo Cedeño, who rose in 1914 in Guárico, in 1918 in the Arauca region and in 1921 in the Amazonas Territory; and also the rising of J. R. Gabaldón in 1928. Arévalo's last attempt began with an invasion from Colombia and met with some success, since he captured the headquarters in Amazonas of the murderer Funes, one of the most sinister figures in the country, whom he tried and shot after taking over his treasury and stores. Probably Gómez was pleased to have this possible rival out of the way. But an unsuccessful march into Apure State ended with Arévalo's final retreat into Colombia.

Gabaldón's revolt was welcomed in foreign newspapers, but it too was crushed. Gómez sent no less than five generals to stamp out the movement which Gabaldón started in the States of Lara, Trujillo and Portuguesa in September 1928. The rebel was a man of honour, governor of the State of Zamora, who resigned in protest against the brutality with which the authorities treated dissident students of the University of Caracas. Gabaldón escaped from a detachment of soldiers sent to arrest him, and took refuge in his native State, Trujillo. There he gathered a numerous band of supporters and opened his campaign, but the five generals and their five columns of troops were too much for the movement.

Yet it was the student protests of 1928 which had the greatest repercussions in the country. For the Student Week celebrations in February Pío Tamayo wrote poems on freedom, and Jóvito Villalba and Rómulo Betancourt (both to become politicians of the first rank in future years) made speeches in the National Pantheon against the dictatorship. The government reacted by imprisoning these young men and a companion, Guillermo Prince Lara. The other students protested, and gave themselves up also to the police. Two hundred and twenty students were imprisoned, and freed again in a few days. But this was the beginning of conspiracies in the form of parties, and indeed the present-day leftist parties of Venezuela began to be formed at that time. There was one action: on April 7th some soldiers, students and professional men tried to assault the presidential palace of Miraflores, but they were defeated by General Eleazar López Contreras, the War Minister. At any rate, from 1928 there was a growing enthusiasm for freedom of a different stamp from that which used to be proclaimed by the *caudillos* for the sake of making war against the government which happened to be in power.

The influence of oil in the destinies of Venezuela is a comparatively recent thing. Oil was of little importance in the world until the later nineteenth century, when in Pennsylvania the first attempts at organised exploitation were made. Oil was known in Venezuela centuries before, and the settlers in colonial times had used it for caulking their boats. But the first commercial enterprise for the exploitation of oil in Venezuela came in 1878, with the Compañía Petrolia del Táchira, in the Rubio district of Táchira State. Fifteen barrels a day was the production about the end of the century, but it rose by 1912 to 60 barrels. The company failed. Important concessions were made in 1907: in February, to Andrés Jorge Vigas to exploit in Colón district, State of Zulia; to Antonio Aranguren in Maracaibo and Bolívar districts; in July to Francisco Jiménez Arráiz in Falcón and Lara States; the same month to Bernabé Planas in Falcón. In 1909 a contract for exploration and development was made with the Venezuela Development Company Limited, represented by John Allen Tregelles, and which covered practically the whole of the country north of the Orinoco. Royalties demanded were one bolívar per hectare of ground, 5% on crude oil produced and 50% on refined products imported. The company went bankrupt.

In 1910 the Bermúdez Company, using influential contacts, gained a concession for exploration and development in the Paria Peninsula, Benítez district of Sucre State, and Pedernales and adjacent islands in the Delta Amacuro territory, all within the lands kept in reserve by the government in the contract with the Venezuela Development Company. The Bermúdez Company was owned by the General Asphalt Company of Philadelphia. The first contract with a foreign company had been for thirty years (but it was declared null later) and the contract with the Bermúdez Company was for forty-seven years. Another company owned by the General Asphalt, the Caribbean Petroleum Company, gained large concessions in 1912, again through influential contacts. This firm was allowed to exploit in the States of Mérida, Trujillo, Zulia, Lara, Falcón, Carabobo, Yaracuy, Sucre, Monagas, Anzoátegui and Nueva Esparta.

The Royal Dutch Shell Group, financed by British and Dutch capital, began operations in 1912 through its subsidiary the Caribbean Petroleum Company, setting up new companies, and arranging to take over concessions granted to Venezuelan citizens. Soon the British Controlled Oilfield Company opened up, with many branches, and was granted large concessions between 1918 and 1920. It was only in the decade 1920-1930 that the North American companies entered the Venezuelan field—Standard Oil, which ramified into the Lago Petroleum Company, Creole Petroleum Company, Standard Oil of Venezuela, Vacuum Oil Company, Richmond Petroleum Company, etc. Creole, set up in 1920, eventually brought under its wing all Standard's operations.

The first well began to be drilled in 1912—Batatui no. 1, in Sucre State—and the first oil was obtained there in 1913. In 1914 the first oil in commercial quantities in the Maracaibo area was produced, at Zumaque no. 1, in the Mene Grande oilfield. In 1917 a refinery was built at San Lorenzo, which now has a capacity of 45,000 barrels a day. In 1922 important drillings were made on the La Paz and La Concepción fields, in the Maracaibo area. So that in the period from 1912 to 1922 exploration was systematised and production was started. On December 14, 1922, in the Santa Rosa oilfield, the Los Barrosos no. 2 well spouted, and in nine days a million barrels flooded out uncontrolled. This was the beginning of the oil boom in Venezuela. In 1929 there were already 73 oil companies at work, with the most important production divided between the Shell group, round Maracaibo, and Standard, in the east of the country. In 1934 twenty million cubic metres of oil were exported, and the figure rose to thirty million between 1938 and 1942. This shows that under Gómez production was not extraordinarily large in proportion to world consumption, but it was still sufficient to bring a complete upheaval to the country's economy. In fact it is only since 1943-44 that production has increased immensely, with a consequent reaction on the country's finances.

The exploitation of oil was started under the terms of the Mining Law of 1910, which was not concerned specifically with oil. The first law governing oil exploitation was promulgated in 1920, when as yet only twelve deposits had been found, and other laws were passed in 1922, 1925, 1928, 1935 and 1936. These laws were favourable to the oil companies. The people involved in the dictatorship—the Gómez family and their friends—made great profits while in power, continuing the custom of peculation which in Venezuela and the other Spanish American countries has not yet been eradicated. Gómez's own fortune, at the end of his rule, was calculated at 200 million bolívares.

What the country itself got out of a national source of wealth which brought exceptional profits to the non-Venezuelan companies handling it was scandalously little, according to Betancourt. An official document of the time just after Gómez's death shows that from July 1919 to June 1936 the Treasury obtained from the oil companies 612 million bolívares, and it was calculated from the production figures and world prices that the companies themselves must have sold the Venezuelan oil for about 8,644 million bolívares; so that the firms had paid about 7% of their gross takings into the Venezuelan national revenue. Since then oil has become the great provider of the national budget.

With the oil boom of the last four decades the economic structure of the country has changed: agriculture no longer has any importance. In 1952 oilfields in production measured 172,000 hectares, there were 10,616 wells, and 75,000 people worked in oil. In 1955 Shell alone produced 246,069,990 barrels, employed 16,318 workpeople, and possessed concessions to the area of 916,790 hectares. These figures will serve to give an idea of the influence of oil, of the presence of a powerful amount of capital concentrated in the hands of foreigners and of very few Venezuelans. This capitalism has permitted the growth of the economy through the one major export—oil—and varied and large imports particularly of luxury and consumer goods. Importation has raised the standard of living; it has made goods more expensive and has increased the salaries of the social groups directly connected with the oil industry. But this has caused a great difference between their standard and that of other parts of the population, who tend to abandon work in agriculture, stock-raising and manufacturing in order to become oil workers.

Oil, then, has imposed one major economic change—the abandonment of agriculture for a single source of income—and one consequent change in the social structure—the concentration of workers specialised in the various functions of the oil industry. This latter fact has particular influence on politics, since governments and politicians must take into account those people who form the most powerful group in the nation. Whereas in the nineteenth century *guerrilleros* and *caudillos* sought the support of the country folk in order to turn them into warriors brandishing matchet, lance or rifle, now politicians seek to win over the oil worker to their parties. Again, since about 1945 new social classes have been coming into being, and these will decide in the near future what happens in Venezuela. These new groups are at least five in number: an aristocracy of wealth consisting of the descendants of the old *mantuanos* (the aristocracy), and immigrants' sons able to make their own fortunes; an educated military class of soldiers who have studied in United States or other academies, and who are open to democratic customs and interested in politics; a lower class conscious of its power and concerned with the question of democratic rights; a class of intellectuals with no political affiliation, but possessing moral influence and alert in the service of culture, trained by universities and scientific disciplines, particularly interested in national politics above parties; and lastly a laborious middle class which is crying out for diversification of industry in both town and country.

One consequence of oil capitalism has been the organisation of political parties which have begun to act as leaders of opinion and as new instruments for gaining power in the government. The first experiment in party government went on from 1945 to 1948, although it could only take place after a military *coup d'état*. The parties have acted rather as forces of opposition and of direction of popular opinion than as the bases of governments.

As for the material wealth which the Venezuelan state now enjoys, it is entirely the product of oil. The Central Bank of Venezuela has calculated the influence of oil on the national revenue in three particular years in order to show this: 1936,

1,500 million bolívares; 1949, 7,352 million bolívares; 1952, 9,158 million bolívares. From 1940 to 1952 the oil firms brought into Venezuela foreign currency to the value of 4,530 million dollars (about 14,000 million bolívares). Part of this money was to pay for goods and services in Venezuela, and part was in payment of taxes and royalties to the government. As the economist and essayist Arturo Uslar Pietri says: 'Now all Venezuela is oil. Not oil sown and transformed into harvests and factories, as it could and should have been; but oil flooding over and carrying away houses, plants and cattle in its path.' At December 31, 1956 Venezuela had 5,038,860 inhabitants. More than half of the population is illiterate and lives in poverty. Is it not time that oil should help to bring so many Venezuelans into cultured, twentieth-century life?

8. LITERATURE SINCE 1830

From 1830 to 1858, from the start of Venezuela's republican life until the Convention of Valencia gathered together the best brains, one generation of writers gave their particular stamp to the spiritual life of the country. José Luis Ramos was severely humanist, Juan Vicente González refreshed Castilian prose, Agustín Codazzi wrote a Geography of the country and prepared an atlas for the scientific inventory of Venezuela's natural resources, and the Liberal leader Antonio Leocadio Guzmán tried to work out a system of social democracy in articles and speeches of a popular nature.

There were four distinct types of literary production: humanist, with Ramos and Andrés Bello, writing from abroad, and other lesser names such as Jerónimo E. Blanco (1823-65); secondly that of political thinkers and stylists, such as Fermín Toro, Rafael María Baralt, Juan Vicente González, Pedro Gual, and Cristóbal Mendoza; thirdly romantic, with José Heriberto García de Quevedo, Abigaíl Lozano and others; and lastly the beginnings of *costumbrismo*, literature using local manners and customs as a vehicle, represented by Juan Manuel Cajigal and others. Rafael Arvelo, the first satirical poet, entered politics, as did the others. He supported Guzmán and later Monagas.

Undoubtedly the greatest intellectual figure of this generation was Fermín Toro, whose work is best seen in his essays such as *Reflexiones sobre la ley del 10 de abril* and articles such as the series *Europa y América*, published in the *Correo de Caracas* from March to July 1839. His speeches in the Convention of Valencia are classic expositions of Venezuelan social and political thought.

Venezuelan *costumbrismo* came to the fore in the violent years between the fall of Monagas and Guzmán Blanco's peace, in the midst of a stream of oratorical and sensational journalism. It began with Cajigal and Luis Delgado Correa, continued with Daniel Mendoza, and reached its best with Nicanor Bolet Peraza and Francisco de Sales Pérez. This movement shaded gradually into traditionalism, bringing the threat of history into literature. Arístides Rojas mingled history and poetry in his *Leyendas* and *Estudios*, and one of his followers, Tulio Febres Cordero, lived until 1930. Eduardo Blanco wrote epic history in his *Venezuela heroica*.

Literary institutions of various sorts were founded in the second half of the nineteenth century: the Academia de Ciencias Sociales y Bellas Letras, 1869; the Academia Venezolana de Literatura, 1872; the Sociedad de los Amigos del Saber, 1882; the Academia Venezolana de la Lengua, 1883; the Academia de la Historia, 1889; and the Ateneo de Caracas, 1892. Some were official foundations, but some reflected the enthusiasm of young men and their desire for organisation and influence—such was the Sociedad de Amigos del Saber, the Society of the Friends of Learning.

In the Academia Venezolana de Literatura were collected the most notable writers friendly to Guzmán Blanco: Eduardo Calcaño, Jacinto Gutiérrez Coll, Amenodoro Urdaneta, etc. But not Cecilio Acosta, who was the most important thinker of that half-century, and whose letters, speeches and essays were an attempt to define the moral nature of the nation.

Notable publications were an anthology of Venezuelan thought, brought out in 1875 by José María Rojas, and the *Exploración oficial* of F. Michelena y Rojas in 1867, an account of an expedition to the territory between the Orinoco and the Amazon.

Besides establishing literary contests, Guzmán Blanco reformed university studies, bringing science and positivism with such teachers as the German Ernst and the native Rafael Villavicencio. These men set up schools and their followings flourished even into the twentieth century. A positivist generation appeared about 1880, which included the critic Luis López Méndez, the historian José Gil Fortoul, the humanist Lisandro Alvarado and the sociologist Laureano Vallenilla Lanz as the most outstanding men of the group.

The lyric poetry of José Antonio Pérez Bonalde (1846-92) was the best Venezuelan poetry of the century. Towards the end of the period Andrés Mata gained fame, now within the new stream called *modernismo*.

This new outlook on poetry (common to Spanish America and begun by the Nicaraguan Rubén Darío) found expression in *El cojo ilustrado*, founded in 1892 by José María Herrera Irigoyen, and *Cosmópolis*, founded 1894. The second journal was especially advanced, and opened its pages to foreign writers as well as native. The modernists were purely literary, but they were working at the same time as the more scientific positivists, and occasionally one figure combined both approaches. The *Cosmópolis* group became known as the Generation of '95, and included the essayist Pedro Emilio Coll, the novelist Manuel Díaz Rodríguez and the novelist, poet and essayist Rufino Blanco Fombona. These were modernists, as were also Luis M. Urbaneja Achelphol and Pedro César Domínici.

The novel about Venezuela began with Eduardo Blanco's *Zárate* (1882), followed with Manuel Vicente Romero García's *Peonía* (1890), and continued with the works of Urbaneja Achelphol and Díaz Rodríguez until, under Gómez's dictatorship, Rómulo Gallegos published his great novels. These works of Gallegos are the books which have been most read in contemporary Venezuela; they reflect the natural and human landscape together with the whole train of problems of Venezuelan society.

In the field of thought, José Gil Fortoul in *El hombre y la historia* and Laureano Vallenilla Lanz in *Cesarismo democrático* have set forth those historical and sociological topics which most demand discussion since they are concerned with fundamental facts of the Venezuelan's political psychology.

The man of letters of today is faced with Venezuela's most complex historical period, with political unrest side by side with overwhelming riches of oil and, now, also of iron ore. Since Venezuela has ceased to be a country of farming and 'pronouncements', the intellectual's task is to cope with the problems of modern culture: capitalism, labour laws, technology and science. The novelists, such as Ramón Díaz Sánchez, find that they must come to grips with actual problems, while the essayists with humanist *nuances*, such as Luis Beltrán Guerrero, Mariano Picón Salas, Mario Briceño Iragorry (died 1958) and Arturo Uslar Pietri, attack those problems in an attempt to find their solution.

CHAPTER VII

Democracy Versus Dictatorship

I. INTRODUCTION

AFTER the death of the dictator Juan Vicente Gómez, Venezuelan history showed various symptoms, some encouraging and others discouraging. There has been a ferocious struggle between democracy and dictatorship in politics, and a constant swinging between poverty and wealth in the economic system. In 1936 the population of the country was 3,364,347, while in 1961 it had reached 7,523,999 without counting the forest Indians, who numbered possibly 200,000.[1] The national budget for the fiscal year from July 1, 1936 to June 30, 1937 was 215,860,785.95 bolívares, and the figure rose to 6,200,000,000 bolívares for the ecomonic year 1963. Oil, iron and politics are the characteristics of modern times. Oil especially became the decisive element in the economy and the history of the country, which became the home of political groups blinded by power and peculation, and a people ambitious for prosperity and peace. Contemporary Venezuela is a wrestling-match between the most aggressive forces and the most healthy aims. Between 1936 and 1945 the road became smoother, a platform was built, democracy was prepared; after October 18, 1945 a political stumbling-block, a continual oscillation, a dictatorship of ever-varying stamp, was thrown across the road of Venezuelan life. But the country works towards the future, struggles in hope. Oil, iron and education will give Venezuela the chance to become a true nation.

This hope is not based merely on patriotism and the speculation of a man of this day and age, but on historical fact: in 1936

[1] See IX Censo nacional de poblaciones, Ministerio de Fomento, Caracas 1961, p. 47.

80 per cent of the population were illiterate, in 1962 only about 30 per cent.

2. TRANSITION TO DEMOCRACY

On December 17, 1935 General Juan Vicente Gómez died a natural death, of old age and illness, after twenty-seven years as president—always constitutional—and as dictator in fact. He died in the town of Maracay, where he lived although the capital was officially Caracas. On December 18th the Minister of War and the Navy, General Eleazar López Contreras, temporarily assumed the executive power after election by the other Ministers, as laid down in the Constitution. Congress on December 31st confirmed the election, and López Contreras therefore finished Gómez's term, until April 19, 1936. López was also elected as president for the term 1936 to 1943, which was, however, reduced to five years by an amendment to the Constitution. And for the first time in the history of Venezuela a president, elected according to the laws in force, governing according to the Constitution, completed his legal term and peacefully handed over his office to his legitimate successor.

Indeed, although it is true that General López Contreras had served in the governments of Castro and Gómez, holding important posts, yet he himself governed according to the law. He established democracy, and respect for legality was the outstanding characteristic of his political and administrative activity.[1] In the field of politics, the new régime began the task of making the transition from dictatorship to democracy—a difficult task, since the revolutionary political leaders desired a radical and violent change. But this reaction was avoided, although at the same time a general amnesty was declared. Thanks to this the political exiles returned to the country, the political prisoners were released from the gaols and the people were able to make their weight felt, even to the extent of violently anarchical acts such as the rioting and looting of February 14, 1936 and the strikes of 1937, including one organised in the oil fields.

Generally speaking, the government of López Contreras followed four main lines. These were, firstly, the creation of a

[1] López Contreras was born in 1883 in the village of Queniquea, Táchira State. See his autobiographical note in his *El triunfo de la verdad (documentos para la historia venezolana)*, México D.F., 1949, pp. XV seq.

nationalist ideology based on the veneration of Bolívar and the exaltation of his ideals. The aim of this doctrine was to prevent the spreading and taking root of some other ideology of foreign provenance, particularly Nazism, fascism or communism. Secondly, there was an effort to bring about a peaceful transition from the dictatorial type of rule which had become traditional in the country to the democratic régime desired by the moderate sectors and established in civilised countries. Thirdly, the government wished to establish freedom of the press and of organisation, and free exercise by the people of their rights and duties; and fourthly, it desired to follow legal methods in all things concerning public affairs: in other words, to set up a truly legal system of government.

Besides positive measures on these lines, the smoothness of the transition required others which the revolutionary opposition considered anti-democratic. In order to avoid civil war or chaos in the life of the nation, López Contreras' government imposed certain legislative, judicial and executive restrictions. For example, a Law of Public Order was issued to regulate the working of Section 6 of Article 32 of the Constitution of 1936 —a Section which forbade propaganda in favour of war or subversion, and specifically condemned communism and anarchism. Left-wing parties with Marxist leaders were dissolved, and forty-seven of these leaders were exiled under the provisions of the Section. Some of them went underground, including Rómulo Betancourt, who for three years lived in hiding among friends and directed the opposition movement, meanwhile organising his Partido Democrático Venezolano (Venezuelan Democratic Party).

On February 21, 1936 López Contreras gave out the programme of his government, methodically exposing the country's needs in a way which showed not only what his own government had to do, but also what successive governments up to the present time must remedy. López's plans were sketched out—his ideas concerning legality of government, public health and assistance, communications, education, agriculture and stock-raising, fiscal and commercial policies, immigration and settlement. In other words, he showed what the nation must do in order to establish itself firmly. Although it enjoyed the collaboration of some men of great talent and capabilities (Alberto Adriani for Agriculture and later the Treasury, and

Arturo Uslar Pietri for Education), yet López's Bolivarian régime produced no immense reforms and fulfilments; but it was
notable for the humanisation of politics, for careful balance,
for legality and the affirmation of peace with no tremendous injustices or criminal repressions. His fight against communism
was not stained by acts of vengeance or useless persecutions; he
did not imprison people brutally nor did his police torture men
whom they arrested.

The president kept the promise he made in his programme:
'In the matter of general policy, the government has the firm
intention of putting into effect, by all the means at its disposal,
a régime based on the rule of law. The law, respected by the
governor and obeyed by the governed, is the pre-requisite of
the freedom of a nation'.

Of course, although the establishment of democracy was attempted, the army continued in the period from 1936 to 1941
to be the 'moral and organic mainstay of the régime', as is the
case with the constitutional period running from 1959 to 1964;
yet the units of the army under López were agreed in their intention to support the Chief of State. López endowed and educated the army, giving it a knowledge of modern techniques,
whereas under Gómez it still possessed some of the characteristics of a feudal levy—indeed, for years the troops quartered at
Maracay were employed as workmen on the dictator's estates.
The improvement in quality and self-respect which the army
gained under López gave rise to a change in public opinion with
regard to the esteem in which the army was held.

In 1941 the constitutional term of the former general of Gómez, Eleazar López Contreras, came to an end. It had, on the
whole, been beneficial. The people of Venezuela had become
used to thinking for themselves; an opposition had been formed, ready to call attention to the government's mistakes. A
spirit of living together and a consciousness of citizenship had
begun to take root. The bases of democracy were assured when
a new constitutional president was elected and when General
López, founder of contemporary democracy in Venezuela,
handed over power in a ceremony which symbolised a truly republican view of the alternation in office of elected leaders.
Mariano Picón Salas, the well-known author, regarded the date
as so important—the year in which the first period of democratic government was completed—that he published a book

beforehand in order to say so.[1] He emphasised: '1941 is therefore a number as significant in the process of our republican life as were 1810, 1830 or 1858'.

López Contreras himself summed up his work: 'I began my government by giving liberty to thousands of political prisoners detained in gaols and labour camps; I authorised the return to their homeland of all the exiles, and gave them the opportunity of working with me; I inaugurated a great number of public works; I permitted the organisation of trades unions and political parties; I allowed freedom of the press and of speech, and supported electioneering—and in the elections, in many cases, the opposition won. I put all my efforts into setting up a system entirely different from the one which had just ended, a new system with all the advantages and privileges of a democratic government.'[2] These words are borne out by history, even in the personal emphasis—the use of the first person—which demonstrates the rule of the presidential system prescribed by the 'organic Constitution' of Venezuela. Venezuela lives and for long will continue to live by the presidential system.

3. ISAÍAS MEDINA ANGARITA

For the constitutional period 1941 to 1946 General Isaías Medina Angarita was elected president by Congress, as provided for by law. Medina gained 130 votes against the thirteen recorded for his rival, the novelist Rómulo Gallegos; and he took office on May 5, 1941. In a manifesto which he had published beforehand, he pledged himself to follow the example of his predecessor and to hand over the presidency peacefully to his duly elected successor at the end of his term, but in fact he was unable to do so since a *coup d'état* brought down his government on October 18, 1945.[3]

Although Medina was the official candidate in the election which brought him to office, being a regular army officer and Minister of War under López Contreras, he quickly became popular and was the symbol of democracy, honesty and ability. No Venezuelan government leader has ever risen so quickly in

[1] *1941: cinco discursos sobre pasado y presente de la nación venezolana.* Caracas 1940.
[2] Eleazar López Contreras, op. cit., p. 31.
[3] Medina Angarita was born in San Cristóbal, capital of Táchira State, in 1897, and died in Caracas on September 15, 1953.

public esteem, and he was able to lead the country towards the longed-for goal of prosperity and freedom. The choice of Congress and the support of the previous government were confirmed within the year by the whole nation's backing for his political and administrative actions.

The Second World War brought special difficulties, which were reflected in the country's economy and international relations. Medina adopted a policy of continental co-operation and solidarity. As a consequence of the Japanese attack on the United States forces on December 7, 1941 and the German and Italian declarations of war, Venezuela applied Declaration XV of the Havana Meeting, and on December 31st broke off relations with the Axis powers. She did not enter the war, but she did not remain neutral. It should be remembered that almost all of the oil used by Great Britain in the war came from Venezuelan wells. Venezuela made an important contribution to the Allied cause, and gave some moral support, thanks to a calm régime and to well-directed public opinion. Certain security measures adopted because of the war did not hamper the régime of freedom, enjoyed fully by the Venezuelans for the first time since they became independent in 1810. López Contreras had rationed freedom in order to save it; Medina put it fully into effect.

On January 31, 1942 Medina announced a Five-Year Plan of Public Works, the fruit of technical studies undertaken for the first time, with the object of directing the country's administrative policy. The president had surrounded himself with the most capable men, scholars and professional men with high scientific and political standards.

Medina gave his first message to Congress on April 22, 1942. In spite of the difficulties caused by the war, Venezuela was full of optimism, and the president could pronounce these words of incalculable importance for a country which had suffered harsh dictatorship: 'The government has not prevented men from coming together in groups according to their own opinions, and political parties have been formed in the shelter of the law, and the frontiers have been and are kept open for all Venezuelans. I can say with pride that there is at this moment no Venezuelan outside the home country or unable to return to it by the effect of or for fear of repressive measures; that in the period under review there has never been a single

An Indian woman of the
Ziruma region, Zulia State

Petroleum worker

iner from the Icabaru
region, Bolívar State

Fisherman from
Chichiriviche Falcón State

8 GENERAL ISAÍAS MEDINA ANGARITA   MARCOS PÉREZ JIMÉNEZ

WOLFGANG LARRAZÁBAL   RÓMULO BETANCOURT

political prisoner, and that there is no fear or doubt in the heart of any Venezuelan on account of any possible arbitrary action of the government.' This was all true until October 18, 1945: not one exile, not one political prisoner, not one case of persecution, no fear or doubt. It was the great period of liberty.

The political group which had, since 1928, been in opposition, firstly, with reason, against Gómez, then, with less cause, against López, and later against Medina because every Venezuelan now had the right to his own opinions, had been legalised on September 13, 1941 and enjoyed complete freedom. Medina kept making reality of the slogans of the opposition: free elections, freedom of association, of the press and of action within the law, administrative honesty; and even the slogans seeking action became decrees. The acid test was the reform of the oil industry, which was fully supported by the opposition party, Acción Democrática.

In the city of Maracaibo, on November 15, 1942, Medina made crystal clear the aims of his administration when, in referring to the basic source of the country's economy, he said: 'The government, in fulfilment of one of its unavoidable duties, firm in its aims and certain in its actions, intends to obtain a juster share for the State in the exploitation of oil and also to ensure that the industrial processes connected with oil shall be a sure source of employment for the Venezuelan worker. I must make it clear that this government, obedient to the law, supporter of the guarantees which are the honour of our Constitution, scrupulous about the rectitude of its actions and most wary of haste, respects legitimately acquired rights and does not regard as adversaries those companies which have brought in capital to intensify the development of our natural wealth; but, animated by a spirit of reason and equity, it deems that Venezuela should receive a share adequate to her character of owner of the raw material which is the true source of the oil industry, and that the industrial processes should in the main be located in Venezuela in order to increase the opportunities for employment of the Venezuelan working man. The government is not making an attack, but is seeking to convince by argument; and it is sure that its object contains just satisfaction for the Nation and stable balance for the industry, for agreements between men are lasting only when they are based on equity and justice. I have said that the government is wary of haste, and when, from the highest post in the Republic [on July 17, 1942, from the presidential Palace of Miraflores, in Caracas], I announced the revision of our oil policy, I did so because I was sure that we should reach it by one road or the other—by the road of agreement and co-operation, or by that of legal steps. If, unfortunately, by the first road we do not reach all, absolutely all, of the results which we expect, the government will abandon its talk of equity and, armed with unanswerable legal and moral strength, it will proceed, in the name of the Republic, to claim what by right belongs to it.'

Reform of the oil industry was the opposition's bone of contention. Now there was nothing else for it but to admit that even this motive for agitation had been snatched away, and this was done when, on November 16th, the Acción Democrática party sent the president a telegram expressing its 'intense satisfaction' with the announcement of the previous day. And again, on the following January 17th, the leader of Acción Democrática, Rómulo Betancourt, spoke at a mass meeting of the party called to give the oil policy its support. His words have a sinister irony in view of the *coup d'état* of October 1945, since he heartily applauded the president's adoption of the new policy, 'which is supported by every honourable Venezuelan who feels duty and responsibility towards the country'.

Political freedom and public tranquility, supported by the beginnings of great prosperity, undisturbed even by the war, allowed Medina to liberalise his administration even to the point of the legalisation of the Communist Party (1945), which had begun activity under the name of Unión Popular Venezolana. The régime showed that the best defence against communism was honest administration and encouragement for material and intellectual progress. Communism, unless imposed by force, only makes headway among peoples who are hungry or demoralised. Medina, therefore, did not attack, persecute or imprison communists; and the Communist Party was a minority party as was, before October 18, 1945, Acción Democrática. In fact the latter was the smaller, with only 20,000 registered members to the Communist Party's 30,000.

Betancourt himself admitted in his best-known book that the years of Medina's government were peaceful,[1] and indeed this

1 *Venezuela: política y petróleo*, México D.F., 1956, p. 134.

opposition leader was entirely free and was able to visit and get to know the whole territory of Venezuela at this time. Soon dictatorship and persecution were to return, however. But during the four years of Medina's presidency the prospects for the establishment of constitutional and democratic political life in Venezuela became brighter. Not only had the people regained confidence in their political co-existence, but the foundations of a higher standard of living for all classes had been laid. There existed a solid programme for finance, industry, the economy and education.

Medina's work is worth summarising here. His foreign relations were successful. Venezuela had been neutral from the outbreak of the world war until Pearl Harbour, when she found herself involved in positive action. The democratic spirit of the people and government, as well as geography and economics, gave the president a clear lead. Relations with Germany, Italy and Japan were broken off in 1942, and in 1945 Venezuela expressed her agreement with the Declaration of the United Nations. Venezuela drew closer to the other American countries in a conscious movement of solidarity, and also showed her status of equality with the most advanced nations. Thus she established relations with the Soviet Union, as the international situation demanded. During nearly the whole of this period, it was fortunate that the Foreign Minister was Dr. Caracciolo Parra Pérez, a man of great experience and culture, undoubtedly one of the most able Foreign Ministers who have served Venezuela.[1]

In internal policies, Medina tried to follow on from López Contreras, whose régime after 1936 brought the freedom long awaited by Venezuela. Medina's aim was to make the freedom secure by improving economic conditions. In his 1945 message to Congress, he showed that his government had gone beyond the old idea that political democracy consisted solely of personal liberty: besides liberty, true democracy must mean consultation of the wishes of the majority and must have as its aim the well-being, progress and security of that majority. Medina therefore directed democracy towards social and educational policies whose effects have been lasting. Laws concerning National Insurance and the pay and conditions of teachers, and

[1] See C. Parra Pérez, *Discursos*, Madrid 1961.

the building of comprehensive schools, were the fruits of Medina's thought. A pro-government party, the Partido Democrático Venezolano, was created and won an overwhelming majority in local government elections in 1945—said to be the 'freest and cleanest elections' ever held in Venezuela, and in fact the official party was never accused of vote-rigging or other sharp practices. Medina, too, was always proud of the record of his administration for not allowing any political imprisonments or exiles, and is the only president the country has ever had of whom this is true. A soldier, proud of his profession, he yet proved to be the outstanding civilian president. Under him, the army did not intervene in politics. It continued to raise its professional standards, and remained where it should, in barracks. In general, the president depersonalised his government and stood by the Constitution, the laws and democratic ideals.

To name the main reforms of Medina's régime will suffice to show its scope. The new Civil Code of laws of 1942, still in force, was an advance in social legislation, especially with regard to the position of the family. There was also the oil reform of 1943, whereby Venezuela as a state entered a new stage of incalculable economic progress. Then came the constitutional reform of 1945, which established direct election of Deputies to Congress (with the result that the political party which gained a majority in the country would, in practice, elect the president), gave the vote to women, eliminated Section 6 of Article 32 of the Constitution (thereby allowing the communists legal standing—in fact the Section had not been applied since 1941, and Marxist doctrines were supported by the Acción Democrática party, the most active opposition), and nationalised the previously chaotic Judicial Power of the nation. Other important measures were the Agrarian Law of 1945 and the Decree forbidding the removal of squatters. This latter implied a peaceful agrarian reform, giving justice to many living on the land.

The relations between the State and the oil companies were regulated by the law of 1938 which had made timid modifications to the out-of-date mining laws. Congress devoted a series of extraordinary sessions to a Hydrocarbons Bill, which became law on March 13, 1943. The nation's interests were safeguarded without harm to the companies which had brought into the country their skill and capital. The Hydrocarbons Law gave the country possession of its own basic wealth, and it is still in force, with a minor modification made in 1955. Venezuela has benefited materially and morally from the new law. Firstly, all the oil companies were brought under one legal administration; but also, the government was empowered to collect technical information from the companies; and the companies were made to pay all general taxes, including income tax—and the royalty was fixed at not less than 16⅔%. The oil pipe-lines became a public service; and the oil itself had to be refined in Venezuela.

A Five-Year Plan of public works was carefully worked out for the period 1941 to 1946. Works begun by the previous administration were completed and new works soon began to transform the country: communications, irrigation, works undertaken for sanitation and for public assistance, and a scheme for education—the most important yet put into effect. This latter included the University City and the Miguel Antonio Caro Normal School, both in Caracas, and a vast plan for building comprehensive schools, beginning some and completing others.

An outstanding figure of Medina Angarita's period was Dr. Arturo Uslar Pietri, the author and politician. Under Medina he served on the presidential staff, in the Treasury and in the Ministry of the Interior, and had great influence on the régime's ideas.

4.   THE REVOLUTION OF OCTOBER 1945

On October 18, 1945, six months before the end of the constitutional term and in the middle of the free political discussion about the candidates for the coming presidential election, a military coup d'état, carried out with the connivance of the Acción Democrática party, brought down the government. The coup interrupted the process of the establishment of constitutionalism and made the country regress to totalitarian systems. As Medina had said in the previous April: 'Venezuelan democracy is not yet strong enough.'

The military conspiracy had its roots in the 'lodges' which had been active in Argentina at the beginning of Perón's revolution. These lodges were formed by small groups of officers who aspired to take part in politics. They spread from Argentina to Ecuador, Bolivia and Peru; and it was to Peru that the Venezuelan officers who led the October coup went to study. Those involved numbered about 150 of the 900 active army officers.

In his as yet unpublished book *Cuatro años de democracia en Venezuela* ('Four years of democracy in Venezuela'), Medina Angarita expressed his surprise at the coup d'état of October 18th, since he had complete confidence in the officers' loyalty 'not to a man, but to the president of the Republic . . ., the Constitution and the laws . . ., which they had sworn to defend.' He explained that he had refused to defend himself and thus start a civil war, but had surrendered as soon as the revolutionary officers had begun to desert him and had seized key points.[1] Accordingly, on October 19th a Revolutionary Junta of Government was set up, consisting of two army officers (Major Carlos Delgado Chalbaud and Captain Mario Vargas), four Acción Democrática leaders (Rómulo Betancourt as president of the Junta, Luis Beltrán Prieto Figueroa, Gonzalo Barrios and Raúl Leoni, who were the top group of the party), and one independent member (Edmundo Fernández).

The Junta at once proclaimed the aims of their movement, beginning with a promise to organise general elections immediately by direct, universal and secret vote, so that the people might choose new representatives, the new Constitution 'which they desire' and a new president. All leaders of past governments since the end of the nineteenth century were to be tried for peculation. Generals López Contreras and Medina Angarita were arrested and were to be made to restore to the nation any ill-gotten gains. 'Stern, implacably stern, will the Provisional Government be towards all those who, sheltered by their positions of power, have become guilty of the crime of enriching themselves illegally.' The cost of living would be brought down and the middle and lower classes would be protected. Civil guarantees were suspended until public order was safely restored. International relations were to be maintained with all democratic countries, 'especially the countries of Latin America, the United States of America, Labour England and the Soviet Union.'[2]

The most important measures of the new régime followed the proclamation's policies. A special Tribunal of Civil and Ad-

---

[1] Señora Irma Felizola de Medina Angarita, widow of the ex-president, is in possession of Medina's manuscript and has authorised Dr. Morón's use of it.
[2] *El gobierno revolucionario de Venezuela ante su pueblo*, Caracas July 1946, pp. 3-5.

ministrative Responsibility was created, which swiftly tried, without any right of appeal to other courts, the two ex-presidents López and Medina and their collaborators, and condemned them for illegal self-enrichment. López and Medina were expelled, together with Uslar Pietri and other politicians. Elections were held for a National Constituent Assembly, which met on December 7, 1946. A new Constitution (1947) and a new Electoral Statute were passed, and the election of the next president was held amid great public unrest. On February 14, 1948 the Junta handed over to the elected president, who was Rómulo Gallegos.

This great Venezuelan novelist was elected president by direct vote. The electoral register contained 1,621,607 voters, who were all over eighteen years old. The vote was in fact given to youngsters and illiterates—majority age generally accepted in law is twenty-one years. The votes were cast as follows:

for Rómulo Gallegos (Acción Democrática) 871,752
for Rafael Caldera (Christian Socialist, COPEI
   [Comité Pro-Elecciones Independientes]) 267,204
for Gustavo Machado (Communist) 36,584[1]

Once more the ever-hopeful Venezuelan people gave themselves over to the task of regaining lost time. The excessively partisan régime made the citizens too politically conscious, and even introduced political sectarianism into the schools. Although many of the measures of the government attempted to justify the coup d'état which had allowed the Acción Democrática party to gain power in 1945, the excess of party zeal brought the people to despair. Therefore the régime fell, without gaining the citizens' support, when the very soldiers who had brought about the coup d'état on October 18th decided to bring Gallegos down on November 24, 1948. Party government was a miserable failure.

5. TOO RECENT HISTORY

On November 24, 1948 a Military Junta of Government seized power, without the slightest struggle. The governing party, Acción Democrática, was dissolved and its leaders went into exile,

---

[1] See A. Arellano Moreno, *El voto directo en Venezuela para la elección de presidente*, in *Política* no. 20, p. 23.

although some parties remained active. The Junta governed until November 13, 1950, when its president, Colonel Carlos Delgado Chalbaud, was assassinated and replaced by a civilian, Dr. Germán Suárez Flamerich.

General elections were held on November 30, 1952. The Unión Republicana Democrática party, led by Jóvito Villalba—a man who since 1928 had been tempered in the struggles of political opposition to régimes of force—was supported by the popular majority, and won with 987,000 votes. Acción Democrática and the Communist Party, in clandestine activity, and also the independents gave their votes to the Unión Republicana Democrática. The Christian Socialist party, COPEI, under Rafael Caldera, was also in opposition and gained minority support. But the government forces refused to accept the results of the elections, and instead Colonel Marcos Pérez Jiménez, in the name of the armed forces, assumed dictatorial power on December 2, 1952.

A legislative farce—the Congress was appointed by the government—declared Pérez Jiménez constitutional president, and from then until January 23, 1958 there was a dictatorship. All political parties disappeared, but their leaders worked underground or in exile in order to bring the régime down. The dictatorship made some important material advances, and economic prosperity continued to grow. But it had two great faults—cruel persecution of its opponents, and the peculation of a group of henchmen of the president and favourites of the régime. On January 23, 1958 it was defeated by a military coup seconded by the people with strikes and demonstrations. The ensuing governments were, first, a Military Junta led by Rear-Admiral Wolfgang Larrazábal, and then a Junta of Government under the presidency of a University professor, Dr. Edgar Sanabria; and this Junta handed over power for the term 1959 to 1964 to a duly elected president, Rómulo Betancourt. Those men who controlled the country in 1958 were inspired by a new spirit. They organised free elections for the presidency and Congress, and sought a truce to political strife by encouraging unity.

In the 1958 election there were three candidates for the presidency: Wolfgang Larrazábal, Rómulo Betancourt and Rafael Caldera. Betancourt (Acción Democrática) won, with 1,284,042, or 49% of the votes. Larrazábal, supported by Unión Republicana Democrática, by the Communists and by the independents, came second with 35%; while Caldera, with the backing of the COPEI and conservative parties, gained 16%. Acción Democrática also won the largest representation in both Chambers of Congress.

For the period up to the present day, it seems wise to leave a blank, since we lack the perspective for an impartial view. Externally, it is easy to relate that Acción Democrática won the elections and began to govern in coalition with Unión Republicana Democrática and COPEI, then, when the former withdrew from the coalition, Acción Democrática continued to govern in alliance with COPEI alone. But there is a real difficulty in attempting to evaluate the present administration. There are certain extraordinary things, as for example the fact that the very day after the new Constitution had been approved all constitutional guarantees were suspended, and the country was ruled for two years with no such guarantees in force. Even when they were re-instituted, the country was governed as if no Constitution existed. Other sorts of problems arise when dealing with, for example, the question of foreign loans and that of the nation's policy concerning oil. The government is under constant pressure from various different quarters, and not the least of the difficulties which have made its policies appear at times variable is the presence not far away of Castro and his Cuba. Contemporary times are complicated and stability is brittle or crumbling.

6.   NOTES ON THE PRESENT-DAY POLITICAL PARTIES IN VENEZUELA

(a) *Acción Democrática* (Democratic Action—known by the initials A.D.)

This party was legally recognised under this name on September 13, 1941. From 1937 to 1941, working underground, it was called the Partido Democrático Nacional (National Democratic Party). The original party was started in 1931, when a group of men exiled by Gómez met in Barranquilla, Colombia, and agreed on a plan for the defeat of the dictator and the establishment of a new order in Venezuela. The signatories were Rómulo Betancourt, Pedro A. Juliac, P. J. Rodríguez Berroeta, Mario Plaza Ponte, Simón Betancourt, Ricardo Montilla, Carlos Peña Uzlar,

Rafael Angel Castillo, Valmore Rodríguez, Raúl Leoni, Juan J. Palacios and César Camejo. After Gómez's death these and others, some of them communists, took part in left-wing politics until all such parties were dissolved in 1937, and the movement went underground. In 1945 A.D. had 20,000 members, but it grew to 700,000 during its three years as the governing party, before it was outlawed in October 1948. It came into the open again after January 23, 1958, and now has about 900,000 members. These are the official figures, and should be regarded as coming from the governing party.

Up to 1931 the original party leaders were communists, but in that year they abandoned international communism while still retaining a Marxist and revolutionary outlook. The Plan of Barranquilla of March 22, 1931 affirms the basic principles of the party:

1. Purely civilian government.
2. Freedom of thought, expression, association, meeting, communication, etc.
3. Confiscation for the benefit of the country of the ill-gotten wealth of Gómez and his followers.
4. Punishment of the criminals of the despotism of Gómez.
5. Workers to be protected against capitalist tyranny.
6. Intense campaign for literacy; technical and agricultural training; complete freedom of the university.
7. Revision of concessions to foreign companies; no foreign loans; nationalisation of sources of water power; control of all industries which are in fact public services.
8. A new Constitution and new laws which will solve the country's political, social and economic problems.

Point 7. should be clarified by the following remark made in the Plan's preamble: 'Standard Oil, Royal Dutch [Shell], the Royal Bank [of Canada] and four or five other companies whose capital is entirely in dollars or sterling control almost the whole of the country's economy.'

In 1936 and 1937 the founders made common cause with the Communist Party, but after 1937 the international communists withdrew and the Partido Democrático Nacional became a purely nationalist party, as was to be its successor, A.D. But the political ideals are Marxist, and the party's philosophy is materialist. Various programmes were adopted in 1958 for organisation, agriculture, economy, trades-unions, etc.

The party's chief men are Rómulo Betancourt, Gonzalo Barrios, Raúl Leoni, and Luis Beltrán Prieto Figueroa. A party split in 1960 took away the younger generation of leaders, who established a new group with the name Movimiento de Izquierda Revolucionaria (Movement of the Revolutionary Left, M.I.R.), alleging that the old leaders were failing to apply the party's socialist principles to government. In 1961 the Acción Democrática party split into two wings, one led by the original leaders, and known as A.D.-Vieja Guardia (Old Guard, V.G.), and the other called A.D.-Ars and led by Raúl Ramos Giménez. (Ars is said to be the initials of an advertising agency active in the democratic period 1945-1948, and which used the slogan 'Let us think for you.' Ars may also be expanded into Asociación Revolucionaria Socialista [Socialist Revolutionary Association]). No exact figure can be found for the percentage of A.D. members who supported these wings. A.D.-V.G. has abandoned its original thesis of social revolution, but not A.D.-Ars.

A.D.'s published thought is socialist but not communist: the state should regulate all facets of public life, such as education, the economy and labour. But in practice these ideas have not been ruthlessly applied in legislation during the two occasions on which the party has been in power. In fact the most important legislative reforms were made in 1941 to 1945, under Medina Angarita, and A.D., when in power, has adopted and confirmed these reforms. The Constitutions of 1947 and 1961 are basically similar to that of 1945, adopted by the Medina régime. A.D. possesses an agrarian doctrine, translated into agrarian reform; but its educational doctrine has not caused any radical change, although the régime has greatly developed education, especially in quantity. A.D.'s labour programme has been reflected in the application of Medina's laws of 1945 and in the general organisation of the Ministry of Labour. In oil legislation, A.D. has applied the law of 1943 with the amendment of 1955, and so far has made no changes in spite of the published views of the party's leaders. As regards foreign loans, A.D.'s views have definitely changed. Now they are to be accepted. In international affairs, the country has been kept within the Western orbit.

(b) *Unión Republicana Democrática* (Democratic Republican Union, known as U.R.D.) This party was founded on March 12,

1946 in order to oppose the régime brought in by the coup d'état of October 18, 1945. Its leaders had similar views to those of A.D., but had differed with them personally. When Rómulo Gallegos fell in November 1948 the U.R.D. was not dissolved, and some of its leaders served in the new government until the establishment of the dictatorship in November 1952. During these two years the party grew and even won the 1952 elections, but it went underground at the accession of Pérez Jiménez, and re-appeared in January 1958. But, while underground, the U.R.D. had great influence in building up the opposition which triumphed in that January. U.R.D. then took part in the coalition government until, in 1960, it went into opposition.

U.R.D.'s outstanding leader, Dr. Jóvito Villalba, was one of the men of 1928. Imprisoned and exiled under Gómez and López Contreras, he was never a Communist Party member. He was the Secretary General of the old Partido Democrático Nacional when it was working underground. Other leaders include Dionisio López Orihuela, Enrique Betancourt Galíndez and Luis Miquelena.

U.R.D.'s theoretical programme is, in general, similar to that of A.D. At present its policy is to work for a so-called government of national integration by means of coalition among the parties and the independents. U.R.D. has not yet had the opportunity to put its ideas into legislative practice, but according to recent information, public and private, if the party did come to power its policies would not be greatly modified.

(c) Christian Socialist Party—*COPEI (Comité Pro-Elecciones Independientes)*. In 1934 Rafael Caldera was a representative of Venezuela at the International Congress of Catholic Youth in Rome at which plans were made for the establishment of Christian Socialist parties in the Latin American countries. Caldera in 1936 led a group of students in Caracas who organised the Unión Nacional de Estudiantes (National Union of Students), splitting off from the Federación de Estudiantes de Venezuela (Federation of Students of Venezuela). This group became in 1946 the Comité de Organización Política Electoral Independiente (Committee for Independent Electoral Political Organisation), COPEI, known now as the Comité Pro-Elecciones Independientes (Committee for Independent Elections). It put up Caldera as a candidate for the presidential election of 1947, won by

Gallegos. But COPEI was able to gain 19 seats in the Chamber of Deputies and six in the Senate, mainly through successes in the States of Táchira and Mérida, where the party gained a majority in local government elections. From the coup d'état of 1948 until 1958, the party was in opposition, and since 1958 it has joined in the coalition government.

COPEI's programme is based on the social doctrines of the Catholic Church. Its immediate policy is to work for real democracy in order to raise the majority of the people from their economic and cultural inferiority. The party is active among young people.

The party's main leaders are Caldera, Lorenzo Fernández, Miguel Ángel Landáez and Víctor Giménez Landínez from the original group of 1936, and others such as Edecio La Riva, Enrique Acevedo Berti and Pedro Pablo Aguilar.

(d) *Partido Comunista Venezolano* (Venezuelan Communist Party, P.C.V.) This was formed underground in 1931 as a section of the Third International. It was suppressed, and its leaders, Rodolfo Quintero, Juan Bautista Tamayo and Francisco José Delgado, in exile, joined other Caribbean Communist Parties. The party began work again in Venezuela in 1936 by means of establishing cells among the oil workers. That year and the next the communist leaders worked with other left-wing politicians in the Partido Democrático Nacional, which, however, they left in 1937 in order to form their own group. The communists were active underground until 1942, especially among students and oil workers; and they even held a clandestine party congress at Maracay in 1937. In 1942 and 1943 pro-communist groups were formed, and in the latter years the party appeared in the open under the name Unión Popular Venezolana (Venezuelan Union of the People), since the Constitution forbade communist parties. The party appeared under its own name in 1945, at the amendment of the Constitution, and remained active after the coup d'état of that October until it was outlawed in May 1950. It was freed again in January 1958, but outlawed again in 1962.

This party's programme reflects the well-known international communist line. Its leaders include Jesús Farías, Gustavo Machado, Pompeyo Márquez, Pedro Ortega Díaz, Héctor Rodríguez Bauza and Guillermo García Ponce.

(e) *Smaller parties.* 1. Movimiento de Izquierda Revolucionaria (Movement of the Revolutionary Left, M.I.R.), made up of leaders of A.D. who have left the main group and cling to Marxist doctrine, communist in practice.

2. Movimiento Republicano Progresista (Progressive Republican Movement, M.R.P.), founded by Ramón Escovar Salom, who was in A.D. until about 1950. It is a minority group supported by some of the middle-class, bankers, merchants.

Other small groups exist, but with little or no practical effect on politics.

(f) *Present-day strengths of the parties.* The only independent figures are those given by the elections of 1958 (see p. 216), and these have since been modified by the split in the majority party, A.D., as well as by normal political shifts.

In Congress the state of the parties is as follows (1962);

	Senators	Deputies
A.D.-V.G.	22	34
A.D.-Ars	3	23
COPEI	6	19
U.R.D.	7	34
M.R.P.	1	
P.C.V.	2	7
M.I.R.	1	13
Independents	9	3
Total		
	51	133

The Universities, especially the Universidad Central, in Caracas, show clearly the state of the parties among the youth of the country. In the 1962 elections by students in the Universidad Central a coalition of U.R.D., Communist Party and M.I.R. won 7,001 votes, 51.29%; A.D.-Ars won 605 votes, 4.40%; and a coalition of COPEI and A.D. won 6,042 votes, 44.31%. The first group, the left wing, was particularly strong among students of Economics.

CHAPTER VIII

The Contemporary Economic Scene in Venezuela

I. INTRODUCTION

THE economist Dr. Manuel Rodríguez Mena, of the Universidad Central in Caracas, has written specially for this English edition a survey of Venezuela's present-day economy, in order to show the situation now, when oil is the supreme factor. As a historical period, this could be called the Age of Oil. What follows is an abridged translation of Dr. Rodríguez's contribution, included for the sake of providing some insight into Venezuela's contemporary affairs as a whole.

Venezuela, with her 352,150 square miles of territory and her 7,523,999 inhabitants at the Census taken in February 1961, for many years the leading exporter of oil in the world and the sixth largest producer of iron ore, has had the highest national product per head of any of the underdeveloped countries (1956 —almost 800 US dollars gross per head of population), and an average income per head comparable to that of some highly developed countries, and almost double the average for Hispanic America. Yet her economy shows important contradictions and, more markedly than many of the other Hispanic American countries, the peculiarities of underdevelopment: her most important exports are raw materials (oil, iron) and fruits(coffee, cacao); her industry is only slightly developed and she imports great quantities of manufactured goods; she still has considerable reserves not fully exploited and has a low per capita productivity; there are great variations in productivity and excessive inequality in the distribution of income; a large proportion of her population is engaged in agriculture, which brings small gain to the national productivity figure; she has a high illiteracy rate (49% in 1950, about 30% in 1962) and a shortage of skilled labour; two millions of her people live in half a million 'ranchos', miserable shacks; lastly, while a small number of industrial and commercial workers and civil servants, city dwellers, can lead an acceptable life, great masses suffer from 'economic anaemia', short of food, clothing, housing and medicine, and in large measure denied the benefits of technical advance and of culture.

Throughout Venezuela's history of international trade, she has never had a diversified range of exports. Her capacity to pay for imports has always sprung from one or two products. From the Conquest to the 1920s agriculture and stock-raising were the mainspring of Venezuela's economy. To begin with the products were tobacco, indigo and cotton; later cacao became supreme until about the 1820s; then coffee was the leading product until the early years of the present century. Stock-raising was always important in the colonial period, but the stock, decimated during the wars of emancipation, took many years to recover. Indeed in 1914 80% of Venezuela's exports consisted of coffee (51.5 million bolívares), cacao (21.4 million) and the fruits of the cattle industry (9.3 million). Production of and trading in these primary products occupied the majority of the country's active population; and of course the largest part of the country's revenue came from the customs duties levied on the imports bought with the foreign exchange provided by the sale of these products abroad. In 1914 these duties amounted to 60% of the 50 million bolívares collected in taxes.

About forty years ago oil suppressed all competition for the first place among Venezuela's exports, and occupied, as it still does, the position of highest importance in the national production and in the country's revenue. In 1960 oil represented 79.4% of the total value of Venezuela's exports, and made up 27.9% of the country's gross production. The revenue gained from the exploitation of hydrocarbons was 60.5% of the total revenue of the country. In recent years iron ore has reached considerable figures in the national production and exports— steel-making has only latterly been started in Venezuela—but iron ore has not approached oil in importance.

This economic evolution over 450 years, based on the production and exportation of raw materials, without diversification, the fact that revenue and the ability to import have always depended on the sale in world markets of primary products whose prices are unstable and tend to fall relatively, the long-standing abstention from industry, which forces the country to buy great groups of manufactured products abroad, all these things have given to the underdevelopment of Venezuela deep historical roots and profound structural characteristics of its own.

2. OIL

Table I shows the production of crude oil in Venezuela from 1914 to 1961. It will be seen that production continues to increase, and that there was a spurt in 1957, due to the closing of the Suez Canal and the consequent rise in demand for Venezuelan oil. In 1960 Russia displaced Venezuela for the first time since 1944 as the country with the second greatest production of oil, the United States being first; in that year Venezuela produced 13.6% of the world total, in comparison with 14.1% in 1959.

Table I
Development of the Venezuelan Oil Industry 1914-1961

	Production of crude oil (Thousands of barrels)	Exportation of crude oil and refined products (Thousands of barrels)
1914	(x)	—
1915	(x)	—
1916	(x)	—
1917	121	57
1918	321	147
1919	305	14
1920	462	0
1921	1,459	1,004
1922	2,262	1,833
1923	4,127	3,410
1924	9,139	8,242
1925	20,046	18,424
1926	36,045	32,762
1927	60,827	56,956
1928	106,056	100,602
1929	135,981	130,566
1930	135,195	134,451
1931	116,517	111,895
1932	116,327	110,470
1933	118,178	113,305

P

1934	135,906	130,222
1935	148,727	138,540
1936	154,218	150,428
1937	185,989	167,994
1938	187,910	178,491
1939	204,881	189,160
1940	183,884	156,999
1941	226,873	222,877
1942	148,020	140,993
1943	179,383	174,264
1944	257,037	249,576
1945	323,403	317,701
1946	388,478	375,290
1947	434,890	423,703
1948	489,999	469,082
1949	482,299	460,013
1950	546,764	519,658
1951	622,195	588,512
1952	660,233	625,782
1953	644,223	606,480
1954	691,788	654,884
1955	787,384	738,628
1956	899,183	846,221
1957	1,014,424	940,311
1958	950,767	889,580
1959	1,011,419	940,868
1960	1,041,675	982,737
1961	1,065,726	

notes: (x) Small production. 1 cubic metre = 6.2898 barrels
          — No figures

Sources: *Petróleo y otros datos estadísticos*, 1961. División de
          Economía Petrolera, Ministerio de Minas e Hidrocar-
          buros de Venezuela.
          Anuario Petrolero de Venezuela, 1950-51, Ministerio
          de Minas e Hidrocarburos de Venezuela.

The Banco Central de Venezuela, discussing the activity of
1960, reported that besides the increase in total oil production,
there were increases in the refining of oil within the country, in
internal consumption of natural gas, and in the incomes of the
oil workers. There were decreases in new exploration and drilling, in internal consumption of oil products, in the hydrocarbon

tax revenue of the country, in employment in the oil industry, and in the earnings of the oil companies operating in the country.[1]

In 1960 51.3 million cubic metres (322.9 million barrels) of oil were refined, or 7.4% more than in 1959. The capacity of the fifteen refining plants operating in the country was 1,003,-500 barrels a day in 1960, and the crude oil processed was in fact 884,700 barrels a day. 30.9% of the oil produced in Venezuela, or nearly one third, was refined in the country. 86% of the refined products were exported, since internal consumption was only 14% of what was produced—this represented a fall of 4.8% from 1959, which was due to a recession in the transport industry, the preference for light vehicles, and the increased use of natural gas in place of fuel oil.

Natural gas production in 1960 fell in total by 1% from 1959 (1960—31,661 million cubic metres), but the decrease was advantageous since more of the gas was used and less had to be released into the atmosphere and wasted. Internally, sales of natural gas rose to 1,686 million cubic metres, or 11.3% more than in 1959, and it replaced fuel oil in new industrial installations, especially in electricity generating plants. Even so, the waste of natural gas is a matter of serious concern: the proportion was 48.8% of total production in 1960, which is the equivalent of about 94 million barrels of oil, or 9% of the annual production of crude oil.

The total wage-bill for the industry was 1,104.6 million bolívares in 1960, or 10.6% more than in 1959, because of a new collective wage contract signed in February 1960. The average oil worker's wage was therefore 27,300 bolívares in the year (about £3,500). 83.3% of the workers are employed in the basic activities of exploration and exploitation, and only 16.7% are engaged in refining.

New exploration was much reduced from previous years, at 3,876,000 hectares; while new drilling reached its lowest level for ten years, with only 456 new wells as compared with 707 in 1959.

Taxes on the hydrocarbon industry in Venezuela are the Exploration Tax, the Initial Exploitation Tax, the Area Tax, the

---

1 These companies are: Creole, Shell, Mene Grande, Mobil, Venezuelan Sun, Richmond, Phillips, Texas, Superior, Sinclair, Varco, San Jacinto, Signal, Petmer, Coro, Caracas, Talon and Corporación Venezolana del Petróleo.

Exploitation Tax (royalty on oil and gas), and the Transport Tax. From these in 1960, 1,631.62 million bolívares were collected, that is 6.3 million less than in 1959. The Exploitation Tax, or royalty, is the most important of these taxes since it is levied at the rate of 16⅔% of oil produced and gas used; it brought in 1,603 million bolívares in 1960.

Besides these taxes, the oil companies also pay income tax, customs duties and other contributions. Income tax on the oil industry was 1,260.28 million bolívares in 1960, 204.63 million less than in 1959, since although production was higher, profits were lower; and therefore the interest on the capital invested in the oil industry fell from 13.1% in 1959 to 11.2% in 1960.

The total revenue from taxes on the oil industry in 1960 was made up as follows:

	millions of bolívares
Hydrocarbons	1,631.63
Income tax	1,260.28
Customs	32.05
Others	78.23
total	3,002.19

Since 1957 employment in the oil industry has fallen from 45,597 to 36,897 workers in 1961. The figure in 1960 was 40,581, and of these 45% were office workers and 55% process workers of all kinds. The fall in numbers employed, according to the Banco Central de Venezuela (1960), is mainly due to the decrease in exploration and to cutting down costs by the companies.

Table I shows how true it is to say that the Venezuelan oil industry is an export activity. This is also obvious from the companies' incomes: in 1960 the industry received a total of 7,396 million bolívares, from exports worth 6,754 million (91.3%), internal sales worth 470 million (6.3%) and the sale of internal services for 170 million (2.3%). Crude oil represented 74% of the sales, and products 26%. These figures prove that the industry is predominantly concerned with exports, and that it produces and exports in the main the raw material, crude oil.

Table II
Total Investment in the oil industry (in millions of bolívares)

year	gross investment (1)	reserves (2)	net investment (1-2)	net investment as %age of gross
1955	10,937	5,288	5,649	51.6%
1956	13,038	6,015	7,023	53.9
1957	15,828	6,826	9,002	56.9
1958	17,218	7,566	9,652	56.1
1959	18,803	8,428	10,375	55.2
1960*	19,627	9,418	10,209	52

* provisional figures

Sources: Ministry of Mines and Hydrocarbons.
  Memoria del Banco Central de Venezuela, 1960, p 223.

From the above Table it will be seen that investment has tended to grow, but that between 1959 and 1960 net investment has begun to fall—in that year there was a disinvestment of 166 million bolívares.

On December 31, 1960 exploitation concessions in force totalled 4,718,445 hectares, which was 1,035,798 hectares less than in 1959. At the same date proved reserves in the country were about 2,759 million cubic metres (about 17,352 million barrels).

In 1960 figures for oil transport were the following: 3,186 kilometres of trunk oil pipe-lines, with a daily capacity of 1,056,828 cubic metres; 1,744 kilometres of gas pipe-lines to take gas to centres of utilisation, 1,192 of the kilometres being administered by oil companies and 552 kilometres by the state oil enterprise, Corporación Venezolana del Petróleo, with a total capacity of 30 million cubic metres daily; the Venezuelan tanker fleet (which is .6% of the world tanker capacity) consisted of six lighters and 25 tankers, the latter of 381,876 tons deadweight and 447,759 cubic metres of capacity; finally, in 1960 there existed for the exportation of crude oil and derivatives 21 terminals with a storage capacity of 78 million barrels.

3. MINING

Iron ore is by far the most important product of Venezuelan mining. These are the figures for 1960:

iron ore	19.4 million tons (metric)
gold	1,432,300 grammes
coal	35,300 tons
salt	70,900 tons
lime	39,500 tons

Most of the iron ore mined is exported, as it has been throughout the period 1951-60:

Table III
Production and exportations of iron ore (thousands of metric
tons)

year	production	exportation
1951	1,269.6	715.4
1952	1,969.8	1,888.6
1953	2,296.4	1,972.8
1954	5,420.6	5,476.4
1955	8,439.5	7,822.9
1956	11,104.8	11,341.8
1957	15,295.5	15,459.4
1958	15,484.6	15,615.8
1959	17,201.3	17,000.2
1960	19,490.4	19,242.5
	97,972.5	96,535.8

Sources: Ministry of Mines and Hydrocarbons.
Memoria del Banco Central de Venezuela, 1960.

In 1960 the 19,242,500 metric tons of iron ore exported went
to the following countries:

United States	14.7 million tons, or 76.6% (Venezuela is the largest exporter of iron ore to the U.S.A.)
Great Britain	1.7 million
Germany	1.3 ,,
Italy	1.0 ,,
Holland	.5 ,,
Belgium } Canada }	small amounts

The internal consumption in that year was only 2,500 tons.
The value of the ore exported reached 524.2 million bolívares,
or 20.4% more than in 1959. That exported to the United States
was worth 44.9% more than in 1959, partly because more in
quantity was sent, but also because of a rise in the price on
April 1, 1960.
The national revenue from iron includes figures for income

tax, export tax, other mining taxes, customs duties and others. It has grown in the following way:

year	bolívares
1956	15,297,529
1957	46,191,875
1958	97,552,458
1959	90,699,827
1960	90,194,155

The largest percentage corresponds to income tax which the companies pay each year according to the previous year's takings. It fell between 1959 and 1960 since, although the companies had higher figures of production and sale than the year before, they also had greater costs and therefore smaller returns.

In 1960 Venezuela became the sixth ranking producer of iron ore in the world, after the Soviet Union, the United States, France, Canada and Sweden, in that order; but Venezuela's ore, at 65%, has a higher figure for purity than that of any country in the first twenty producers, except for India and the Union of South Africa, which equal her, and Brazil, which surpasses her with 70%. Yet in spite of this, Venezuela has no steel industry as yet. On July 9, 1962, however, the Orinoco Steelworks were opened, in their first stage, with a capacity of 700,000 tons of steel and 650,000 of finished articles per year (seamless tubes, wire, galvanised wire, galvanised barbed wire, nails, girders, rails and other railway equipment, bolts and plates, in steel; and, in iron, pipes and foundry products). The works are to be enlarged to produce 1,200,000 tons a year. They have so far cost 1,200 million bolívares. In their first stage they will employ about 6,000 workmen.

4. MANUFACTURING

The importance of manufacturing industry for Venezuela is shown, among other things, by the proportion it provides of the national revenue. In 1959 the national revenue was 19,921 million bolívares, to which manufacturing contributed 2,396 million and in which it came fifth in size, after oil (3,929 million), commerce (2,809 million), government (2,651 million), and rents and interest (2,578 million); but much above services (2,082 million), much more above agriculture (1,380 million) and other branches such as building (1,075 million), transport and communications (577 million), electricity (248 million) and mining (196 million). It is worth note that the excess of commerce over manufacturing, fairly well marked here, is another characteristic of underdevelopment, as is the preponderance of the oil industry, especially when, as in Venezuela, it is mainly concerned with producing the raw material for export.

Table IV   Manufacturing industry
Production of certain goods—1960

Articles	Unit	Production
Sugar	metric tons	193,970
Wheat flour	,, ,,	199,273
Pasteurised milk	thousands of litres	155,885
Farinaceous pastes (noodles etc.)	metric tons	40,231
Oils	,, ,,	23,131
Cattle carcases	,, ,,	147,223
Beer	thousands of litres	241,114
Cigarettes	thousands	6,839,591
Cotton cloth	metres	33,168
Knitted fabrics	kilogrammes	1,776
Woollen cloth	metres	1,347
Cloth made from artificial fibres	,,	27,191
Leathers	thousands of square feet	12,611
Cow-hide	metric tons	5,104
Paints	,, ,,	15,084
Cement	,, ,,	1,487,008
Tyres	units	752,768
Inner tubes	,,	604,783
Passenger vehicles	,,	6,452
Commercial vehicles	,,	3,882
Oil derivatives	cubic metres	29,228
Tin cans	metric tons	273,690
Vehicle batteries	units	50,701,699

Source: *Memoria del Banco Central de Venezuela*, 1960, p. 300.

In 1960 manufacturing employed 163,000 persons (2.5% fewer than in 1959), and capital greater than 4,000 million bolívares, which brought about 2,898 million bolívares to the gross product of the country.

There was in 1960 a fall in total demand, so that manufacturing fell by something over 3% in comparison with 1959; although gross industrial output increased by .6%. Various sections of industry were affected differently: for example the production of durable goods fell by almost 14%, on the average, although there were some sectors—such as the timber and furniture industries, and the building, assembly and repair of vehicles —which fell by more than 25%. On the other hand, the production of non-durable goods—consumer goods and raw materials not connected with capital goods—grew by almost 4%, with tobacco production increased by over 55%, whilst ready-made clothing and skins and leathers fell by 14% and 13% respectively.

Latin America was one of the regions which in 1960 showed low industrial growth, and Venezuela's development is in consonance with that of the region. Industrial production per inhabitant decreased in 1960, since although the rise in population probably went on at the average rate of 3 to 4% per year, industrial production rose by merely .6%, with the result that production per inhabitant must have fallen by about 2 or 3%.

The comparison between the production of non-durable consumer goods and that of durable consumer goods and capital goods emphasises the type of underdevelopment suffered by Venezuela, for while considerable quantities of some of the former goods are produced, in the second category production is much lower, and in the case of capital goods it is almost nonexistent. This is pointed out by the Banco Central de Venezuela (*Memoria 1960*, p. 300): 'Whilst 194 million tons of sugar are produced, and almost 200 million tons of flour, 156 million litres of milk, 241 million litres of beer, 147 million tons of meat and 6,840 million cigarettes, not one radio or television set is produced, for example, nor one machine-tool. In this type of goods production is practically confined to the assembly of automotive vehicles'.

The number of firms which used less than 35% of their installations was considerable, and the Directorate of Industries of the Ministry of Development concluded, as a result of an investigation made in mid-1960, that it was common for the proportion of installed capacity in use to fluctuate between 35% and 70%.

The final value of manufacturing industry in 1960 was 7,325 million bolívares, and of this 6,078 million (84%) was the final value of the production of non-durable goods (food, drinks, tobacco, textiles, ready-made clothing, paper and cardboard, graphic arts, skins and leathers, chemical industry and products derived from oil), whilst only 16% (1,152 million bolívares) corresponded to durable goods (industries of timber and furniture, rubber, non-metallic mineral products, metallic products, building assembly and repair of vehicles).

Looking a little closer, we find a predominance of products derived from oil, with 2,548 million bolívares (35% of the total); food, drinks and tobacco also form a high proportion (26%), whilst there is only a small contribution from metallic articles, machinery of all types and vehicles (a mere 7%), and it must be remembered that in the case of vehicles the operation is reduced to the assembly of imported parts.

Again, of the total final value of production in 1960 (7,326 million bolívares), 65% (4,747 million) corresponds to the raw materials and half-finished products incorporated in the finished goods. The refining of oil weights this figure, since this industry gives 35% of the final value, and its raw materials have a high value. If we include the refining of crude oil in the total sum, then foreign contributions in raw materials and half-finished goods reach only 27%; but if oil is excluded in order to give a truer picture of the level of Venezuelan manufacturing industry, then we find that imported raw and half-finished materials used in Venezuelan industry amount to no less than 49% of the total such materials, and therefore that Venezuelan production is greatly dependent on foreign materials. This, in turn, means that Venezuelan industry is not so influential as might be hoped in creating local employment, in consuming local raw materials and in creating processes for goods in intermediate states of completion; while at the same time the foreign countries whose goods are imported enjoy some or all of these benefits. This is the reason why some Venezuelan industries can be called 'artificial'—that is, those which only complete the last or the last few stages of manufacture, and import articles almost completely finished in order to make the final small transformation inside the country. Such industries are far less effective as generators of employment than if the whole process were carried out in the country, and are completely useless as creators of demand for raw materials. The Banco Central de Venezuela has stated: 'Dependence on foreign countries for raw materials and half-finished goods may cause instability in the development of industry and could cause strong pressure on the balance of payments, and it is therefore necessary to encourage the growth of the production of half-finished goods, at least in those sectors such as metal articles, for which the country is specially well endowed.'

The Venezuelan economic crisis is felt in the manufacturing industries, which confront the main problems of the contraction of demand and the scarcity of finance. Their activities fell by 3% between 1959 and 1960, as has been pointed out above, and at the same time employment fell by 2.5%.

5. AGRICULTURE

In spite of the preponderance of oil and the greater development of other sectors of the Venezuelan economy, such as commerce, agriculture is still important since it provides much employment (833,000 persons in 1959), and since it supplies a considerable proportion of the vegetable and animal products which feed the people and provide raw materials for industry. In 1960 agriculture provided 1,806.6 million bolívares, or 6.8% of the total, in the gross territorial product. The foodstuffs were supplemented by the importation of 685,304,000 kilogrammes of food, worth 523,348,000 bolívares. For export, the most important products are coffee, with 27,712 metric tons (1960), worth 73.16 million bolívares, and cacao, with 11,988 metric tons, worth 30.50 million. The products of the cattle and timber industries made up a mere 1.2% of agricultural exports.

Table V

Agricultural production and its value at current prices—1960

	Production	value (thousands of bolívares)
Total agricultural production		1,832,602
Vegetable produce		1,035,979
Cereals:		146,322
rice (husked)	71,862 metric tons	43,117
maize	439,440 ,, ,,	102,829
wheat	836 ,, ..	376

	Production		value (thousands of bolívares)
Leguminous grains:			64,780
peas	1,627	,, ,,	1,155
French beans	49,842	,, ,,	38,079
black beans	29,448	,, ,,	23,470
pigeon peas	3,397	,, ,,	2,076
Roots etc:			186,912
celery	9,147	,, ,,	5,671
sweet potatoes	15,329	,, ,,	4,062
dashee (a type of yam)	19,612	,, ,,	9,531
yams	44,655	,, ,,	19,738
tania	69,409	,, ,,	29,291
yucca	340,248	,, ,,	64,647
potatoes	133,594	,, ,,	53,872
Fibrous and oil-bearing plants:			72,027
sesame	24,868	,, ,,	27,355
raw cotton	24,947	,, ,,	28,065
copra	7,742	,, ,,	7,866
groundnuts (in shell)	1,587	,, ,,	1,746
sisal (fibre)	9,993	,, ,,	6,995
Fruits and other vegetables:			174,171
cambur (a type of banana)	452,778	,, ,,	94,178
other fruits	76,000	,, ,,	15,200
onions	23,163	,, ,,	11,442
tomatoes	49,340	,, ,,	26,545
other vegetables	40,800	,, ,,	26,806
Coffee, cacao, etc:			391,767
cacao	9,222	,, ,,	24,530
coffee	8,485	metric tons	169,126
sugar cane	55,072	,, ,,	81,083
unrefined sugar	2,133,758	,, ,,	34,669
bananas	44,505	,, ,,	32,514
tobacco	235,609	,, ,,	49,845

	Production	value (thousands of bolívares)
Animal produce		679,325
Milk	420,863 thousand litres	214,640
Cattle and fowls:		426,749
cattle	1,003,881 head	305,605
pigs	855,478 ,,	69,263
goats	70,000 ,,	700
sheep	51,612 ,,	319
fowl	6,954,000 ,,	50,852
Eggs	189,300 thousand	37,936
Fishing		
fish	85,851 metric tons	50,238
Forest products		67,060
Timber:	276,441 cubic metres	64,310
fine woods	64,223 ,, ,,	24,405
hard ,,	40,361 ,, ,,	14,126
soft ,,	171,857 ,, ,,	25,779
Other products:		2,750
balata	111 metric tons	266
charcoal	12,108 ,, ,,	2,332
fire-wood	1,663 ,, ,,	83
chicle	69 ,, ,,	69
dividivi fruit (for tanning)	quantity unknown	

Source: *Memoria del Banco Central de Venezuela*, 1960.

Table V gives the quantities and values of the main products for 1960. Vegetable products were up by 13% over 1959, but since the cultivated area was up by 21% this means that the average production per hectare was lower. Cereals were particularly buoyant, being 41% up on the 1959 figure.

145,842 tons of cattle and pig products were used. The consumption of meat is low in Venezuela—in 1958 only 22½ kilogrammes per inhabitant, that is about sixty-two grammes per day. If one remembers that apart from the rich, certain groups of workers such as oil men and civil servants consume several times the sixty-two grammes per day, one must conclude that many Venezuelans eat almost no meat at all; and this is true of some other basic items of diet.

In 1960 8% more leguminous produce was grown than in 1959, but even so 22,443 metric tons had to be imported; that is 21% of the apparent consumption. Production of rice and of maize was the greatest for some years. The potato crop was the biggest ever in the country, yet 7,151 metric tons had to be imported, 5% of the apparent consumption. The consumption of goat flesh is bigger than production every year, so the herds constantly decrease; and the number of sheep also fell between 1958 and 1960. More fish was brought in than for some years, with 85,851 tons, most of which was eaten fresh. 4% more timber was produced than in 1959.

The general characteristics of Venezuelan agriculture today, according to the conclusion of the Venezuelan Agrarian Reform Commission (Comisión de Reforma Agraria de Venezuela) are the following:

1. Low productivity per hectare, save for a few exceptions. This is because the techniques used are very backward. Too little capital is employed, and methods are usually primitive. Also, much farming is for subsistence only, and in small units. The land is badly divided: 2.5% of the estates account for 82% of the land farmed (1956); much of the rest is held in too small units; farming is therefore largely carried on by employed labourers, whose productivity and standards of living are low, while the social system is highly stratified.

2. The relative importance of agriculture is declining in Venezuela, as other industries grow more rapidly. Agriculture's low rate of growth is a brake on the whole expansion, since the agricultural population (40% of the economically active) and the total rural population (40% of total population) have low purchasing power and form only a small market for the other industries. Therefore, the difference between the standards of living of the agricultural and the other populations is becoming more accentuated.

3. Under-employment of the land is normal, with large areas of permanent crops and natural pasture. Crops are usually in small, subsistence parcels; while cattle-raising is carried on in extremely large individual areas. The land is not conserved: slope farming and slash-and-burn favour erosion and harm the climate of certain regions. The absence of seasons and the ability to grow crops at any time of the year are not taken advantage of, so that really intensive farming takes place on a very

small proportion of the land: there are 7.2 hectares of natural pasture for every one of sown pasture.

4. Agricultural products never suffice for the country's needs: the rise in productivity (5% in the last ten years) is not sufficient to keep pace with the rise in demand. Much agricultural produce is therefore imported (more than a third the amount produced), and prices are considerably higher than average.

5. The agricultural population has tended to become stable in numbers over the last twenty years, so that it is falling in proportion to total population. Emigration takes place from the countryside to the industrial areas.

6. The conditions in which the rural population lives are lamentable: huts with straw roofs, walls of palm leaves, mud floors, water from the nearest spring or river, no sanitation, food consisting of scraps of meat and spoonfuls of milk. 79% of these people over fifteen years of age cannot read or write. Their homes are chock-full of people, and their family life begins with concubinage.

7. The labour force is much bigger than is needed, and therefore wages are low. What increase in agricultural production has taken place has been due to increased productivity of the soil in certain regions, and not to increased output per head of labourers.

8. Management is usually inefficient, as is seen from the low productivity. Lack of education and of technical training keep management unqualified. On the small-holdings the owner is illiterate, with rudimentary notions of farming.

9. Marketing is poorly organised, distribution costs are high and losses in the process of marketing are great. There is a shortage of good and well-placed stores. The producer therefore makes very low profits. The whole farming system works against the establishment of a more efficient marketing system.

10. Financial backing is insufficient, and in any case many of the farmers are ignorant of the use of credit or are nervous about contracting debts.

11. Oil concessions create doubts about validity of tenure of the farmer on the surface, and this inhibits investment and kills incentive.

12. System of inheritance: because of the legal situation whereby a property may be the inheritance of a large number of persons, some estates are scarcely farmed owing to the diffi-

culty of making the necessary decisions with so many co-proprietors, some of whom may be absentees.

13. Unequal distribution of human and land resources: crops are mainly concentrated in the central and western regions, whereas stock-raising is mainly carried on in the *llanos*.

Because of the situation described above, it has for long been thought that agricultural reform was needed in Venezuela. The Law of Agricultural Reform promulgated in March 1960 is in operation, and its object is 'the transformation of the agricultural structure of the country and the incorporation of its rural population into the economic, social and political development of the Nation by replacing the system of large estates by a just system of ownership, tenancy and use of the land based on the equitable distribution of the same, the adequate organisation of credit and complete aid for farmers, in order that the land shall constitute for him who works it the basis of his economic stability, the foundation of his progressive social well-being and the guarantee of his liberty and dignity' (Article I). The Law gives country workers the right to ownership of lands granted to them, the right to certain loans, to help with the marketing of their produce, and to public services in general.

Of the ninety-one million hectares of the country's area, twenty-three million were in private hands. On the other hand, the Census of 1961 gives the rural population as 2,818,711. Including lands distributed since the Law was passed and those given out in various reforms since 1937, by September 1961, 569,462 hectares had been given to 35,622 families. The average rural family consists of five persons, therefore this means that about 178,110 people have been affected, or a mere 6.32% of the rural population. Of the land in private hands, so far only 1.69% has been affected by the Reform, since the National Agrarian Institute has acquired for distribution 167 farms with a total area of 389,564 hectares. Coffee is grown on 34,000 of these, and cacao on 70,000, by the work of 150,000 families (750,000 persons) of country people.

6. COMMERCE AND SERVICES

Commerce and services are very important as creators of employment, since between them they give work to over a third of Venezuela's labour force. Commerce brings in 15%, and services 14%, of the gross territorial product. But information on this sector of the country's economy is deficient, and the figures of the Statistical Directorate of the Ministry of Development must be treated as provisional.

Lately, commerce has been difficult. In the Federal District (where the capital is situated) sales have fallen 30% from 1959, and in some lines 45%. As the economic crisis has grown, pharmaceutical products, iron-ware and hardware, building materials, vehicles, radios, refrigerators, etc. have been hit; and the contraction of demand has affected food, textiles and foot-wear, although not so strongly since these are basic necessities.

Venezuelan commerce shows the country's underdevelopment also in the fact that a high proportion of the goods handled is either imported or made in the country from imported materials.

There has been a real advance in the educational services. In 1950 only 3.8% of the population had received primary education, and only 23,696 persons had completed a year of university studies. The great effort made since then has produced the figures shown in Table VI, and the following facts: in the academical year 1960-61 27,000 students were receiving secondary or higher education, and in the same year the number of primary students was 15% greater than in the previous year.

Table VI

Number of educational institutions, pupils and teachers

	1959	1960	% increase
number of institutions	10,242	12,519	22.2
number of pupils	1,265,231	1,456,534	15.9
number of teachers	41,607	48,297	16.1

Source: *Memoria del Banco Central*, 1960, p. 340.

Yet there are also high figures for failures (25% of those in the first primary year in 1959-60) and for students who abandon their course (27% in the same year). Many students begin education at an advanced age, and many schools only cover a part of the whole primary course, and these facts partly account for the high proportion of abandoned courses. Only 20% of schools teach the whole primary course. Also, about 25% of the first year primary pupils are between ten and fourteen years

Q

old, while over 3,000 (out of 431,905 at this stage) were over fourteen in the year 1959-60.

The total student population in 1960-61 was divided as follows: 1,253,068 in primary schools; 102,955 in secondary schools: 31,641 in teachers' training schools; 41,419 in technical schools; 27,451 in universities. Total: 1,456,534.

There was some contraction among the services. Hotels dropped 15% of their gross takings, and beauty salons 8%; yet the takings of barbers, laundries and dry cleaners rose by 9%.

93% of the receipts of the amusement industry come from cinemas (98.7 million bolívares) and horse-racing (197.7 million). Radio's receipts went up 1% and those of television 8%, but those of publicity fell by 2%.

7. BUILDING

This sector has been hardest hit by the present crisis, after a great boom in the first two-thirds of the '50s, which brought the industry's employment up to 95,000 in 1959 and endowed it with much capital and modern machinery. It came second in economic activity, after oil. But in 1960 its contribution to the gross national product was only 5.5% of the total, with 1,443.5 million bolívares; and its activity had fallen 15% from 1959— private building fell by 6%, but public building fell by no less than 18% since public works were reduced in an effort to economise. It should be noted that public building for many years has represented about three-quarters of the total building.

Private building fell off because it became difficult to finance houses as credit contracted, while costs were very inelastic. Also the atmosphere of unease limited the desire to invest in houses. A further fall in this sector is likely, since there is no solution to the financial problem. Public building, which fell from 2,066 million in 1959 to 1,732 million bolívares in 1960, has ceased to be occupied with prestige works and has been concentrated on useful construction likely to bring in greater social benefit in one form or another.

The price of building land fell in the country except for the metropolitan area and Departamento Vargas, where it rose by 11%. In Caracas and district land is worth about 200 bolívares per square metre, although in some specially favoured areas prices have become prohibitive even for the well-to-do middle class. Some social classes who could afford medium prices are unable now to enter the market, even though there has been some fall in building prices, possibly at the expense of the companies' own profits, since labour costs are maintained at about 35% of the total, and costs of materials have not changed a great deal.

In 1950 there was a need for 128,000 more houses, and the figure in 1960 had risen to 250,000. But it should be remembered that in 1950 there existed 408,000 shacks, and therefore adequate housing is needed by about 42% of the total population. This situation gets worse since demand increases every year, and new building only covers 61% of the demand.

Low-income groups have no way of financing housing. Mortgages are very expensive, which makes house-buying difficult and sends up rents. Even so 90% of real property is mortgaged, according to the estimate of the Chamber of Real Property. Housing in Venezuela is fairly expensive, either to buy or to rent: rents normally take about a third of a family's income. In order to deal with this situation the Workers' Bank (Banco Obrero) was created, and it built in 1960 5,363 houses, 702 appartments and fifty-six communal improvements, for a total of 6,121, or double what it built in 1959. Also, a plan for providing the most necessary services is engaged in bringing such things to areas occupied by shacks and in distributing plots of land so that the shacks may be progressively replaced by better houses. Technical help and materials are supplied to the plot-owners so that they can build their own houses.

8. ELECTRICITY, GAS AND WATER

Table VII

Production of electricity (thousands of kilowatt-hours)

1953	952,650
1954	1,081,037
1955	1,275,985
1956	1,501,284
1957	1,908,028
1958	2,250,262
1959	2,718,735
1960	2,972,595

From the Table it will be seen that consumption of electricity continues to rise, and it should be noted that the proportion of electricity generated by water power has fallen each year, from 15.4% in 1953 to 3.3% in 1960. In use of energy, the Federal District is the most electrified area (1,201 million KWH), followed by the central zone (793 million), the east with much less (140 million), and lastly the south (only thirty-four million). All of the 200 biggest towns have electric power, and 55% of those with from 2,500 to 5,000 inhabitants. Generating capacity in 1960 was 1,178,000 Kw, or over six times as much as in 1950, and various schemes exist for increasing this figure, by both hydro-electric and thermal plant. The state organisation for electricity, CADAFE, plans to raise its capacity to half the total for the country by 1964.

Production of natural gas reached 31,561 million cubic metres in 1960, 51.18% of which was used and the rest lost—in 1953, it should be noted, 73.79% was lost. Natural gas is employed to reinject into oil-bearing layers, in industry and for domestic purposes. The country has a network of 1,726 kilometres of gas pipe-lines, almost a third of which belongs to the national Corporación Venezolana del Petróleo.

Use of water in 1960 reached 187 million cubic metres, and an average growth of 12% per year has taken place in the demand between 1953 and 1960.

9. TRANSPORT AND COMMUNICATIONS

Transport and communications employed 86,000 persons in 1960, and their contribution to the gross national product was 1,000 million bolívares, or 4% of the total.

Up to 1959 6,000 million bolívares had been invested on roads and communications equipment, including 18,018 kilometres of metalled roads. Venezuela has thirty-one kilometres of roads per thousand square kilometres, in comparison, for example, with Argentina's 36.2, Brazil's 61.8, Colombia's and Mexico's 69.6, U.S.A.'s 580 and France's 1,506. In 1960 there were 369,474 vehicles, with the capacity of 1,555,000 passengers and 320,000 tons, distributed as follows: passenger vehicles 6,800, motor cars 268,693 (88% of them private), and 93,981 load-carrying vehicles.

In contrast with this, the railways amount to 474 kilometres of track in service, with twenty-three locomotives, twenty-seven passenger cars and 481 wagons. In 1960 the railways carried 24.6 million passenger/kilometres and 19.6 million ton/kilometres. The railways have been declining for thirty years, and now the capacity is over double the actual use, partly because few routes are served, the equipment is old, slow and poor (except on the Barquisimeto-Puerto Cabello branch), and the costs are higher than in the case of road transport.

Even though the receipts in 1960 of the Gran Ferrocarril de Venezuela and the Puerto Cabello-Barquisimeto lines were 16.6% greater than in 1959, they still only amounted to 1.5 million bolívares, and since outgoings came to 13.1 million (12 million for wages, salaries and other remunerations for the staff), the result was a considerable loss of about 12 million bolívares.

As regards water transport, Venezuela in 1960 had thirty-four ports, eleven of them with installations capable of handling international traffic. There were 102 ships of over 100 tons, with a gross tonnage of 330,238, although the total fleet—including pleasure boats and special craft such as floating cranes—consists of 8,863 units.

Venezuela has fifty-four airfields, four of them engaged in international traffic, one of which, Maiquetía, is able to handle any type of modern aircraft. Four of the most important national companies have sixty-five large passenger aircraft, one small plane and fourteen freight aircraft. In 1960 there were 821,844 passengers, 749,025 internal and 72,809 international; 25,152 tons of cargo were carried, 16,811 internally and 8,341 abroad. Gross receipts from passengers came to 73.05 million bolívares, and from cargo 28.04 million.

Communications employ 16,062 persons and had in 1960 gross receipts of 160 million bolívares. There are 6,400 radio stations in the country, set up by private enterprises in zones where the public service is poor. Telex has partly displaced cable traffic in international communications. There are 65,595 telephone lines to private houses and 54,595 to businesses. The postal service uses 803 offices spread throughout the country.

10. FOREIGN TRADE

In figures, Venezuela's balance of trade has improved. In 1960 gross imports fell by 22.3%, while her exports rose by 2.4%, and in total her gross excess of exports over imports amounted to 4,894.14 million bolívares. Yet the exports are very dangerously specialised (oil, then iron, coffee and cacao), and imports are very diverse (foodstuffs, drinks and tobacco; non-comestible raw materials; lubricants and fuels, and connected products; vegetable and animal oils and fats; chemical products; manufactured articles; machinery and transport equipment; live animals, etc.) The composition of Venezuela's foreign trade is another index of her underdevelopment, since it shows her to be an exporter of raw materials and an importer of capital goods, manufactured articles and superior raw materials. The result is that for every unit of exportation Venezuela obtained only .824 units of importation, owing to the terms of international trade. It is generally accepted that capital goods and the manufactured articles exported by industrialised countries tend to rise in price, while raw materials and produce exported by underdeveloped countries tend to fall in price.

The dependence of Venezuela's economy on foreign trade (shown by the ratio between the total volume of exports plus imports and the national income at current prices) has fallen in the last three years, from .81 in 1957 to .61 in 1960. This is still high, since the coefficient tends to diminish as a country develops and replaces by its own products articles previously imported.

In 1960 the total value of exports was 8,446.57 million bolívares, the highest figure so far, and imports were 3,552.43 million bolívares, continuing a tendency to decrease which has existed since the record high point in 1957. The United States has the highest figures of trade in both directions: 51.7% of imports and 40.9% of exports.

Imports in 1960 can be classified: consumer goods 29.8%, fuels and lubricants 1.1%, raw materials and half-finished products 23.6%, capital goods 45.5%. This last figure shows the great effort being made to industrialise the country, even though the proportion was 47.8% in 1959 and as high as 58.7% in 1957, and even though a part of this figure is attributable to the oil industry. Yet there has been some success, since the amount of imports of consumer goods has fallen from a maximum of 35.5% in 1952, and the imports of raw materials and intermediate products has risen, which shows that there is now some finishing industry in the country.

In 1960 Venezuela had favourable balances with the United States (1,611 million bolívares), Great Britain (426 million), Brazil, Argentina, Canada (80% more than in 1959), France, Spain and Holland; and unfavourable balances with Germany (228 million), Italy, Belgium and Denmark, among other countries.

The imports were distributed as follows: America sent 57.8%, Europe 36.2%, Japan 3.6%. In the first group, the United States had the highest figure with 51.7%, then Canada with 3.7%. In Europe, the greatest provider was Germany with 8.8%, followed by Italy, 6.3%, and Great Britain, 6.0%, as the nearest rivals.

II. FOREIGN INVESTMENTS

Table VIII

Gross foreign investments classified according to their origin—
1959
(accumulated values in thousands of bolívares)

United States	13,784,673
Holland	4,502,192
Great Britain	1,862,461
Canada	79,239
France	63,383
Spain	52,381
Panama	50,438
Italy	42,104
Switzerland	41,083
Brazil	26,146
Argentina	25,624
Sweden	24,018
Uruguay	18,246
Germany	10,802
Colombia	7,595
Belgium	6,908
Portugal	6,478
Jamaica	3,132
Mexico	2,791
Cuba	2,634
Africa	1,700
Chile	1,667

Peru	1,037
Denmark	951
Costa Rica	807
Austria	567
Other countries (*)	2,188

Total 20,621,245

(*) Ecuador, Australia, Bolivia, El Salvador, Liberia, Monaco, Nigeria, Tangier, Andorra, Laos, British Colonies, Norway, Luxembourg, Hong Kong, Guatemala, Libya, Nicaragua, Lichtenstein and Dominican Republic.

Table IX

Foreign investments in Venezuela on December 31, 1959
classified by activities
(accumulated values in thousands of bolívares)

	Direct	Portfolio	Totals
Oil	17,321,810	127,638	17,449,448
Mining	1,286,395	2,442	1,288,837
Commerce	599,601	115,583	715,184
Industry	453,144	196,840	649,984
Services	151,587	21,055	172,642
Building	138,833	16,636	155,469
Banks	93,793	45,890	139,683
Insurance	42,270	7,728	49,998
	20,087,433	533,812	20,621,245

Source (for Tables VIII and IX): *Memoria del Banco Central de Venezuela*, 1960.

As is seen from Tables VIII and IX, the countries with the largest sums invested in Venezuela, considerably above the rest, are the United States, Holland and Great Britain; and oil and mining, especially the first, are the greatest fields for this investment. A high proportion of the foreign investments is direct, that is these are in companies established in Venezuela and are made by companies or persons residing abroad, who control 50% or more of the shares. Of a total of 20,621,245,000 bolívares of foreign investments on December 31, 1959,

20,087,433,000 were direct, and the rest, 533,812,000 bolívares were portfolio investments; that is, investments made by the acquisition by foreigners of shares, bonds, etc. issued by Venezuelan limited companies and official organisations. These latter investments remain under the control of persons residing in Venezuela. The gross accumulated foreign investment in 1950 was 8,892 million bolívares, and in 1960 it had risen to about 20,621 million. Foreign investment continued to increase until 1957, since the companies' policy was to increase their capital, and new enterprises were also founded; but with the political changes of 1958 the economic crisis arose and opened a period of readjustment, which is still continuing. Investments therefore fell off, until in 1959 there were more disinvestments than investments in some sectors.

The United States is not only the greatest gross total foreign investor, but she is also the biggest foreign investor in all economic sectors: 11,178 million bolívares in oil (64.06%); 1,286 million in mining (99.81%); 536 million in commerce (74.96%); 435 million in industry (67%); 150 million in services (87.20%); 109 million in building (70.3%); 51 million in banks (36.62%); and 23 million in insurance (46.93%).

The gross foreign investment in commerce in 1959 (599,601,000 bolívares) was distributed thus: vehicles and refrigeration 169,161,000 bolívares; dry goods 58,272,000; building materials 57,920,000; food and drinks 50,646,000; chemists shops 30,591,000; hardware and iron ware 16,663,000; others —department stores, importation, exportation, representation, distribution—216,348,000.

In manufacturing industry the distribution was: electric energy and light 130 million bolívares; chemical products 127 million; metals 38 million; tobacco 54 million; textiles 24 million; cosmetics and paints 17 million; food 15 million; cement 15 million; bottling and canning 8 million; cardboard and paper 6 million; rubber and derivatives 5 million; drinks 3 million; others 4 million.

In the services the distribution was: gas 44 million bolívares; accounting machines 37 million; scientific research 27 million; oil services 16 million; transport 10 million; dredging, excavation and drainage 8 million; distribution, representation and commissions 4 million; storage 174,000; representation of aluminium industries 544,000; hotels and tourism 84,000.

The profits on foreign investments in the various sectors in 1959 were: industry 17.76%; mining 17.19% oil 16.12%; commerce 14.04%; insurance 11.19%; building 10.33%; services 10.23%; and banks 7.67%.

Bibliography for Chapter VIII

Acosta H., Eduardo A., *La Industria petrolera desde el punto de vista nacional*, paper presented at the Congreso Centenario del Colegio de Ingenieros de Venezuela, Caracas, October 1961.

Anuario Petrolero de Venezuela, 1950-51, Ministerio de Minas e Hidrocarburos de Venezuela.

Banco Central de Venezuela, *Memoria correspondiente al ejercicio anual 1960*.

Carta Semanal, Ministerio de Minas e Hidrocarburos de Venezuela, Vol. V, No. 1, January 6, 1962.

Censo General de Población 1961. Resultados preliminares. Ministerio de Fomento de Venezuela.

Comisión de Reforma Agraria. Subcomisión de Economía, *Informe*, Vol. II, T. I, Caracas, 1959.

De la Plaza, Salvador, *Evaluación de la Reforma Agraria. El Nacional*, July 29, 1962, p. 4.

El Nacional. July 8 and 21, 1962.

Furtado, Celso, *El desarrollo reciente de la economía Venezolana*, Caracas, August 1957. Mimeographed by the Oficina de Coordinación y Planificación de Venezuela, February 1960.

Ley de Reforma Agraria de Venezuela. Promulgada el 5 de marzo de 1960. Gaceta Oficial de la República de Venezuela. No. 610, *Extraordinario*.

Malave Mata, Héctor, *Petróleo y desarrollo económico de Venezuela*, Caracas, 1962.

Mayobre, José Antonio, *Problemas de desarrollo económico de Venezuela*, read before the Comisión Económica para la

América Latina (CEPAL) at Panama (plenary session, 15 May 1959).

Maza Zavala, D.F., *Dos notas sobre la economía venezolana*, Caracas, 1961.

Ministerio de Fomento. Dirección General de Estadística.

Pérez Alfonzo, J.P., *Venezuela y su petróleo. Lineamientos de una política*, Caracas, 1960.

Petróleo y Otros Datos Estadísticos, Ministerio de Minas e Hidrocarburos de Venezuela, Caracas, 1961.

Petroleum Press Service, Vol. XXIX, No. 7, July 1962.

World Oil, August 15, 1961.

General bibliography

Besides the following list, the enquiring reader should consult the monumental *Biblioteca de la Academia Nacional de la Historia, Serie Sesquicentario,* 53 vols. of texts and secondary works published to commemorate the 150th anniversary of the movements of independence in 1810; and also the *Serie de Fuentes para la Historia Colonial de Venezuela,* the first 10 vols. of which are to be published by the end of 1962.

Academia Nacional de la Historia, *Archivo del Mariscal, Juan Crisóstomo Falcón,* 5 vols., Caracas 1957-1960.

Acosta Saignes, Miguel, *Estudios de Etnología antigua de Venezuela,* Caracas 1961.

Alvarado, Lisandro, *Historia de la revolución federal en Venezuela,* obras completas, vol. V, Caracas 1956.

Arcaya, Pedro Manuel, *Estudios de Sociología Venezolana,* Madrid (s.f)

Arcila Farías, Eduardo, *Economía Colonial de Venezuela,* México D.F. 1946.

Arcila Farías, Eduardo, *El régimen de la encomienda en Venezuela,* Sevilla 1957.

Arcila Farías, Eduardo, *Historia de la Ingeniería en Venezuela,* 2 vols., Caracas 1961.

Archila, Ricardo, *Historia de la Medicina en Venezuela,* vol. I, *Época Colonial,* Caracas 1961.

Arellano Moreno, A., *Fuentes para la Historia Económica de Venezuela,* Caracas 1950.

Armellado, Fray Cesáreo de, *Fuero indígena venezolano. Segunda parte,* Caracas 1954.

Baralt, Rafael María *Resumen de la Historia de Venezuela*, Brujas-París 1939.

Betancourt, Rómulo, *Venezuela: Política y petróleo*, México D.F. 1956.

Bierck, Harold A., junior, *Vida pública de Don Pedro Gual*, Caracas 1957.

Blanco Fombona, Rufino, *El conquistador español del siglo XVI*, Madrid (s.f.).

Bolívar, Simón, *Obras completas*, 3 vols., Caracas 1950.

Briceño Iragorry, Mario, *Obras Selectas*, Madrid 1954.

Castro, Américo, *La realidad histórica de España*, México D.F. 1954.

Colección Muñoz, Real Academia de la Historia, Madrid.

Cortés, Santos Rodulfo, *Antología documental de Venezuela*, 1492-1900, Caracas 1960.

Díaz Sánchez, Ramón, *Guzmán, eclipse de una ambición de poder*, Caracas 1953.

Dupuy, Walter, *El Indio en el mapa de Venezuela*, in *Tierra Firme* no. 15, Caracas May 1953.

Felice Cardot, Carlos, *La rebelión de Andresote*, Caracas 1952.

Fernández, Pablo Emilio, *Gómez, el rehabilitator*, Caracas 1956.

Fundación Eugenio Mendoza, *Venezuela Independiente*, 1810-1960, Caracas 1962.

Gandía, Enrique de, *Límites de las gobernaciones suramericanas en el siglo XVI*, Buenos Aires 1933.

García Chuecos, Héctor, *Estudios de historia colonial venezolana*, Caracas 1937.

García Chuecos, Héctor, *La Capitanía General de Venezuela*, Caracas 1945.

García Chuecos, Héctor, *Siglo XVIII venezolano*, Caracas 1947.

Gil Fortoul, José, *Historia Constitucional de Venezuela*, t. I, Caracas 1942.

González Guiñán, Francisco, *Historia Contemporánea de Venezuela*, 15 vols., Caracas 1909.

Historia de la Cultura en Venezuela, 2 vols., Publicación de la Facultad de Humanidades y Educación. Universidad Central de Venezuela, Caracas 1955-1956.

Lecuna, Vicente, *Crónica razonada de las guerras de Bolívar*, 2 vols., New York 1950.

Lecuna, Vicente, *Bolívar y el arte militar*, New York 1955.

Lecuna, Vicente, *La entrevista de Guayaquil*, Caracas 1952.

Madariaga, Salvador de, *Bolívar*, 2 vols., México D.F. 1953.

Magallanes, Manuel Vicente, *Partidos políticos venezolanos*, Caracas 1959.

Materiales para la historia del periodismo en Venezuela, durante el siglo XIX, Ediciones de la Escuela de Periodismo, Caracas 1951.

Morón, Guillermo, *Los orígenes históricos de Venezuela*, t. I, Madrid 1954.

Navarro, Monseñor Nicolás E., *Anales eclesiásticos venezolanos*, Caracas 1951.

O'Leary, Daniel Florencio, *Memorias: Narración, 3 vols.*, Caracas 1952.

Parra León, Caracciolo, *Filosofía universitaria venezolana*, Caracas 1933.

Parra León, Caracciolo, *La instrucción en Caracas, 1567-1725*, Caracas 1932.

Parra Pérez, Caracciolo, *Moriño y la Independencia de Venezuela*, 2 vols., Madrid 1954.

Parra Pérez, Caracciolo, *Historia de la Primera República de Venezuela*, Caracas 1939.

Parra Pérez, Caracciolo, *El rébimen español en Venezuela*, Madrid 1932.

Pensamiento Político Venezolano del siglo XIX, 15 vols., ediciones Presidencia de la República, Caracas 1960.

Perales, Pablo, *Manual de Geografía económica de Venezuela,* Caracas 1955.

Picón Febres, Gonzalo, *La literatura venezolana en le siglo XIX.* Caracas 1906.

Picón Rivas, Ulises, *Índice Constitucional de Venezuela (1811-1936),* Caracas 1944.

Picón Salas, Mariano, *Obras Selectas,* Madrid 1953.

Picón Salas, Mariano, *La pintura en Venezuela,* Caracas 1954.

Planchart, Enrique, *Tres siglos de pintura venezolana,* Caracas 1948.

Polanco Martínez, Tomás, *Esbozo sobre Historia Económica Venezolana,* 2 vols., Madrid 1960.

Rondón Márquez., R.A. *Guzmán Blanco, el autócrata civilizador, (Parábola de los partidos políticos tradicionales en la historia de Venezuela),* 2 vols., Caracas 1954.

Roscio, Juan Germán, *Obras,* 3 vols., Publicaciones de la secretaría general de la décima conferencia interamericana, Caracas 1953.

Salas, Julio C., *Etnología e historia de Tierra Firme,* Madrid (s.f).

Simón, Fray Pedro, *Noticias Historiales de las conquistas de Tierra Firme en las Indias Occidentales. Primera parte, Bogotá,* Bogotá 1882.

Tratados públicos y acuerdos internacionales, Ministerio de Relaciones Interiores, Caracas 1957.

Uslar Pietri, Arturo, *Obras Selectas,* Madrid 1953.

Vallenilla Lanz, Laureano, *Cesarismo democrático, ed.* Caracas 1952.

Vallenilla Lanz, Laureano, *Disgregación e Integración,* Caracas 1930.

Vila, Pablo, *Geografía de Venezuela. Volumen I: El Territorio Nacional y su ambiente físico,* Publicaciones del Ministerio de Educación, Caracas 1960.

Yanes, Francisco Javier, *Historia de Margarita,* Caracas 1948.

Some books in English

Hasbrouck, Alfred, *Foreign legionaries in the liberation of Spanish South America*, New York 1928.

Hussey, Roland D., *The Caracas Company 1728-1784*, Cambridge, Mass., 1934.

Lieuwen, Edwin, *Petroleum in Venezuela: a history*, Berkeley, Cal., 1954.

Lieuwen, Edwin, *Venezuela*, London 1961.

Masur, Gerhard, *Simón Bolívar*, Albuquerque 1948.

Robertson, W. S., *The life of Miranda*, Chapel Hill 1933.

Trend, J. B., *Bolívar and the independence of Spanish America*, London 1946.

INDEX

R

GEORGE ALLEN & UNWIN LTD
London: 40 Museum Street, WC1

Auckland: P.O. Box 36013, Northcote Central, Auckland N.4
Bombay: 15 Graham Road, Ballard Estate, Bombay 1
Barbados: P.O. Box 222, Bridgetown
Buenos Aires: Escritorio 454-459, Florida 165
Calcutta: 17 Chittaranjan Avenue, Calcutta 13
Cape Town: 68, Shortmarket Street
Hong Kong: 44 Mody Road, Kowloon
Ibadan: P.O. Box 62
Karachi: Karachi Chambers, McLeod Road
Madras: Mohan Mansions, 38c Mount Road, Madras 6
Mexico: Villalongin 32-10, Piso, Mexico 5, D.F.
Nairobi: P.O. Box 4536
New Delhi: 13-14 Asaf Ali Road, New Delhi 1
Sao Paulo: Caixa Postal 8675
Singapore: 36c Prinsep Street, Singapore 7
Sydney, N.S.W.: Bradbury House, 55 York Street
Tokyo: 10 Kanda-Ogawamachi, 3-Chome, Chiyoda-Ku
Toronto: 91 Wellington Street West, Toronto 1

RUN SOFTLY, DEMERARA
ZAHRA FREETH

Demerara: to English readers the word has long meant sugar and rum, but the past thirty years have seen the rise of an important new industry in British Guiana—the bauxite industry. Mrs Freeth spent four years in the bauxite-mining town of Mackenzie, fifty miles up the Demerara river. Her life not only gave her opportunities for excursions into the tropical forests and upland savannahs, but also brought her into close contact with the negro section of the country's population. She has some shrewd observations to make about the strangely mixed inhabitants of this 'Land of Six Peoples' and the peculiarly complex problems which face them in their aspirations to political maturity.

Mrs Freeth's approach to Guiana and the Guianese was one of frank and lively curiosity and she touches on many different aspects of the Guianese scene. She tells of the birds, beasts and butterflies of the colony; of Georgetown, the capital; of the early settlers and of the Amerindians, remnants, for whom there now seems no place in modern Guiana. This in an engrossing book for all who love tales of life in remote places.

Demy 8vo   21s. *net*

TROUBLE IN GUYANA
PETER SIMMS

An Account of the People, Personalities and Politics as they were in British Guiana

For fifteen years the story of British Guiana is of demonstrations, riots and of an ever increasing violence that came closer to being civil war.

Trouble in Guyana looks beyond the immediate causes, to the deep rooted feelings of the six peoples, many of whose ancestors were brought over as slaves or, what was almost the same, as indentured labourers. It also relates the Guianese problems to those in the present world-wide struggle between the Communist nations and the West.

For many years it was the Marxist premier Dr Cheddi Jagan and his American born wife who led the movement for independence. Their aim, it was said, was to create a 'Communist beach head' in South America and the West Indies. The author who knew them, and other political leaders, has shown the political development of the colony through their decisions and against a background of clashes between personalities and ideas. For ten years before he went to Guiana, the author held appointments in Thailand and Burma. In South East Asia he saw what it meant to a relatively small country to be beset by world politics. In Guiana he found much that was superficially similar and it was, in trying to understand the Guianese viewpoint, that he came to write this book.

Demy 8vo   *About* 30s. *net*

BRITISH HONDURAS
STEPHEN L. CAIGER

British Honduras is perhaps the most neglected of all English colonies. Even the larger histories of Colonial development barely mention it. The author has now told the story of this interesting country from the early days of its settlement by the logwood-cutters and buccaneers up to the present.

Beginning with the discovery of British Honduras by the Spanish Conquistadores, he describes the growth of the colony under its occupation and settlement by British adventurers, and consolidation by the buccaneers after the 'conversion' of Harry Morgan. He gives an account of the early quarrels with the Spaniards which were later followed by controversies with neighbouring Central American republics especially Guatemala. The dispute with Guatemala ended in the territorial Agreement of 1859, but the aftermath of diplomatic strife remains to the present day, and may be referred to U.N.O.

The concluding chapter deals with the Colony today with special emphasis on its economic and commercial status and recent Government proposals for development. The writer shows that its agricultural and other resources have been gravely neglected, and that this fertile land could maintain a population many times its present size.

Frontispiece. Demy 8vo   18s. *net*

HISTORY OF THE BRITISH WEST INDIES
SIR ALAN BURNS

While many authors have dealt with particular periods of West Indian history or with the history of individual colonies, there is no work yet published that covers the whole ground and the whole period. Sir Alan Burns attempts to give, in this single volume, a complete picture. He covers all the British colonies and former colonies in and near the Caribbean; trade and warfare in this area before and after the founding of British colonies; the aboriginal inhabitants; the discoveries of Columbus and the establishment of Spanish rule; and the colonies of other nations.

The first two chapters give a general description of the West Indies and of the races which have lived there, while the next three deal with Spanish exploration and administration. Another sixteen chapters continue the history to the year 1900, while a final chapter, added for this second edition, brings the story down to 1964.

The book is enriched by the sympathetic understanding for colonial peoples and their problems which is characteristic of Sir Alan's distinguished career as a colonial civil servant. It is illustrated by a number of line maps, and there are several appendices.

Mr Alec Waugh, in his recent book *A Family of Islands*, has referred to this history as 'required reading for any student of the area'.

Second Impression.   Small Royal 8vo.   856 pages.   70s. net

THE CONQUISTADORS
JEAN DESCOLA

Four hundred and fifty years ago there set out from Spain across 'the Dark Sea,' a handful of men intent on reaching 'Cipango' (as Japan was then known) by the Western route. Instead they discovered a world—the New World—and drew in their train a host of adventurers who feared nothing and spared no one, who spread out from the islands of the Caribbean westwards and southwards to conquer and convert, and, not last, to make their fortunes. Gold lured them on, and by fire and sword and torture they got it, and then passed on in search of more. And by fire and sword and torture they Christianised the natives too. The great civilisations of Mexico and Peru, each with a clearly defined culture and a highly organised political—religious-military system crumbled before the advance of a few hundred Spaniards with a few score of horses and even fewer cannon.

Demy 8vo   *30s net*

DAILY LIFE IN PERU UNDER THE LAST INCAS
DAILY LIFE SERIES
LOUIS BAUDIN

The Inca Empire that was long established in Peru prior to its discovery by the Spanish conquistadors is one of the most astonishing pieces of racial organization the world has ever seen. Through the eyes of a man of the twentieth century, daily life in the times of the last Incas gives the impression of having been organized once and for all as a piece of mechanism of sad but surprising perfection. The absolute and the permanent reigned without opposition. The common people had nothing to learn, nothing to foresee, nothing to desire. They knew, to the last detail, what would be their lives from birth to death. There was for them no inner withdrawal, no outer radiance. The Inca Council, and they alone, constituted the brains of this immense collective personality.

How did the people spend their days? What were their clothes like, what were the degrees of society, what were their tools, what were their dwellings like, what was their religion? The answers to all these questions, among many others, are here.

Demy 8vo   *28s net*

GEORGE ALLEN & UNWIN LTD.